HOMER'S MEDITERRANEAN

Homer's Mediterranean

From Troy to Ithaca
Homeric journeys

by Wolfgang Geisthövel

Translated from the German by Anthea Bell

HAUS PUBLISHING

This English translation first published in Great Britain in 2008 by
Haus Publishing Ltd, 26 Cadogan Court, Draycott Avenue, London
SW3 3BX
www.hauspublishing.co.uk

First published in German by Patmos Verlag GmbH & Co. KG Düsseldorf,
in 2007 under the title *Unterwegs mit Odysseus durch das Mittelmeer.*

Copyright © Patmos Verlag, Düsseldorf 2007

English translation copyright © Anthea Bell 2008

A CIP catalogue record for this book is available from the British Library

ISBN 978-1-905791-39-2

Designed and typeset in Garamond by MacGuru Ltd
info@macguru.org.uk

Printed in China by SC (Sang Choy) International Ltd.
Cover illustration: private collection

For the child in Berlin

Contents

The queenly nymph sought out the great Odysseus –
the commands of Zeus still ringing in her ears –
and found him there on the headland, sitting, still
weeping, his eyes never dry, his sweet life flowing away
with the tears he wept for his foiled journey home.

Odyssey, Book 5, 165

And he went away.
As the rocks of Ithaca
Gradually vanished from sight
And he set all sail on his westward course
To Iberia, to the Pillars of Hercules –
Far away, in any event, from Aegean waters –
He felt alive again
As he shook off the burdensome chains
Of familiar things and household matters,
And his heart, lusting for adventure,
Rejoiced, cold as it was and empty of love.

The Second Odyssey, Constantine Cavafy

Foreword

IF WE REGARD travel and all its ingredients – the initial idea, the preparations, the journey itself and its aftermath – as an essential element in our lives, and have discovered that such travels can be wonderfully enhanced and enriched by the many reflections of landscapes and places in the works of writers and poets, then it is only a question of time when – rather than whether – we set out to make the journey on which Homer (see *Notes*) sent the hero of his *Odyssey*: the greatest travel adventure in the dawn of our culture, described in 'the basic text of European civilization'.[1] One author may see the driving force of the *Odyssey* as the final, mutual recognition of Odysseus and Penelope, husband and wife; another will interpret the epic as the story of Telemachus' search for his father and his successful initiation into the adult world. Meanwhile, readers of the poem who enjoy travel may feel impelled to turn their attention to the places that feature in both the hero's wanderings and his son's journey in search of a father who has been absent for twenty years.

But this book is not intended as another attempt to locate the places visited by Homer's wandering hero in the real world. There have been almost ninety such attempts since the age of classical antiquity, when Homer's contemporary Hesiod is said to have undertaken to provide geographical details of the adventures. Not that we need deny the existence of any real background to the journeys of Odysseus and Telemachus. There are good reasons to assume that a kernel of reality can be found in accounts of the wanderings of Odysseus, even though they often partake of the nature of fairy-tale, owing that element to the treasure-chest of pre-Homeric tales of seafarers and home-comings with Odysseus as the central character, shot through with seamen's yarns and enriched by a motley array of monsters, giants and cannibals. The search for real places that Homer might have had in mind need not be dismissed out of hand. But theories that it may be possible to identify them have proliferated since antiquity, and so have doubts or outright denial of any such possibility, often linked to a certain wish to ridicule assumptions about the reality of those places. One of the earliest and wittiest attacks on supporters of the theory that they can be identified was made by the Alexandrian scholar Eratosthenes of Cyrene, who lived in the third century BC. We shall have to find the cobbler who sewed the sack to contain the winds of Aeolus, says Eratosthenes, before the places to which Odysseus travelled can be discovered.

So this is not another attempt, whether more or less convincing, to prove that the geography of the *Odyssey* is anchored in reality and thus not merely mythological. Here I may say that I am the beneficiary of two recent works giving scholarly accounts of a Homeric geography: *Celebrating Homer's Landscapes*, by John V. Luce,[2] emeritus professor of classics at Trinity College, Dublin; and *Die wirkliche Reise des Odysseus* [The Real Journey of Odysseus], by the historian Professor Armin Wolf and his brother Hans-Helmut Wolf.[3] Luce examined the landscapes of Troy and Ithaca by studying what can still be seen of them today through the lens of the Homeric text, and concluded that Homer had known the places mentioned in the epics well, describing fictional events against authentic backgrounds. Wolf and Wolf took as the subject of their research the question of whether it was possible to work out a real itinerary from the account of the wanderings of Odysseus on his way home from Troy to Ithaca. In their opinion the *Odyssey* is based on geographical knowledge, so the question can be answered in the affirmative. Of the more recent attempts to locate the hero's wanderings in real places, the theories put forward by the Wolf brothers seemed to me the most probable, since they have been very thorough methodically, not least because of their plausible thesis that, given the temporal proximity of Greek colonization to the west in southern Italy and Sicily from about 770 BC onwards with the composition of the *Odyssey* in about 720 BC, the epic can be seen as an account of a voyage around Sicily. However, the Wolfs are careful to point out that we must take account of historical refraction, always remembering that we are looking at the ideas of Homer the poet, not a real journey by Odysseus. As the French scholar Louis Moulinier had already made clear, it is not a case of 'finding locations for the myth of Odysseus, but discovering where Homer set his story.'[4]

For Odysseus, surely the best-known figure in Greek mythology, who to this day brings the human mind into many different kinds of cultural discussion, was not an individual, historically identifiable person. Vividly as he came into the world in the *Iliad*, even more so in the *Odyssey*, and soon after its composition in the visual arts as well, with works in pottery, stone, and other materials echoing the written word and passing the story on to later generations, his image had been influenced for hundreds of years before Homer by myths and legends made up of human experience, human values and wishful thinking. The name 'Odysseus' itself, containing no Greek stem, points to the pre-Greek period. The bearer of the name was probably a native figure of legend closely connected with seafaring, whom the Greeks came to know after their emigration took them to the southern peninsula of the Balkans, and whom they then took over, along with the nautical knowledge and seafaring stories of the indigenous population, assembled over the centuries and all coming together in the character of Odysseus.[5]

Homer was able to draw on this fund of stories to develop the figure of Odysseus as an archetype in which 'the collective memory of extraordinary deeds, of the exploration of distant lands, of the bold and wily art of survival [was] graphically intensified and depicted.'[6] Here was a prototype looking to the future, announcing the advent of modern man, yet he is also a lively and highly individual character. The *Odyssey* has been praised, and rightly so, as a poem of world-wide resonance in its all-embracing presentation of human life. It is also to a considerable degree a travel story, the tale of the long, dangerous and eventful voyage home of Odysseus as seen by the poet Homer's imagination.

In their wanderings, Odysseus and his companions meet no other ships and no human beings, more particularly no Phoenicians, despite Greek contacts with that seafaring people. The Greeks certainly knew them at the time and were indebted to them. Could it be that Homer's idea was to create, in the figure of Odysseus, an exemplary Greek character for the aristocratic society that he served at a time of renaissance[7] when it was looking back to the great Mycenaean past? As if he were a focal point, the hero unites the praiseworthy qualities of intelligence, cunning, eloquence, a thirst for knowledge, audacity, energy, a gift for survival and an inflexible will, all summed up in the term *politropon* by which Odysseus is introduced to us in the first lines of the programmatic *prooimion* ('prologue', 'introductory song') of the epic. It is variously rendered by translators into English as *the man of many devices* (A. T. Murray), *that resourceful man* (E.V. Rieu, revised D.C.H. Rieu), *the man of twists and turns* (Robert Fagles).

We know no details of what the poet saw with his own eyes, what was passed on to him or what sources were available to him. Since communication and recollection were confined to oral exchange and oral transmission, our information about knowledge in the Greek world up to the composition of the two epics the *Iliad* and the *Odyssey* is bound to be extremely sketchy. But we may doubt whether an author whose work presents such a richly detailed world, and whose approach was so realistic, refrained entirely from incorporating at least fragments recording some traces of geographical fact into the poems. If we assume that ancient experiences of travel, including some from the pre-Homeric period, have come down to us in the character of Odysseus, it cannot be categorically denied that the wanderings of the Homeric hero, given poetic form a few decades after the great Greek colonization of southern Italy began, reflect those conquests – admittedly with many interludes which are more like fairy-tale. The Wolfs go so far as to say that the Homeric account allowed them 'to identify the places named with *sufficient* clarity', and conclude that 'the supposition that Homer was referring to geographical facts is extraordinarily plausible.'[8]

Warnings against assigning actual locations to the wanderings and adventures of Odysseus may be understood as intended to protect the poetic, mythological substance of the work from prosaic reference to reality. But the literary cosmos of the modern period shows that making use of real places – often the small world of a province or just a town – need not impair quality. Far from it; it can be regarded as a prerequisite for creating a major work with very wide reference, as Flaubert, Proust, Faulkner, Svevo, Joyce, Doderer, Uwe Johnson, and more recently Pamuk, to name only a few, have shown in their writing. Virgil proved the same to good effect in his 'Roman Odyssey', the *Aeneid*. No one would claim that the *Aeneid* lacks poetic magic, yet it is full of references to real places and landscapes that can still be easily found today.

If we understand Goethe's celebration of the Homeric landscapes of south Italy and Sicily – 'Only now that all those coasts and promontories (...) are present in my mind does the Odyssey seem truly alive to me' – as describing his own experience of having his eyes opened, then a reading of the *Odyssey* cries out to be complemented by the sight of certain places and landscapes which, we may speculate, might possibly have inspired Homer.

Surely the understanding of many literary works, including the Homeric epics, with their special aura and stylistic nuances, together with our confidence in the truth of the fiction is actually increased, as it was for Homer's first audiences, if we have a concrete idea of real places as possible backgrounds for the story? If we set out on a literary trail, that means trying to find those places and landscapes that the author (or at least his informants) knew, places whose unique charm and beauty appealed to his poetic imagination. Of course it would be foolish to begin such a search expecting to find that literary and 'real' truth were just the same. The *Odyssey* is a work of fiction composed more than 2,700 years ago. Any effort to pin places down precisely must be made knowing that categorical statements are not just futile but also problematic and vague. However, a traveller's impressions of real features of the landscape as possible models for the poet – straits, mountains, caves, coastlines, volcanoes, rivers, lakes – can symbiotically enhance the text of the *Odyssey,* with images that endow such places with the beauty of the poetic text, and conversely by satisfying the senses lend the text vivid clarity. 'How brilliant, however, did the poem appear to me when I read its cantos in Naples and in Sicily!' [10] Goethe's comment can just as easily be made of many other places connected with the *Odyssey.*

In his epics Homer left us such an extensive, graphic account of the world of his time and its cultural institutions, as well as the Greek landscape, that his works can be taken as a 'compendium of the knowledge of his time'.[11] Looking for real details – places, landscapes – that interest the enthusiastic traveller in this compendium can be a very stimulating venture. Then, if we leave aside the real landscapes and look back at the poems, wondering how those places are reflected in them, we have an incentive to take many journeys that all revolve like satellites around their fixed star, the *Odyssey,* and are linked by the waters of the Mediterranean Sea washing around the coasts of the Troad, Greece, Italy, North Africa, and the islands in between.

So in this book I shall try to follow the wanderings of Odysseus, which are certainly literary but also very probably contain references to real places. My journey, starting with empirical principles – going to see all the places mentioned in the hero's travels from Troy to Ithaca – will trace its way back to the poetry. And it may even become something else: a journey through a densely woven network in which personal perception and reading, topography and the imagination, authenticity and fiction all mingle.

The scene of the action

Troy – *Truva*

ZEUS AND MOUNT IDA. Beyond the little town of Evciler on the forested slopes of Kas Dağı in western Turkey, lush vegetation borders the narrow, rising road. A grey-bearded old man in a woollen cap sits on a wooden crate; he wears a knitted waistcoat over a check shirt, his right arm rests on a stick. He is sitting under a tree heavily laden with apples, like thousands of trees in the orchards of this well-watered valley. Poplars accompany the river, coniferous forests grow and flourish on the mountainsides. Myriads of red globes nestle in the soft green foliage of the trees. The abundant apple harvest goes to the transshipment centre of Evciler, packed in crates. We don't have to scrump an apple or so in passing; the old man gives us plenty from one of the many crates in his orchard.

Round a few more bends, and then at the place called Ayazma a twilit paradise opens up in a ravine between tall rocks with a stream running past them, tumbling over megalithic boulders, swirling, fast-flowing, taking its cool waters down to the valley and the apple orchards. The trees have to reach very high to find the light that gives their leaves a diaphanous glow, like stained glass windows in a cathedral.

The mountain stream, escaping from a steep wall of the ravine a little way above, is divine. No, not in the metaphorical sense but in reality, or at least the reality of myth. It is one of the main headstreams of the river officially known as the Kara Menderes, but famous as the Scamander or the Xanthus, names that have endured through the ages. It springs from several sources in the Kaz Dağı, and flows into the Dardanelles north-west of Troy. Only a few kilometres lie between the mountain torrent at Ayazma and the peak of the Kaz Dağu.

The great deep-swirling river immortals call the Xanthus, mankind calls Scamander (I, F 20, 88), river and god, *the strong, whirling Xanthus sprung of immortal Zeus* (I, F 21, 2) had its source here, and was very close to the god who brought it forth. For although this mountain range where the sources of the Scamander rise is officially called the Kaz Dağı, its name through the centuries has been Mount Ida. Ida was the mountain of the father of the gods, Zeus the Cloud-Gatherer, the Thunderer, also addressed as *Zeus ruling over us all from Ida* (I, F 24, 364). He came down to the heights of his mountain to watch the Achaeans fighting the Trojans. On a clear day it is possible for a human eye, let alone a divine one, to see from Mount Ida to the Troad, the country around Troy, about 60 kilometres away. Homer could therefore easily make his audience and readers believe that the father god was stationed on Mount Ida, sending down thunder and lightning on the Achaeans, much to their alarm, in the changing fortunes of war.

Mount Ida was also the backdrop to less martial scenes than the appearance of Zeus the Thunderer. For if we are to believe the geographer Strabo, the incident that ultimately led to the Trojan War, the wrath of Achilles, the fall of Troy and Odysseus' ten-year journey home to Ithaca took place in a ravine on the southern slopes of Ida: it is the tale of the judgement of Paris in the beauty contest between the goddesses, and its fatal outcome when he awarded the apple to Aphrodite. We may agree to this day that he made the right decision – for if he had chosen Hera or Athene, Helen would never have been abducted, and without the Trojan War the *Iliad* and *Odyssey* would not have been written. Mount Ida was also the place where Apollo spent some time in the shape of a herdsman, and *herded his shambling crook-horned cattle/along the spurs of Ida's timbered ridges* (I, F 21, 512). It was also the birthplace of Aeneas, reputedly the son of Aphrodite and the Trojan Anchises, and the delightful setting for the love-making of Hera and Zeus in a captivating scene of marital seduction, in which the goddess tires her husband out so much that he calls a halt to his partisan backing of the Trojans, at least for the time being.

> With that the son of Cronus caught his wife in his arms
> and under them now the holy earth burst with fresh green grass,
> crocus and hyacinth, clover soaked with dew, so thick and soft
> it lifted their bodies off the hard, packed ground ...

Folded deep in that bed they lay and round them wrapped
a marvellous cloud of gold, and glistening showers of dew
rained down around them both.

(I, F 14, 413).

POSEIDON AND THE PEAK OF FENGARI. Homer, an Ionian who
may have been born in Smyrna, obviously made use of his geographical knowledge in allotting another lookout post with a fine view to
Poseidon, whose support for the Greeks sometimes brought him into
conflict with his brother the father of the gods. Poseidon's choice
fell on a place with panoramic views, presumably known to the poet
and to many of his hearers and readers from their own experience:
the peak of Fengari on Samothrace, visible from the Troad on a clear
day. It is 1600 metres above sea level, and thus the highest place on
the island and in the entire northern Aegean. Does it owe its name
of Fengari, 'moon', to its position closer to the heavenly bodies than
any other place in this part of Greece, or the fact the upper reaches of
the mountain chain of which it is part are of astral bleakness, and its
rock shines in the moonlight on nights of full moon?

But the mighty god of earthquakes was not blind.
He kept his watch, enthralled with the rush of battle,
aloft the summit of timbered Samos facing Thrace.
From there the entire Ida ridge swung clear in view,
the city of Priam clear and the warships of Achaea.

(I, F 13, 12).

Homer deliberately stations Poseidon on a mountain peak with a
view of the Troad, and perhaps even the Kaz Dağı, given particularly good visibility. The eye can sometimes see as far as the island
of Thassos and even Mount Athos. From this vantage point, Homer
allows the god to watch the battle raging outside Troy and the desperate situation of the Achaeans, who have already been driven back
to their ships.

Terms such as *timbered* and *the mountain's rocky crags* reinforce
the assumption that Homer had detailed knowledge of the island he
calls *Samos facing Thrace*. Here he was probably alluding to the still
densely wooded area of the south of the island, facing the Turkish
mainland. For Samothrace was and still is *timbered*, at least in parts.

This is most obvious in approaching the island from Alexandroupolis, the seaport in the far east of Greece. The forest is visible from some distance away, with the trees lying like dark shadows over the granite rocks. The magnificent woods of wild plane trees are the glory of Samothrace. Walking in the shimmering twilight under their broad canopy of leaves, past mighty and often bizarrely shaped tree trunks with streams and rivers cascading down between them, waterfalls finding their way to the sea through beds that have filled up with great rocks polished to round, oval and polygonal shapes, you feel compelled to go on until your head is hot and throbbing and your feet are sore. Then you can enjoy the luxury of bathing in a natural stone basin under a waterfall, discovering the wonderful effect of clear, cold water on a heated body.

In crystalline, inorganic contrast, the Saos mountains rise above the lush splendour of the woods that are watered by those cool springs. When you see the mountain range fully revealed at evening, viewed from a southerly aspect, there is no need to shrink – with Homeric lines in your head – from calling it a sublime sight: you may see a flock of sheep on a stubble field in hilly country, with bushes and an olive grove nearby, while higher up the massif rises, its steep slopes and rugged crags sharply outlined against the sky and dominated at the centre by the pyramidal shape of Fengari, all bathed in the light of the setting sun that transforms the fleece of some of the black sheep to warm tones of umber and sienna brown.

Poseidon, then, was *aloft the summit*, first merely as an observer, then anxious as he saw the Achaeans threatened by defeat, finally angry as Zeus sided with the Trojans. Something had to be done – in spite of the promise extracted from his divine colleagues by Zeus in Book 8 that they would favour neither the Trojans nor the Achaeans. With four great strides he hastened to his palace in the depths of the sea and drove his chariot and horses out to the coast, near the camp of the Achaean ships. Assuming the shape of the seer Calchas he mingled with the Greeks, spurring them on to fight.

If you visit the Sanctuary of the Great Gods in Palaopolis at mid-day, when there is almost no one there, you soon feel sure that this is one of the most beautiful excavated sites of Greek antiquity. At the northern foot of the Saos mountains and on both sides of a ravine through which a mountain stream flows (although its bed dries up in summer), many terraces supported by masonry lie on the densely forested slopes. These terraces were built for a wide variety of buildings:

temples, arcaded halls, theatres, porticos, altars, a complex of sacrificial pits, precincts sacred to the gods, a huge gymnasium – it dates from Roman times – and not least a niche containing the replica of a monument that has made Samothrace famous in modern times: a female figurehead standing on a plinth shaped like the prow of a ship. The statue once adorned a basin here, and as one of the finest exhibits in the Louvre, where the original now stands, is better known to art lovers and museum visitors as the Nike or Winged Victory of Samothrace. Wherever you go in this great sanctuary, sacred to the deities known as the Cabeiri, you are almost always in natural surroundings close to the sea, which can be glimpsed between and above the treetops, and close to the mountain peak above the holy places, unchanged since the times when the mystery cult of the Cabeiri was celebrated here. At the time these wonderful natural sights were accompanied by ceremonies performed only at night, by torchlight, in what for many must have been a moving personal experience.

MOUNT OLYMPUS. Now that Mount Ida (or Kaz Dağı) and Fengari have been introduced as sites sacred to the gods, we must not forget the mountain that was the home of Zeus, Poseidon and all the other many Greek divinities: Mount Olympus is a real as well as a mythological place. It is easy, with the mighty massif of this highest of all the Greek mountains before your eyes, to think that once again Homer was drawing on his knowledge of the real place in creating the mythological version. You should see it on a sunny day when there are only a few clouds; these clouds do not concentrate somewhere above as clouds usually do but cling to the peaks of Olympus, preferring the highest of them, Mytikas. Climatologists can easily explain why: the high mountains form a barrier to moisture rising from the nearby sea. But if you do not have a climatologist with you, such a phenomenon calls for a different explanation. To the storyteller, a poet familiar with the myths, these lofty peaks, which are covered with snow for many months of the year, will easily have become the residence of the gods where the greatest of them, Zeus, sat enthroned, and it was understandable that the blessed spirits would sometimes wish to withdraw from the eyes of mortal men. The peaks were veiled from sight when Zeus gathered the clouds close around his palace and the dwellings of the other gods. The weather on Mount Olympus can change quickly, and then a storm with thunder and lighting may break (if you are walking in the region, be warned) – Zeus is speaking a word of power, flinging lightning bolts from his thunderclouds on Olympus.

To the seaward side on the Thermaean Gulf, the Olympus range begins with the magnificent canyon of Enipeia, set in front of the seat of the gods like a gigantic version of the monumental type of entrance known as a propylaeum. In Book 8 of the *Iliad*, when the gods meet on Olympus, Zeus commands them all to be neutral towards the two sides locked in combat outside Troy. He himself, however, intends to harm the Greeks, and goes to Mount Ida. Hera and Athene are firmly determined to support the Greeks. Unwilling to watch the downfall of their protégés and do nothing, they decide to set off for Troy. The two goddesses have already raced down from the Olympian heights in their flaming chariot drawn by a team of horses in golden harness, and have reached the outermost gates of Olympus. But the disobedience of his wife and daughter has not escaped the notice of Zeus on distant Ida. He tells Iris, the messenger of the gods, to warn both goddesses off on pain of severe punishment. On both sides of the outer gateway to the citadel – and it is hard to imagine a more magnificent entrance to the mountain of the gods, or one better suited to display their powers, than the rocky canyon of Enipea – the eye is drawn to the steep green slopes of the ravine, then up to the assembled peaks of the central group, the most striking being Mytikas and Stefani. Many travel guides still call Stefani, which rises almost vertically like half of a disc from the rubble field below it, Olympus or the Throne of Zeus. But to my mind that is a better term for Mytikas, which is nine metres higher and presents a triangular steep rock-face as it turns towards Stefani. Homer could not have known the peaks in detail; the first ascent was not made until 1913. The cluster of peaks, nine in all, with tall, jagged rocks and deep crevasses between them, are well described at the beginning of Book 8 of the *Iliad*:

> Now as Dawn flung out her golden robe across the earth
> Zeus who loves the lightning summoned all the gods
> to assembly on the topmost peak of ridged Olympus.
>
> (I, F 8, 1).

Homer provides even more telling evidence of his geographical knowledge in describing the route taken by Hera when, as the fighting goes on, she makes another attempt to stand by the Greeks and tries to keep Zeus from favouring the Trojans, at least for a while, by seducing him on Mount Ida. This erotic passage, wonderfully described in Book 14, is a delightful interlude in a story mainly concerned with men and their favourite occupation of war. Hera's flight from Olympus to Ida is so precisely described, (I, Greek original 14, 225) that you can follow it by running a finger over the map and trace her journey over land and sea: first from Olympus over the region of Pieria that has borne the same name since Homer's time, with its modern capital of Katerini, and the plains of *lovely Emathia*, with their many marshes, then along the Thermaean Gulf to the massif of Pangaion in Thrace, *over the Thracian riders' snowy ridges*, past the eastern flank of Mount Athos to the islands of Lemnos and Gökceada (Imbros in the ancient Greek period), from there over Cape Baba (Cape Lekton in antiquity) and the Gulf of Edremit, and up to Kaz Dağı/Ida. Athos, Lemnos, Imbros, Lekton – Hera passes them all on her journey through the air, and Homer calls them by their names.

SCAMANDER AND FALSE TROY. To the west of Evciler the Scamander meets other rivers flowing from *the slopes of Ida streaming with springs*, and together they form a quiet lake in a hollow at the foot of Skepsis, as it was known in the ancient world, surrounded only by sandy banks and fields and without any human settlements nearby. The outline of the Kaz Dağı range is visible in the distance, veiled in a soft grey haze. Later, the river can be seen among plantations after sinking into the broad and fertile Bayramic and Ezine basin, through which it flows peacefully on westward without boulders in its bed, rapids or sharp bends – lord of the plains, accompanied by trees on its banks. They owe their flourishing growth to the river, as trees already did in the great days of Troy, which drew most of its provisions from this area.

On reaching Ezine the Menderes – to give the river its modern name, which derives from the ancient version – turns north-west and runs through the last foothills of the Kaz Dağı. Here the river can rest where, aeons ago, it cut a way with tireless patience through the rocky resistance of the mountains, until at last it reached the valley floor after carving out the Araplar ravine.

The result was to create a wonderful oasis, still almost shut off from the world today. Rocky heights on both sides, narrow strips, sometimes widening into fields, of the fertile alluvial land that comes to an end on reaching tall, steep wooded slopes rising to a height of several metres. Two large flocks of goats are going along the opposite bank. In this lonely valley with only a field path running through it we make contact with the goatherds, waving and calling. to show that we are harmless and well-disposed. They wave back. The goats perform a two-part tune for us with their bells, and the wind joins in, rustling the leaves in the right key. The goatherds make their contribution to this pastoral piece by clicking their tongues, and the goats add further rhythm with a kind of staccato coughing as well as their characteristic bleating, known even to us city folk, at least by hearsay.

Then the valley opens up ahead. The self-contained image of the idyll is broken at a place where a huge stone quarry is eating its way into the rock, with all the machinery required for the job. The mountains fall to the plain. It was once thought, at the time when modern research into Troy began, that Priam's city stood here, where the last bastion of the mountains on the left is Balli Dağ, 150 metres above sea level, in what is now the village of Pınarbaşı. Was this holy Troy, sacred Ilium? For almost 90 years the theory, first put forward by the French classical scholar Jean Baptiste le Chevalier, seemed plausible, until excavations carried out by the Austrian scholar and diplomat Johann Georg von Hahn, and later by Schliemann showed that a Bronze Age site could be ruled out. Since then Balli Dağ, whose remains date from the classical Greek period, has been nicknamed 'False Troy'.

THE SCAMANDER FORD. The last part of the course of the river Menderes, running close to the real site of Troy, leads through the plain that the river helped to create. For many millennia it carried down the valuable gift of soil that extended the coastline to the north from around 4000 BC, making the northern part of the Troad – the country west of the Biga peninsula between the Dardanelles and the Gulf of Edremit – an excellent grain and vegetable-growing region. Once it reaches the flat land of the plain, the Menderes can follow a leisurely, winding course between its low or only slightly rising sandy banks. The landscape of the river includes a number of small islands and sandbanks which give the Menderes a picturesque and diversified look, despite embankments built in the middle of the last century.

Willows, elms and tamarisks grow and thrive here, welcoming little ringed plovers and little bitterns to their branches. Grey herons and little egrets can also be seen. They do not like being photographed, or not at close quarters, and let you know it by rising in the air to fly a few rounds at their leisure, with stately elegance, coming down again with as much dignity as they took off.

A few kilometres further towards the sea, not far from the village of Kalafat south-west of Troy, a footpath through the fields leads down to the Menderes and continues on the opposite bank. Now, in autumn, the ford here can be crossed even on foot when the water is fairly low.

Is this the setting for two scenes in the *Iliad*, different but both very dramatic? They are connected with a ford over the Scamander or Xanthus River, which according to Homer's account lay between Troy in the east and the camp of the Achaean ships in the west. Achilles, joining the battle again to avenge his friend Patroclus after days in his tent, sullen and withdrawn, rages among the Trojans, spreading indescribable terror, and drives them back. Some of the fleeing men fall into the waters of the Xanthus:

> But once they reached the ford where the river runs clear,
> the strong, whirling Xanthus sprung of immortal Zeus,
> Achilles split the Trojan rout ...
>
> (I, F 21, 1).

There follows a scene which, despite all the horrors we see daily in the modern world, can still make us shudder at the merciless and murderous thirst for revenge shown by Achilles. He sees Lycaon, one of Priam's sons, whom he himself had captured some while before and had sold as a slave on the island of Lemnos. The young man had recovered his freedom by various means and was home again twelve days later. Now he falls into the hands of the son of Peleus once more. But this time the situation is different. Hector has killed Patroclus, and Achilles has sworn revenge on all the Trojans.

Lycaon, without armour or weapons, is in effect executed by Achilles, who then takes the corpse by the foot as if it were a dead animal, throws it in the river, and sends Lycaon's body on its journey to the sea with words of the utmost contempt, spoken in jubilant tones:

Lie there! Make your bed with the fishes now,
they'll dress your wound and wash it clean of blood –
so much for your last rites! Nor will your mother
lay your corpse on a bier and mourn her darling son –
whirling Scamander will roll you down the sea's broad bosom.

(I, F 21, 139).

'The orgy of mourning is followed by an orgy of vengeance,'[12] culminating in the shameful dragging of Hector's body after the chariot of Achilles. Here we have a telling early image of the way that love, disappointed or robbed of its object, can turn to a form of destructive rage that spurns all civilized instincts. Rudolf Hagelstange, in his fictional account of the similarly brutal murder by the Greeks of young Polydorus, another of Priam's sons, makes his imagined Paris say in revulsion, 'Had I not seen them send the defenceless boy to death with my own eyes, I would refuse to believe that battle-hardened men and princes of a noble house were capable of such an act, or would permit it.'[13]

In Book 21 of the *Iliad* Homer also describes the flourishing plant life near the Scamander, mentioning elms, thickets of willow, tamarisks, sedge and galingale, many of the details closely resembling the flora still found there today. It is not surprising that the poet, as an Ionian, knew the local plant life, particularly that of the Troad, and made it into something that would relate to what his hearers and readers knew. In fact Homer's integration of real details into his work goes much further. We can 'find a wealth of real items here, a variety of objects used in religious ritual, ordinary household goods such as furniture, jewellery and weapons, as well as buildings, monuments, roads through the landscape and places in it, all described so knowledgeably and in such rich detail that the poet himself must surely have seen them or heard about them from eyewitnesses.'[14]

Standing on the slight rise of the embankment, you can easily trace the further course of the Menderes past the trees on its banks, following it in an unbroken line through the plain. There are fields to left and right all the way to the Dardanelles. As you approach the straits you can hear, still some distance away, the slow murmur of the engines of the big ships, and soon they are visible between trees, as if in a peepshow. The Menderes still has its playful character; although it is wild and tumultuous near its source, it takes its leave of us in relaxed and friendly mood at its delta in the Dardanelles, the natural channel between Europe and Asia. In the *Iliad* it is called the Helle-spont, the Sea of Helle, after a character from a dramatic mythologi-cal legend who drowned in its waters. Homer describes it as broad, rich in fish, and with a strong current, and he knew that the Helle-spont divided Thracian land (on European soil) from the kingdom of Priam (on the Asian side). We can see that, as elsewhere in the topography of the *Iliad*, the poet know a great deal about major fea-tures of the landscape.

KARA TEPE AND KESIK TEPE. The Dardanelles in the north, the foothills of Kaz Dağı in the east and south and the Aegean in the west are the borders of the central 'Homeric' landscape of the Troad, divided diagonally by the Menderes running from the south-east to the north-west. The eastern region is marked by a mountain ridge gradually sinking from east to west. At its western end the hill of Hisarlik, in Turkish 'place of the castle', with the ruins of Troy, lies 33 metres above sea level. Approaching Troy on the main road from the north, we can survey the mountain ridge from its origin in a hill called Kara Tepe in the densely wooded foothills of the Kaz Dağı all the way to Troy. Kara Tepe is traditionally identified with the Callicone of the *Iliad*.[15] Its gentle rise could have inspired Homer in the battle of the gods in Book 20, where the Olympians temporar-ily fight on the sides of either the Achaeans or the Trojans, and the poet describes the divine supporters of the latter using the hill as an observation post and operational base:

> Their divine opponents also sat down on the brow of Callicone on the
> other side, round you, Apollo, and Ares, sacker of cities.
>
> (I, R 20, 151).

The plain of the Menderes and Hisarlik are certainly clearly visible from the top of Kara Tepe.

Now, in autumn, the little river Dümrek at the northern foot of the mountain ridge is dry. We see just one puddle with midges swarming above it, in the shade of dense foliage; otherwise the river bed is full of leaves, stones and rubbish. But in winter and spring the Dümrek brings down so much water that its deposits were able to form alluvial land joining the deposits of the Menderes west of Troy, just as the two rivers themselves join near the coast. Homer seems to have known that when, in Book 5, he describes *the place where the rivers Simois and Scamander meet* (I, R 5, 774); the Simois is thought to be the modern Dümrek. Even the dry bed of the river, quite wide as it approaches the sea, allows us to guess how much water must come pouring down from the mountains in the rainy season. The torrents of water can be so strong that Homer imagines the larger river Scamander begging its little brother the Simois for help in taming the murderous Achilles as he storms over the plain:

> Oh, dear brother, rise! Both of us rush together
> to halt this mortal's onslaught! (...)
> Beat him back, quickly! Deluge all your channels
> from all your gushing springs – muster all your torrents –
> raise up a tremendous wave ...

(I, F 21, 350)

It seems natural to conclude, from this passage, that the fight took place when the season brought plenty of rain.

From the village of Kumkale, a path along an embankment fringed with reeds leads across a bridge over the Menderes, the only bridge in the part of the Troad west of the river apart from the southern one at the foot of the Balli Dag. From the viewpoint of the epic, we are approaching an area that for years was mainly under the control of the Achaean attackers, and the gods who were on their side needed a suitable observation post. The gods who supported the Trojans had theirs on Callicolone, so where was the lookout post of the divine partisans of the Achaeans? It had to have a clear view of the fighting, which as imagined by Homer probably took place in the plain through which the Scamander flows, between Troy and the Greek ships' camp on the coast.

The gravel road, now used by farmers, curves as it approaches a chain of hills along the steep coastline of the Aegean, the Yeniköy Ridge, called after the village of the same name and traditionally known as the Sigeum Ridge. Its eastern part, at the entrance to the Dardanelles, is a prohibited military area and is thus surrounded by a fence, which seems superfluous in view of the tall, prickly thistles and the bushes densely covering the hill. Very close lies Kum Tepe, the oldest human settlement in the Troad and dating from the end of the sixth millennium BC. At that time it was directly on the western edge of a bay reaching far inland, and around 2920 BC the city to which we now refer as Troy I stood directly opposite it on the eastern side.

A few kilometres to the south a smaller hill, approximately the shape of an isosceles triangle, rises on the coast. I make for it, crossing a stubble field. A delicate, easily overlooked weed with tiny pink flowers makes its protest against the uniform colour of the field, winding everywhere and discreetly triumphant as it flowers among the stubble. In strong contrast is the bright red of tomatoes that fell in this field after the tomato crop from the field next to it was loaded up. Only a short, steep climb, hardly fifteen metres – and up at the top, like a wisp of mist dissolving, everyday reality disappears. Time stands still, the fabric of the present is removed from ordinary life and enriched by the historical and mythological past pressing in on it. I feel sure that I shall remember such moments. The sea is smooth, with a faint haze still lingering over it in the morning air, and the precipitous coast, still in shadow, is not yet entirely free of the night. But over the fields, reaching from the hazy distance of the eastern hills to the sharply outlined top of the cliffs, day has spread. The plain of the Menderes, a geometrically patterned landscape of agricultural colour, reminds me of Pau Klee's colourful landscapes with their scarf-shaped areas of yellow, brown, ochre and green.

Looking from Kesik Tepe, there is nothing in the way of the view of the coast, the river plain, Troy, the foothills of Mount Ida and the hilltop of Kara Tepe. An ideal and panoramic lookout for either men or gods intending to intervene in such human concerns as battles. Am I standing on the hill where the gods who backed the Achaeans planned their campaign?

During the international excavations carried out in the Troad since 1982 under Manfred Korfmann of Tübingen, the distinguished classicist and ancient historian, many drill samples were taken in investigating the geomorphological changes in the alluvial plain of the Menderes. Some remarkable discoveries were made, particularly about the coastline north-west of Troy on the Dardanelles. The Ice Age and then the melting of the Polar ice zones on one hand, and alluvial deposits of sediment left by the Menderes on the other, have both affected the coastline over the millennia. The sea level rose, the sea level sank again. If the sea and the bay reached about thirty kilometres further south in 5000 BC than they do today, going as far as the place where the river flows down from the mountains, then by the time of the 'Trojan War' around 1250 BC – archaeologically speaking, the period of Troy VI to Troy VIIa – it had fallen back to several kilometres north of Troy, along a line drawn between the village of Kumkale and prehistoric Kum Tepe to the west of it. The bay of Troy at the time can thus be visualized as a southern incursion of the Dardanelles, bordered to the west by an irregularly shaped peninsula, with the northern part of the Sigeum ridge reaching as far as the cliffs, and to the east by land falling gently to the bay.

This is where Luce[16] visualizes the camp with the Greek ships, the base for their ten-year siege of Priam's city, while the battlefield would then be in the adjoining plain of the Scamander between the Sigeum Ridge and Troy. In this plan of the terrain, observers on Kesik Tepe would have had an excellent view of the plain beneath – especially if they were Olympian observers. Luce therefore thinks that this natural tumulus, further formed later by human hands, was the observation post from which the gods supporting the Achaeans followed the fortunes of the battle, and could see their opponents within the divine family on their own lookout on Callicolone directly above the citadel of Troy.

Luce sums up his reflections on the topographical landmarks thus: 'Antithetical viewing points are named on either side of the Trojan plain, and the rival groups of gods look down from them on the city soon to be sacked by Ares. Homer is not merely setting the scene but also deftly concentrating our attention on the theatre of war that lies between the heights on either side.'[17]

Sitting on Kesik Tepe among tall blue and yellow thistles, surrounded by a landscape so full of history and myth, on one side the endless sea, on the other the plain of Troy, with only the occasional flash from the window of a vehicle left somewhere far away in the fields to remind me of ordinary modern life, it takes something drastic to disturb me enough to drive me from this spot – and I get it in the form of an attack by ants!

THE TOMB OF ACHILLES. This is another place of great importance for the history and archaeology of Western Anatolia and Troy, as well as for Homeric studies. A bird's-eye view shows it as a semi-ellipsoid bay with a sandy beach and a low belt of dunes, to the north side of a low-lying promontory. Beyond this headland, on its southern side, a long, shallow bay curves out into the sea. A few hundred metres inland, on rising ground, stands a regularly shaped hill. An island lies in the background. This in brief is the way the topography of a striking coastal area about 8 kilometres south-west of Troy can be described. In today's terms, we have here the foothills of Beşik-Yassıtepe, Beşıka Bay to the south, the tumulus of Beşik-Sivritepe, and the island of Bozcaada. What is hidden behind those names, what lies beneath the surface?

Information on 7000 years of human history became available once Korfmann first dug a spade into the earth in 1999 not far from the coast, at Sivritepe. Time had destroyed the early settlement, but not the material it was made of; in the early Hellenistic period the earth was re-used to erect the tumulus that is now called Sivri Tepe. As early as the 1980s, Korfmann's team had already found that there was a settlement of the early 3rd century BC near the headland of Yassı Tepe by the shore, founded at the same time as the first Troy. Ever since navigation of the Aegean began, ships had found a natural harbour to the south of the bay, with an inlet that, at the time, ran several hundred metres inland, so that prehistoric Sivri Tepe can really be thought of as lying by the sea. It was on the leeward side of the spur of the Yassı Tepe headland, and thus well protected from the *meltemi* wind that blows from the north-east for many months in summer.

The path from the village of Yeniköy leads down to the Beşik-Yassı Tepe headland and to Beşıka Bay. So let us go through cotton fields, through the stubble fields where the grain has been harvested, and so up to Sivritepe, where a pleasant wind soon blows away the sweat of the climb. There is nothing to be seen now of the deep shafts of the 1999 excavations on the eastern side. The conical form of the tumulus has been restored, and with it, its dignity as the grave mound of one of the heroes of the Trojan War. Of the supreme Achaean hero, Achilles himself. Not Achilles the berserker, who went out to avenge the death of his friend Patroclus, returned to the battle, and raged with such murderous frenzy among the Trojans on the Xanthus, nor of 'the beast Achilles' as Cassandra calls him, in revulsion, in Christa Wolf's novel,[18] but the glorious ancestor of Alexander the Great, for so the young Alexander himself regarded him. On his campaign against the Persians in the year 334, Alexander visited Troy. In fact his visit became something of a pilgrimage; he is said to have slept with a copy of the *Iliad*, which he revered, under his pillow. Because of its proximity to the settlement of Achilleion on Yassı Tepe, founded by immigrants from Lesbos in the 6th century BC, the old mound of the settlement was venerated as the tomb of Achilles. Alexander therefore stopped to see it, anointed the tombstone, and arranged races around the hill.

The memory of Achilles the murderer, however, revives when we remember another terrible story set at his tomb: the tale of the slaughter of Priam's daughter Polyxena by Neoptolemos, euphemistically presented as a sacrifice. Carrying out the wish of his father Achilles, Neoptolemus slit her throat before the assembled army at the dead hero's grave mound. Was this a case of a scorned lover wanting revenge, or was it the fervent wish of the dying Achilles, mortally wounded in his heel, to take the woman he loved into the next world with him, even though she had betrayed him? Although she did not see it as betrayal; she could not forgive Achilles for his brutal killing of her young brother Troilus. Revenge was due to her, and when her chance came she took it. Achilles had fallen passionately in love with her when he saw her in the temple of Thymbrian Apollo, which both Greeks and Trojans regarded as neutral ground. There were negotiations with Priam over the conditions on which he would consent to the marriage. At her wish, they were that Achilles was to come to a sacrifice in the temple unarmed and barefoot, and Polyxena now succeeded in discovering the secret of his vulnerable heel. Hidden behind the statue of a god, Paris shot a poisoned arrow, and the dying Achilles asked Odysseus, who entered the temple at this moment, to sacrifice Polyxena on his tomb once Troy had fallen. The killing is shown on both sides of a very impressive marble sarcophagus of 480 BC found a few years ago in a tumulus in the Troad, near the provincial capital of Çanakkale. 'Depicted in the finest late archaic style, the terrible sacrifice at the tomb of Achilles is carried out. The tumulus is crowned with a kind of cippus, before which a tripod as the prize of victory reminds us of funeral games.'[19] If you admire this sarcophagus in the Archaeological Museum in Çanakkale, with its many figures and the extreme delicacy of the carving, you can almost forget the horror of the event itself.

At the age of twenty-eight the German poet Hölderlin expressed the utmost admiration for Achilles. 'He is my favourite among the heroes, strong and tender, the finest and most transient flowering of the heroic world.' And of Homer, Hölderlin says: 'But most of all I love and admire that poet among poets for the sake of his Achilles. The love and intelligence with which he has studied, understood and depicted the character is unique. Take the old lords Agamemnon,

Ulysses and Nestor, with their wisdom and their folly, take Diomedes the brawler, take raging Ajax, and set them against the brilliant, all-powerful, melancholy and tender son of the gods Achilles, that *enfant gâté* of nature (...) and you will find that the character is a miracle of art.'[20]

These quotations are from two short texts written by Hölderlin, with the title 'On Achilles' added by another hand, and they are eloquent with ardent idealism and the enthusiasm for Greece in the Europe of Hölderlin's time as exemplified by the great German scholar and art historian Winckelmann. But perhaps it is fair to think that Hölderlin's aesthetic feeling suspended his moral judgement here. Otherwise it is hardly imaginable that he would not have mentioned his great hero's frenzied rage and abandonment of all the moral rules of war. Instead he metaphorically described Achilles' rejection of all that he himself had previously considered right conduct as the onslaught of a terrible thunderstorm breaking, after which peace and calm return, and the hero is even reconciled to Priam. 'This last scene is heavenly, after all that went before.' At least we cannot but agree with that last remark; the meeting of Priam and Achilles once the latter has recovered his humanity and equilibrium is undoubtedly a very moving episode.

The factor disregarded in Hölderlin's aesthetic judgement is described by the American psychiatrist Jonathan Shay, in an extensive study of 'Combat Trauma and the Undoing of Personality' (the wording of the subtitle of his book) as the state of mind of American soldiers in the Vietnam war, which he compares with the devastation wrought in Achilles by the Trojan war, at least intermittently.[21] In both cases, something similar happened: the warrior was transformed into a berserker who kills indiscriminately and with joy, desecrates corpses, rejects every kind of softer feeling, throws every vestige of pity overboard and leaves behind all the stirrings of conscience. A prerequisite for such a transformation, says Shay, is the fundamental violation of decent behaviour, in the case of Achilles the mortal insult offered to him by Agamemnon when he withdrew the gift of the maiden Briseis. Then the killing of his friend Patroclus acted as the trigger of violence.

But here, on the tumulus named after the Greek hero, we can forget bloodthirsty associations in reading the passage on the tomb of Achilles in Byron's *Don Juan*:

There, on the green and village-cotted hill, is
(Flank'd by the Hellespont, and by the sea)
Entomb'd the bravest of the brave, Achilles;
They say so – (Bryant says the contrary):
And further downward, tall and towering still, is
The tumulus – of whom? Heaven knows, 't may bed
Patroclus, Ajax, or Protesilaus,
All heroes who if living still would slay us.[22]

Byron spent several weeks in the Troad in 1810. He made notes of
his impressions of the landscape in letters and journals, and brought
them into his great verse epic *Don Juan.* In the parenthesis he briefly
refers to the great dilemma in Homeric studies, one that has lasted to
the present day: is there any historical basis for Troy and the Trojan
War? Does the *Iliad* have any real background or is it pure fiction?
In a dissertation of 1796, Jacob Bryant rejected all theories that the
Homeric epic had any historical value or indeed contained any local
references, thus incurring the righteous anger of Byron the great
Romantic poet. Even then, when Troy/Hisarlik had not yet been
discovered, the plain of the Scamander was regarded by many as the
scene of Homer's story, and for Byron its reflection in the epic was
beyond question. Eleven years after his visit to the Troad he could
still write angrily of the pedantic scholar Bryant: 'We do care about
"the authenticity of the tale of Troy". I have stood upon that plain
daily, for more than a month, in 1810; and if any thing diminished
my pleasure, it was that the blackguard Bryant impugned its veracity
(...) But I have still venerated the great original as the truth of *history*
(in the material facts) and of *place*. Otherwise it would have given
me no delight.'[23]

'The authenticity (...) of *place*' is an encouraging idea for those
trying to distinguish the realistic basis of Homer's poetry from its
transformation into the epics. In his study of the landscapes of Troy
and Ithaca, Luce aims to show that the 'authenticity of place' is a
vital part of Homer's work.'[24] If it is true that the poet Homer, who
was presumably acquainted with the Troad, described images of its
landscape in the *Iliad*, then Homeric views are offered all around the
place known as the tomb of Achilles, modern Sivri Tepe. They extend
from Hisarlik with the citadel of Pergamos of *sacred Ilion,* over the
sea to the island of Bozcaada, in antiquity Tenedos, from the outposts
of the mountains and Kesik Tepe as the observations posts of the

gods, over the river plain of the Scamander, and all the way to the nearby coast with the Fort of Heracles, and Beşıka Bay as the probable site of the Bay of Troy.

THE BAY OF TROY. The bay traces a crescent running south-east from Yassı Tepe. Already well positioned on the leeward side of the tongue of land, in earlier times it was even better sheltered from the *metelmi* or *Etesian* wind blowing strongly from the north-east because it ran a good deal further inland. Beşıka Bay was a natural harbour on the Aegean coast of the Troad – and presumably also the model for the Achaean camp and ship station in the *Iliad*. The appearance of the thousand ships of the Greek armada sailing towards the coast must have been breathtaking – at least, if we imagine a sight like that depicted in Wolfgang Petersen's 180-million-dollar film *Troy*, although in that case a few model ships were enough for the computer-enhanced image of the thousand-strong fleet, just as a few extras in armour did duty for a fighting force of ten thousand men.

As well as the early settlement on Yassı Tepe, Korfmann's excavations uncovered a large cemetery of the late Bronze Age near the coast, containing the graves of men, women and children. If we assume that Beşıka Bay was the harbour of Troy VI, it would be natural to locate the Achaean ship station here too. We may suppose that in his own period Homer knew the harbour that had been in use so long, and described it as it then existed as the place where the Greeks beached their ships in epic. One must always remember that the poet was composing his work for a public which believed in the historical authenticity of the Trojan War, and expected a realistic background which might even be known to some hearers or readers from personal experience. The problem of whether the *Iliad* can be regarded 'as a contemporary source for the location of Troy' was answered by Korfmann after many years of excavations thus: 'We can say today that all Homer's facts, so far as archaeology can evaluate them at present, are roughly correct. No one – and I refer to those interested in Homer and/or his informants, as well as modern visitors – could expect more of a place that is now in ruins.'[25]

A glance down to the flat, sandy bay from Yassı Tepe, where deep shafts are still left from Korfmann's excavations, shows that there would have been plenty of room for a large fleet of Achaean warships – which depending on their shape and weight could have been hauled up on shore by human hands without too much trouble – and that a coastline running several hundred metres inland before the terrain began to rise slightly was a good place to range them in rows behind each other:

> First ships ashore they'd hauled up on the plain
> then built a defence to landward off their sterns.
> Not even the stretch of beach, broad as it was,
> could offer berths to all that massed armada,
> troops were crammed in a narrow strip of coast.
> So they had hauled their vessels inland, row on row,
> while the whole shoreline filled and the bay's gaping mouth
> enclosed by the jaws of the two jutting headlands.

(I, F 14, 30).

The contingents brought by Odysseus and Agamemnon were in the middle, those of Achilles and Ajax at the sides. A large defensive wall surrounded the ship station and the dwellings of the camp that were erected as the years went on. On the other side of the wall, facing Troy, according to the *Iliad*, a trench secured with stakes was dug to act as a barrier to the Trojan war chariots.

Luce, as mentioned above, prefers to see the site of the camp with the beached ships on the slope below Kesik Tepe, which falls away slightly to the plain of the Menderes. However, one factor in favour of Beşika Bay is the nautical conditions prevailing in the Dardanelles, known to have existed there ever since shipping first used the strait: a surface current of fresh water coming from the streams flowing into the Black Sea makes for Aegeas at a speed of up to five knots, and meets a deep and very salty counter-current flowing towards the Sea of Marmora. Every summer, in addition, from May to September, the whistling Etesian winds rise, dry and generally blowing from the north-east, dying down only for a few days. It was only on such days that Bronze Age ships, which were unable to sail against the wind, could have run into the Dardanelles and the bay reaching almost all the way to Troy.[26] Few long sea voyages were made in the months of October to April during antiquity because of the possibility of storms. How sensible would it have been for the Achaean attackers to choose to draw their ships up on land and make their camp in a bay that they could leave only in certain conditions, and to which they could return only with difficulty? Surely Beşika Bay would have been a better point of departure for the Greeks as they mounted attacks on the islands off the countryside of the Troad during the long years of the siege.

THE TOMB OF FESTUS. If the Greek hero Achilles had been a shining example to Alexander the Great, Alexander of Macedon himself was an example to the Roman emperor Caracalla. Because the nearby tumulus was thought to be the tomb of Achilles, Alexander had regarded Beşıka Bay as the Greeks' harbour and landing place near Troy, and therefore so did Caracalla later. And since Alexander's great hero Achilles had organized such lavish funeral games for his dead friend Patroclus, Caracalla too had to hold a funeral ceremony when he visited Troy as a tourist. In fact his companion and friend, his favourite Festus, was not yet dead, far from it. But as there can be no funeral games without a funeral, Caracalla had Festus poisoned, arranged a magnificent funeral for his dear friend and buried him in an existing stone structure converted into a grave mound. The tumulus of Festus, now known as Üvecik Tepe, lies south-east of Sivri Tepe, divided from it by some strips of fields and small woods. You leave the road going to the village of the same name, passing a tumble-down enclosure for goats covered with corrugated iron, devoid of any pastoral charm but for the white, black and piebald goats themselves, who stand at several long drinking-troughs knocked together from wooden planks and placed on stones in the adjoining open terrain, you cross a field and go through some bushes up to the small rise of the tumulus, from which there are many different views of the Troad.

Üvecik is a village like many in the Troad, similar to Yeniköy, Kumkale, Halileli, Dümrek, Tevfikye, Ciplak, Kalafat, Pınarbaşı. There is much seasonal activity in these villages. At harvest time the village squares and main streets are full of tractors, trailers and trucks. You see crates upon crates of tomatoes, big jute sacks brimming over with white cotton. The men are busy, groups of women wait by the roadside to help bring in the harvest. Old ladies sit on the ground outside their front doors and watch the hurry and bustle. School is out, and the boys and girls run home. In their smart school uniforms they are a striking contrast to the women, most of whom still wear traditional dress and are almost as colourful as the *çingene* people, the Turkish gypsies, who can be seen here and there, for instance camping beside a garbage tip on the outskirts of the village of Kalafat. At a swift glance the eye is caught by gypsy women and girls in flower-patterned skirts and brightly coloured headscarves, not pulled as far down over their foreheads as the village women wear them. Attractive reed baskets made for shopping stand around. A man sitting on a shabby rug is weaving a basket, sheltered by a handsome sunshade also made of reeds and adorned with red flowers. But on closer inspection the poverty of the gypsies is soon obvious. No caravans, no cars; poor huts, rickety wooden structures, covered with sheets of plastic or tarpaulin for the short time the gypsies will stay.

THE WASHING PLACE. Schliemann looked in vain for anywhere that could be identified with the famous washing place of the Trojan women. Homer describes it in presenting a contrast between peace and war:

> ...washing pools
> where the wives of Troy and all their lovely daughters
> would wash their glistening robes in the old days,
> the days of peace before the sons of Achaea came ...
>
> (I, F 22, 150).

The time of peace in Troy before the war is briefly conjured up as a melancholy memory when the pursuit of Hector by Achilles is moving towards its tragic climax. Achilles thrusts his spear through the Trojan prince's throat as the two of them, in their fourth wild circuit of the city wall, reach the springs and the washing place. Luce thinks it is possible that these springs may have been those of the Pınarbaşı stream in the village of the same name near the Balli Dağ – still known locally today by the poetic name of Kirk Göz, 'forty eyes'. Four of them look at you from a rocky slope near Pınarbaşı, where quiet, silvery springs run down and change the terrain at the foot of the hill into a little garden of Eden, beginning with moss and grass bravely growing on the edge of a pool where the ground underfoot is still stony, and continuing past islands of water plants to the other side of the pool, where reeds sway, tall poplars grow, and there is a green field nearby.

However, even leaving aside the enormous distance that Hector and Achilles would have had to cover fast and on foot – some 79 kilometres in all, given the distance of ten kilometres between Troy/ Hisarlik and Pınarbaşı – a discovery made in 1997 suggests another site for the Homeric 'springs and washing pools'. A few hundred metres outside the citadel of Troy, where the ridge of the hill of Hisarlik falls gently to the south-west and the plain, Korfmann and his team found a system of water-bearing tunnels and caves, with stone hollows on the outside, and already laid out in the early 3rd century BC. A fig tree with dense foliage stands here. In its shade lies the entrance (walled up except for a small opening after the end of the excavations) to a cave with springs and a tunnel driven at least 160 metres into the rock, an aqueduct ensuring the city's water supply.

Outside the entrance, there are four hollows in the rock, and on the ground a narrow channel leads to a basin of water dating from Roman times. In Korfmann's opinion this place could well be described as a washing pool, or at least used for that purpose.[27] He thinks that the cave with the spring was still in use in Homer's time, and it is easy to imagine the scene.

TROY. Now we come to the last location in the Troad, on the spot that Homer may have envisaged as a gallery from which the Trojan aristocracy could watch the course of the battle, the famous lookout post where they looked down from the walls, and where the heartrending scenes that accompanied the death of Hector took place. I mean the area around citadel gate VI U of Troy VI, a few metres in front of the largest and best preserved building in the lower ring of terraces, palace VI M. Its sloping supporting wall, divided up by four jagged edges, gives a clear idea, even to an eye without much archaeological experience, of the structure of Trojan palaces, as they have been graphically shown, at least in virtual terms, in recently published computer-simulated images.[28] The city wall ran parallel to the wall of this palace. Strategically speaking, its gate (VI U), the way out to the plain of the Scamander, was the best place for an attack on the citadel area. For at this point the buffer zone of the lower city, between the open plain and the wall of the acropolis, was at its narrowest, and in addition, as earlier excavations had already shown, the ancient wall must have been in poor condition. In Korfmann's opinion that fact must also have been obvious to Homer's contemporaries centuries later.[29] The archaeologist Dorpfeld also suggested that the place in the wall which Andromache recommends to her husband Hector as offering the best protection (Book 6, 433) could have had a real-life counterpart in the same part of the wall around Gate VI U.

Is the gate in the south-west of the city wall of Troy VI, dating from the thirteenth century BC and so unassumingly labelled by that archaeological abbreviation, the model for the legendary Scaean Gate in the *Iliad*? Schliemann identified the Scaean Gate with the entrance in a wall of the citadel reached by way of the famous stone ramp that is one of the most impressive sights to have been found in the excavations. But he had not uncovered the Troy of the 'Trojan War'; according to the later system of classification, he had excavated Troy II, which is 1250 years older. The Scaean Gate of the *Iliad* cannot have been here. But not far away, about 40 metres to the south-west, is Gate VI U, walled up later. The patchwork job done on the masonry here is obvious even to the layman's eye. There are good arguments for seeing this as the Scaean Gate and the wall described in Books 3, 6, 21 and 22 of the *Iliad*, although it is true that there was no tower in this section of the fortifications.

Stirring scenes take place at the Scaean Gate. Seeing the attacking Achaeans, Andromache pleads with her husband Hector not to go into the battle, for Achilles has already killed her father and all her seven brothers earlier in the poem. Hector, with his strong sense of duty, tells her that he can do no other but *take my place in the front line* (I, R 6, 446). However, it is clearly hard for him not to do as she wishes. In a touching scene Hector says goodbye to his wife and his little son Astyanax, who screams with fright at the sight of his father's great plumed helmet.

> And his loving father laughed,
> his mother laughed as well, and glorious Hector
> quickly lifting the helmet from his head,
> set it down on the ground, fiery in the sunlight,
> and raising his son he kissed him, tossed him in his arms.
>
> (I, F 6, 562).

Also deeply moving is the scene describing Priam and Hecuba on the wall, wailing and lamenting, tearing their hair and shedding tears as they bare their breasts in their attempt to keep their son Hector from a fight that he cannot win against Achilles; they have to watch him chased three times round the city by his powerful enemy, past the washing pools with the springs which, when he reaches the place for the fourth time, will be the scene of his death.

No less fascinating, if in a different way, is the so-called 'viewing from the wall' or teichoscopy of Book 3. No fighting between the opposing armies has yet taken place, and there is a proposition that the war should be decided by single combat between Menelaus and Paris. Priam and the city elders sit on a tower by the Scaean Gate, where they consult together while keeping an eye on what has happened. Helen appears, to the admiring murmurs of the assembled crowd. Priam asks her, in friendly tones, to tell him the names of the Greek heroes who can be seen from the city. Helen replies, *That man is Atreus' son Agamemnon, lord of empires*, and she also points out Ajax and *godlike Idomeneus*. The old man asks again, *Come, dear child, tell me of that one too – now who is he?* (I, F 3, 191).

'That one', Odysseus, is described at much greater length than the others, almost as if Homer were intentionally announcing that he would be the central figure of a second epic. Homer describes him not just from the narrator's viewpoint but from that of three different characters. Helen gives a short account of his salient qualities and his country of origin:

> That's Laertes' son, the great tactician Odysseus.
> he was bred in the land of Ithaca. Rocky ground,
> and he's quick at every treachery under the sun –
> the man of twists and turns.

(I, F 3, 241)

Priam, on the other hand, give his immediate impressions of the physical presence of Odysseus. He is:

> Shorter than Atreus' son Agamemnon, clearly,
> but broader across the shoulders, through the chest.

(I, F 3, 234)

Finally, old Antenor, remembering an earlier visit to Troy by Menelaus and Odysseus to negotiate for the return of Helen, is emphatic about Odysseus' skill with words, which he says was in contrast to his initially unimpressive, almost sullen or stupid appearance:

> But when he let loose that great voice from his chest,
> and the words came piling on like a driving winter blizzard –
> then no man alive could rival Odysseus! Odysseus ...
> we no longer gazed in wonder at his looks.

(I, F 3, 266)

So now we have a literary picture of the man who had not really wanted to take part in the Trojan War at all, but who then, after ten years of the unsuccessful siege of Priam's fortress by the Achaeans, brought Troy to the point where it could be stormed by using the trick of the Wooden Horse, and who thus ushered in the downfall of the city. After it had fallen, he put to sea, to go home to Ithaca at long last and take his wife Penelope in his arms. But we know that his wish was not to be so easily fulfilled. He would have to spend another ten years far from his native land, pursued by the vengeful wrath of Poseidon, he would have to perform superhuman feats to survive the many kinds of dangers to which he found himself exposed on his wanderings.

Mention of the Wooden Horse reminds us to look at another scene, one that reappears at the beginning of the voyage home of Odysseus' squadron. There is a wide view of the landscape of Troad from the western wall of the citadel over the Scaean Gate, all the way to the mouth of the Menderes in the Dardanelles and the Segeum Ridge on the coast of the Aegean, a view of the rising land of Yass Tepe, Sivri Tepe and Üvecik Tepe. Green and yellow fields are spread out in rectangles, divided by the green strips of trees on the river banks, and beyond, to the south-west, we can see the outline of the island of Bozcaada.

The ancient name, Tenedos, can still be read on the modern map and tourist brochure for this small island only a few kilometres south-west of Beşıka Bay, as well as its modern Turkish name. Myth and history go back a long way. If Herodotus is to be believed, its first inhabitants were Pelasgians. One King Tenos ruled on Tenedos when the Achaean fleet approached Troy and first cast anchor off the island. To prevent an occupation, he threw blocks of stone down on the Greek ships from a cliff. Achilles immediately responded by killing the king. He then swam ashore, and the Greeks, following him, laid Tenedos waste. From this base, a delegation consisting of Menelaus, Odysseus and Palamedes set out for Troy to demand the return of Helen. When the Trojans refused, the Greeks moved their fleet to the Trojan coast, and the siege of sacred Ilion began. It ended ten years later, as ordained by the will of the gods, with the storming and destruction of Troy.

It was Odysseus' idea to make the Trojans believe that the Greeks, frustrated by the failure of their siege, had destroyed their own camp and set off for home, leaving a great wooden horse on the shore as an offering to Athene. In fact, on the directions of Odysseus, Agamemnon moved the entire Greek fighting forces to the coast of the island of Tenedos that did not face Troy.

The horse was hauled into the city on Priam's orders, in spite of urgent warnings from his daughter the priestess Cassandra and the priest Laocoon. At a secret sign from a beacon lit by the tomb of Achilles, the ships set out from Tenedos to the Trojan shore. The soldiers moved swiftly forward, the gate was open, and a blood-bath ensued, a massacre, rapes, destruction, the city was burned and its people enslaved. It was the end of sacred Ilion.

Athene, offended by the rape of her priestess Cassandra by Locrian Ajax in her temple, now sowed discord between Agamemnon and Menelaus. There were angry quarrels in the council they held about the timing of the Achaean army's departure. While the Atreides brothers were still at odds, Nestor and Odysseus sailed to Tenedos, where they sacrificed to the gods. However, Odysseus and his men turned back as a favour to Agamemnon. After hundreds of cattle had finally been sacrificed to mollify the angry goddess Athene, all those who were still on the Trojan shore put out to sea.

Unlike the other groups Odysseus and his squadron of twelve ships, with crews comprising some five hundred men, did not sail straight for home, but went first to Ismarus, the city of the Cicones. Since antiquity this has been considered to lie near the Alexandroupolis district in the easternmost part of Greek Thrace, close to the Turkish border.

But the victors were not blessed with good fortune any more than the vanquished. From the first, their homecoming was under an unlucky star. It is only later, in the *Odyssey* (Book 3, 132), that we learn of the fate of the Achaeans after the fall of Troy, when Menelaus tells the story of their departure from the Trojan shore to Telemachus, who is visiting his court in Sparta to see if he can discover any clue to the whereabouts of his father Odysseus. Only King Nestor of Pylos, presented as the sole humane and god-fearing character among the leaders, came home to a happy ending. The other heroes of the war died either while they were still in Troy or on the voyage, while some met with an unnatural end soon after coming home, or ate the bitter bread of exile, or reached home only after long and laborious years of wandering. Among these last were Menelaus and Helen, whose voyage lasted eight years before they returned to Sparta, and Odysseus, who came home only ten years after the fall of Troy.

BOZCAADA. Half an hour's journey by ferry from the coast of the Troad brings us to the main town on the island of Bozcaada. We do not know quite what to expect – perhaps a poor fishing village on a rocky, deserted island? On coming closer, the view is one of a lively harbour full of small steamers, fishing-boats and sailboats, surrounded by neat houses and dominated by a fine castle with well-maintained, handsome walls. And once on land we have the pleasure of wandering along alleys with attractive shops alternating with pleasant bars – and a series of shops offering plenty of the main product of the island, wine. But let us leave the lively little harbour behind and cross the island until a gravel path brings us to its westernmost point, where there is a lighthouse at the end of a row of huge windmills with their white sails turning. An almost white line of cliffs falling precipitously to the sea borders the flat area of the island in the west where the windmills stand, moves curving on, bay after bay – one of them with slopes of grapevines growing in a gently rising hollow – to the south-eastern point of the island. The eastern coastline up to the harbour of Bozcaada is full of so many curving bays and foothills that from above it must look like a festoon.

But only the bays on the western coast of Tenedos would have offered concealment from view – the land rises a good hundred metres above sea level – and at the same time shelter from the Etesian winds. Here the Greek squadrons would have been well hidden from keen Trojan eyes looking for them. After landing at Hebbele Plaji or Sulubahce Plaji or Ayazma Plaji, they would also have had a good opportunity to fill their leather wineskins. The vineyards are not far away, and Turkish viticulturists, who took over from the old tradition of Greek wine-growing in 1920, have used the Greek growers' experience. You can taste some excellent vintages here.

In the evening, we sit on a folded fishing-net in the hurry and bustle as the ferry is prepared for departure. The muezzin calls to prayer, but hardly any of the crowd remember their Muslim duty, which is hardly surprising in view of the cheerful comings and goings in the streets and inns and the lavishly stocked wine shops. And what a sight the trucks are, brimming over with plump, dark grapes! Could Odysseus and his companions have taken advantage of similar offers? Perhaps, if it was the vintage season, they could even have joined in the vigorous treading of the grapes, and shouted with glee to see the red liquid spurt – juice this time, not blood. At least they would have had a good chance to stock up well with wine. If they did, they might have enjoyed one last happy and carefree celebration after all the slashing, stabbing and murdering. For once they had set sail, a journey with a deadly end lay ahead. Only one man was to escape alive, Odysseus himself, the hero whose homecoming Homer describes in the *Odyssey*. The poet could draw on the whole complex of stories about Odysseus that had come down to him from a long oral tradition of singers, making them into his own version of the tale with supreme skill. And over 2700 years after the composition of that great poem, Odysseus is still alive to us today. Writers and poets from the time of classical antiquity to the present day have celebrated, questioned or condemned that complex character in many meditations on his story and reflections of it, as a theme for allegories and parallel stories, as a paradigm of the archetypal hero, the exile, the Utopian, the unscrupulous egotist or the bold inquirer.

Achaean Bandits

Ismarus – *Alexandroupolis*

ALEXANDROUPOLIS. A flock of hundreds of gulls, swooping furiously through the air above the silvery foam-topped waves in our wake, accompanies the ferry from Samothrace to Alexandroupolis. Chains of hills rise behind the harbour town, coming right down to the sea: the outlying parts of the Rodopi mountains. In front of them lies a strip of fields extending east and north in the belt of wetlands along the great river Evros – Ergene in Turkish – that forms the frontier between Greece and Turkey. This part of the countryside is patterned in green and light brown. Are the light brown parts stubble fields and the green ones vineyards? In antiquity, Thrace was known far and wide for the horses bred there, its fertile soil and its good wine. If Homer meant Thrace, not far from the Troad, when he spoke of the land of the Cicones, and identified the Cicones themselves with a Thracian tribe, he put high praise for the vintages grown there into the mouth of his protagonist. The scene comes at the court of the Phaeacian king Alcinous, and Odysseus is describing the crucial part played by the wine of Ismarus when he and his men escaped from the cave of Polyphemus:

> I picked out my dozen finest fighters
> and off I went. But I took a skin of wine along,
> the ruddy, irresistible wine that Maron gave me once,
> Euanthes' son, a priest of Apollo, lord of Ismarus.

(O, F 9, 216)

What an aroma wafted from the bowl, Odysseus tells us; it was *a drink fit for the gods,* and it is praised by the Cyclops himself as *nectar, ambrosia – this flows from heaven!* before Odysseus gets him drunk on it as a prelude to putting his eyes out.

It is disappointing, on close examination of the agricultural land surrounding Alexandroupolis, to see not a single vine. But it seems that there were still many vineyards half a century ago, hence the still traditional summer vintage festivals, although no local wines are drunk. So in one of the many bars along the harbour promenade we have to make do with the delightful illusion that we are enjoying a *drink fit for the gods* made in the area – although drunk neat and not, like the wines of Homeric days, which must presumably have had a much higher alcohol content, diluted with water, usually in a proportion of 1:20 – and watching the people who, on a Saturday evening, crowd along the wide street reserved for motor traffic in the daytime on the way home. This is the *volta*, the leisurely ritual of an evening stroll. There is not a free seat left in the many open-air restaurants looking out on the harbour, with a giant wheel turning colourfully in front of the sea.

The place was not always as peaceful and cheerful as it is this Saturday evening. It was a black day for the people of Ismarus when Odysseus and his companions, on their way from Troy, fell on the town like bandits. The townsmen were murdered,

> ... but as for the wives and plunder,
> that rich haul we dragged away from the place –
> we shared it round so that no one, not on my account,
> would go deprived of his fair share of spoils.
> Then I urged them to cut and run, set sail,
> but would they listen? Not those mutinous fools,
> there was too much wine to swill, too many sheep to slaughter
> down along the beach, and shambling longhorn cattle.
>
> (O, F 9, 46).

The priest of Apollo with his wife and children were spared, for the sake of the god, and he showed his gratitude with many gifts, including twelve wine pitchers. On the only pictorial representation of the Ismarus episode – on an elegant red-figure crater or mixing bowl of about 370 BC in the Museum of Lipari – we see the priest Maron giving Odysseus a full wineskin. Odysseus has spread his arms to receive the gift which was to mean survival in the adventure with the Cyclops.

Word of the attack soon spread. The Cicones, well-practised in fighting on foot and from chariots, gathered and prepared to inflict a bitter defeat on the Achaean robbers and murderers. Six of the crew of every one of the twelve ships on which they had put out to sea from Troy were left for dead on the field of dishonour. The others fled to the ships.

THE EVROS DELTA. The losses might have been even greater if Odysseus and his men had not (undeservedly) been lucky enough to get a north wind that helped them to escape from the danger area of the beach of Ismarus. But cloud-gathering Zeus did not send a pleasant, favouring wind – the men who laid waste cities, slaughtered men and raped women were not to escape him so easily. Instead, a mighty hurricane drove black clouds over land and sea, made it look as if night were falling, and ripped the sails of the ships to shreds. Rowing hard, they reached *the nearest shoreline* (O, F 9, 82). Homer does not give the name or location of this part of the shore.

We may picture it as a nearby country area where the men soon found shelter from the raging sea in the bend of a waterway or in a lagoon – for instance, somewhere in the extensive Evros delta southeast of Alexandroupolis. Today this place, one of the largest and most important biotopes in Europe, is designated a specially protected wetland area, full of countless waterways, and with lagoons and lakes offering permanent habitats to forty-six species of fish, forty different mammals, twenty-eight species of reptiles and amphibians and three hundred and sixteen bird species, as well as resting and overwintering places for millions of migratory birds. Might it not also have been a good place for the fugitives from Ismarus to wait for the hurricane to die down?

Agriculture is still possible on the outskirts of the delta, where cotton, vegetables and tobacco are grown. Then the salt-marshes begin, with two main arms of the waterway flowing through them, and many channels fed by lagoons which provide food for the fish that grow up there and return to the freedom of the sea to spawn – a biological chain living on the exchange between sea-water, the river and rain-water. This region is not really spectacular. Its beauty lies in its broad extent, all the way to the distant Turkish hills and the sea, and the peace and isolation to be found here. At one place, where paths divide, there is a locked log cabin, and beside a lagoon an empty house that looks deserted may perhaps be used only occasionally by the fishermen whose boats rock on the water here. For a long time I am entirely alone on my way to the delta, and then as I walk through t along the paths on the embankments. Then I see a truck standing by the broad, slowly flowing western arm of the Evros just before it reaches the sea. The driver sleeps in his cab until a boat puts in beside the sandy bank. The fisherman wakes the driver, gives him his catch, two crates of assorted fish that are put on ice at once, and the man lies down to sleep again until the next boat arrives.

Where pelicans, flamingos, swans, many other birds and even the imperial eagle feel at home, it is easy to imagine an emergency camp for seamen who must find shelter from stormy seas and wait there awhile. There are plenty of sheltered shorelines on the banks of the Evros and the lagoons that connect with the sea. Odysseus and his men had to wait two tedious days and nights.

> When Dawn with her lovely locks brought on the third day,
> then stepping the masts and hoisting white sails high,
> we lounged at the oarlocks, letting wind and helmsman
> keep us true on course ... And now at long last
> I might have reached my native land unscathed ...
>
> (O, F 9, 85).

But as we know, that hope was deceptive. The same wind that had saved the men homeward bound from potential annihilation would soon prevent their safe return, and, and the author was to send Odysseus on a ten-year journey.

This wind will have been one of the Etesians, the 'annual winds' that regularly blow over the Aegean from the north during summer, sucked in by the thin air over the southern Mediterranean and the North African deserts, and now letting out their hot breath high above. Perhaps it was the north-easterly Gregotramounta, or its neighbour the Tramountana blowing only from the north – the Boreas of classical antiquity, and it is in fact called *boréis* in the *Odyssey* – that finally blew the ships right across the Aegean. By what route? And how long did it take? Homer says not a word about that. We are told only, laconically, in the lines directly after the passage above:

> But just as I doubled Malea's cape, a tide-rip
> and the North Wind drove me way off course
> careering past Cythera.
>
> (O, F 9, 87).

CAPE MALEA. Odysseus was now approaching the southern end of the eastern protrusion of the Peloponnese, where the Parnon mountains run through it. The massive block of the mountainous promontory known as Minoa in antiquity – with what today is the Byzantine settlement of Monemvasia on its southern slope – lay on the starboard side, with sharply ridged Cape Malea. In good conditions it would have been easy for the ships to navigate around the cape, pass Aphrodite's island of Cythera and reach the Laconian Gulf, passing first the supposed site of Hades, Cape Tainaron, and then Cape Acritas, and thus reaching home waters, the Ionian Sea, and come into their home harbour of Ithaca at long last.

But up to the age of steam Cape Malea often proved perilous to seamen, and it still demands respect even from big modern container ships. Tricky currents and strong winds frequently forced vessels of course, or even flung them on the steep, sharp rocks and shattered them. The Greeks still call Cape Malea 'swallower of wood' because of the many ships stranded there.

Odysseus and his companions had a strong north wind at their backs when they drew level with the cape. Here a current running east to west also met them sideways on, as sea charts show. Hard as they might row or reef in their sails, there was nothing the men homeward bound from Troy could do to counter this combination of the power of nature. They were driven south-west, past Cape Malea, past the safety of the channel into the Laconian Gulf, past Cythera.

Cape Malea, even today, is remote, as isolated as in Greece of the heroic period, far from humanity. Gythion, the last little town on the Laconian Gulf, nestles between the sea and the Koumaros Hills; the little island of Marahonisi, ancient Cranai, is in its district. This island was a transshipment centre for the Phoenician trade in purple and was the place where Paris and Helen spent the first night of their famous love affair after Helen's abduction from Sparta. Long beaches and fertile coastal plains reach to the little provincial town of Neapolis, with the foothills of the Personas mountains rising above them. The village of Aghios Nikolaos in the interior of the peninsula is the last place to which buses and taxis go. Aghia Marina, a few kilometres further on, is a collection of a few huts with only the basic necessities, with some sheds and pigsties among the rocks and in the caverns of a ravine reached here by the sea. Two bearded men are tending the goats gathered around tin troughs filled with water: poor relations of Eumaeus, Odysseus' swineherd, with his well-tended pig farm.

A rust-brown rubble road passes through the sparse *macchia* covering the steep flank of Mount Chinovracha for a while. Then there is only a narrow path winding away to its destination, visible in the distance between grey boulders, the white church of Aghia Irini. Finally, above a steep rise, we see the green of bay trees, larches, tamarisks and opuntia or Indian fig. Cube-shaped houses shelter in their shade, with the bright white dome of Aghia Irini towering up beside them on a rocky substructure that has been smoothed to form a plateau.

A flight of steps leads to a high terrace built on to the dome, the location of the free-standing belfry. It arches form airy white frames for pictures made of nothing but lucid colours, not bound to any design, and if you lean forward you have nothing around you but sea and sky in every shade from royal to Byzantine blue. It is a place where, standing high above the sea with a strong wind in your face, you can easily conjure up, from the broken cisterns lying around, a lofty sense of what we may call the cosmic. You feel jubilation, a nameless sense of happiness to which you abandon yourself, well knowing that it will pass quickly but also that it will always be memorable.

The one day in the year when the isolation here gives way to cheerful hurry and bustle is 15 June, when St Irene's Day is celebrated. Then pilgrims come on foot or by boat to this place, to abandon themselves to heavenly sensations that can quickly change to the earthly variety, and they have no difficulty in reaching a condition, light of hand and later in the day light of foot, which merges the heavenly and the earthly as one.

It would be good to be here that night, drinking and dancing, and then celebrate another notable day, if in unusual surroundings, 'Bloomsday', 16 June. Those who would like to pay tribute at Cape Malea not just to St Irene but to the sainted Homer and the sainted Joyce as well, or indeed first and foremost, can easily bridge the gap, for our destination is Cape Malea, which is not yet entirely explored once you have reached the church of St Irene. After a visit to the tiny interior of the church we must go on.

A little way further on, the path leads to a rocky barrier falling away to the sea. This really is Cape Malea. You suddenly find yourself facing a little church in a hollow, a building with no windows and spotlessly whitewashed walls, nestling among the grey rocks between which a few isolated brown and green bushes grow. Beyond the slope of the rocks lies the deep blue sea, rippling slightly, and far away there is a tiny white speck, a sailing boat that seems to be mocking all the sayings about the 'wood-swallowing' cape, so confidently has it entrusted itself to the sea. It sails on safely and unharmed.

Sweet Temptation

Land of the Lotus-Eaters – *Djerba*
Land of the Cyclops – *island of Kerkennah, Matmata region of Tunisia*

'At the moment when a storm blows Odysseus off course from Cape Malea, the most southerly point of his way home from Troy to Ithaca, and into the open sea, he (unlike the wandering Menelaus) reaches a world that is no longer part of reality but of the imagination,' writes A. Heubeck in his introduction to the *Odyssey* in the Tusculum Series.[30] Such a dismissal of the idea that any Homeric geography lies behind the wanderings of Odysseus, a geographical system going further than the passage that Odysseus missed taking between the mainland with Cape Malea and the island of Cythera, which at this point still relates to reality, expresses an opinion widely held by those who consider that there is no basis for seeing real places reflected in the poems.

But why, we may ask, would Homer have given real locations to some of the scenes in his epics, if all the other places between Cythera and Ithaca are to be seen as purely the product of the poetic imagination? Does it not seem strange to make Odysseus go from Troy, a real place, to Cape Malea, another real place, then send him on a long journey existing only in fairy-tale and fantasy, and finally provide him with real ground under his feet again back in Ithaca? The classical scholar Uvo Hölscher, although he does not support the theory that Homeric geography can be fully reconstructed, still postpones entrance into the world of fairy-tale until Odysseus reaches the Polyphemus adventure, and even sees the real wanderings as beginning only with the Aeolus episode,[31] three stages after Odysseus drifts off course at Cape Malea. What idea did Homer's audiences and readers have of direction, what sense of space and landscapes? Did they not want to know how the journey went on? Is it outlandish to suppose that after a public reading, Homer may have been asked questions: just where was his hero, where might Odysseus have landed after missing his route around Cape Malea?

The *Odyssey* tells us that after ten days at sea, Odysseus and his companions reached the land of the Lotophagi, the Lotus-Eaters. Where can it be? As the names of Crete, Egypt and Libya – mentioned elsewhere by Homer and thus presumably connected by him with some idea of great distance – do not occur in the Lotus-Eaters passage, those regions can be ruled out. In antiquity, Sirte was generally agreed to be the home of the Lotus-Eaters. But which Sirte? Greater Sirte? This is the large gulf between Benghazi and Miṣrātah in Libya, when after hundreds of kilometres of anonymous steppes as flat as a pancake, where frequent mirages seem to offer drivers the chance of driving through a shimmering haze of silver straight into the sea, the landscape finally comes to life with palms and olive trees, growing sparsely at first, then more densely until, after the magnificent ruins of the Phoenician and Roman seaport and trading centre of Leptis Magna, they form magnificent forests. Or is it Little Sirte, between Tripoli and Sfax in Tunisia? That is the general opinion, and was backed by the satirical Eratosthenes, who gave the even more precise information that the island of Djerba was the homeland of the Lotus-Eaters.

Arriving at Cape Malea, Odysseus intended to sail west around the Peloponnese by the usual route between the cape and the island of Cythera, but he was unable to do so.

> And now at long last
> I might have reached my native land unscathed,
> but just as I doubled Malea's cape, a tide-rip
> and the North Wind drove me way off course
> careering past Cythera. Nine whole days
> I was borne along by rough, deadly winds
> on the fish-infested sea. Then on the tenth
> our squadron reached the land of the Lotus-eaters,
> people who eat the lotus, mellow fruit and flower.

(O, F 9, 87).

After waves (*kima*) and the current or rip-tide (*róos*), Boreas (*boréis*) is mentioned, the sometimes stormy north wind of summer, and these are certainly the crucial factors in the parallel forces converging on Odysseus and his ship, driving it south-west across the sea until, if it did not sink first, it would surely come ashore somewhere – and that, given the geographical conditions, would be on the North African coast.

We may easily assume that such a thing happened not just in the fiction of the *Odyssey*, but again and again in real life once more and more vessels were travelling this way under the flag of Greek colonialism. And it is easy to picture seamen who survived such dangerous adventures talking about them after their safe return and exaggerating their experiences, exciting enough in themselves, to make a tale with imaginative embellishments. We also know the facts of Phoenician-dominated seafaring in the Mediterranean and then the Atlantic, with the founding of trading settlements and colonies first on the north African coast in the 9th century BC, then more particularly on Sardinia and to a lesser extent on Sicily and Malta.[32] Phoenician expansion in the Mediterranean area was followed by the great movement of Greek colonization in southern Italy and Sicily, ultimately stimulated by the close contact that the Euboean cities of Eretrea and Calcis as well as the island of Cyprus had built up with the Phoenicians, particularly in the form of the trading settlement of Al Mina that they built near the present city of Antakya (Antioch in ancient times).[33] Even before 775 BC, the close physical contact caused by common economic interests, with the demands of running the ports and the conduct of trade and commerce, led to adoption by the Greeks of Phoenician consonantal script, which they then turned into the phoneme script enriched by five vowels still in use today.

With such close contact, would we not expect other areas settled by the Phoenicians to have been mentioned as well now and then, for instance North Africa or the islands of the central Mediterranean? And would not such nautical and geographical information have come to the poet's ears? If so, it seems likely enough that when he took old fairy-tales and seamen's yarns, with their wealth of strange figures and mysterious, threatening incidents, he would have used that information to link his story to the world that his hearers knew by referring to real places.

Odysseus was driven the wrong way for nine days. *Nine days*, according to Hölscher, means just a round number of uncertain size – or is it to be understood as chronological time after all? At an average speed of 2.7 to 3 knots, Odysseus and his ships[34] could have travelled 600 to 650 sea miles in nine to ten days, just about the distance between Cape Malea and Cythera, and Sirte near Djerba.

So let us trust Eratosthenes, who with many other supporters both ancient and modern of the theory that Homeric geography is real believes it was the island of Djerba where the men succumbed to the sweet temptation of the lotus fruit. If we assume that Odysseus and his men were coming to the island from the north-east they could have made an easy landing on a whole series of beautiful beaches. Or at least, to revise that statement slightly, they could have done so up to forty years ago. When just two or three hotels stood along the twelve-kilometre beach of Sidi Mahrés, the choice would have been very wide – today there will soon be three streets with a hundred hotels. One of those original two or three hotels bore the name of the Ulysses-Palace, another the beautiful name of the island of Al Jazeera, which has entirely different connotations today. At that time only the Club Méditerranée raised its tourist head on the beach of La Seguia in the east of Djerba, a place now overwhelmingly occupied by all-inclusive club complexes. Somehow one cannot picture Odysseus mooring his ships off the beaches of Sidi Mahrés or La Seguia. But there was a better place for the wanderers to land: Ras R'mel, the promontory jutting like a hawk's beak into the sea on the north coast of Djerba, to which it is linked by a beaten mud road that is sometimes flooded or covered with sand. Ras R'mel is uninhabited, unexploited in spite of its long, sandy beaches and a dune landscape that would be just the place for romantic couples. But walking up and down the beach in the morning I see only one man, washing and grooming his horse, which obviously feels happy in the sea, another man preparing to throw out a fishing net, and two anglers sitting beside the rods they have driven into the sand. It is fine, pale yellow sand, with delicate rims of sea-foam moistening it in calm weather, and when the seas are rougher long tangles of brown seaweed are washed up.

The shore here is a perfect place to receive the seamen who were driven off course:

> We disembarked on the coast, drew water there
> and crewmen snatched a meal by the swift ships.
> Once we'd had our fill of food and drink I sent
> a detail ahead, two picked men and a third, a runner,
> to scout out who might live there – men like us perhaps,

who live on bread. So off they went and soon enough
they mingled among the natives, Lotus-eaters, Lotus-eaters
who had no notion of killing my companions, not at all,
they simply gave them the lotus to taste instead ...
Any crewmen who ate the lotus, the honey-sweet fruit,
lost all desire to send a message back, much less return,
their only wish to linger there with the Lotus-eaters,
grazing on lotus, all memory of the journey home
dissolved forever.

(O, F 9, 94).

For a meal, they could resort to their own provisions, and there was no lack of wine either. But where could they find water in the dry land of the Lotus-Eaters? That was no problem – it would have come from one of the 3770 wells and 2224 cisterns still in existence on Djerba, at least in the 1960s, quite apart from two artesian wells going 250 metres down, all of them necessary on an island where there are no springs of fresh water. Today a pipeline laid from the mainland at great expense provides enough fresh water for the wash-basins, showers, lavatories and swimming pools of the hotels and the grass, which is always green on the golf courses. There is some left over for the villages too; tankers call at isolated farms.

So the meal had been eaten, and now they wanted to find out about the land and its people. Odysseus sent three men out. Soon they met peaceful, friendly native inhabitants of the place, sitting under strange trees with tall, bare trunks from which long branches like wing feathers hung down. They offered the newcomers some of the fruits they were eating – from the tree above us, perhaps they mimed. Here was a cheerful company in which the Achaeans at once felt very much at ease after the long years of war and their strenuous and dangerous voyage since leaving Troy. And how delicious the fruits tasted, sweet as honey! After a while they felt increasingly relaxed. Their minds were freed from concentrating on orders, everyday reality and the insecurity of their situation. Their limbs relaxed. Sensations of happiness that they had not felt for a long time surfaced in them. And the three forgot what they had been sent to do, forgot to return, until Odysseus roughly wrenched them away from their psychedelic bliss, and they were taken back to the ship and thrown below decks, tied up like prisoners.

How did they come to forget their duty? Was it the effect of a drug?

What botanical species did Homer mean by the lotus, the fruit-bearing tree of the Lotus-Eaters? Was it *Celtis australis*, the hackberry or lote tree, which provides good material for wood-carving but has no special reputation as an intoxicating substance? *Ziziphus jujuba*, the Indian jujube? As a close relative of the Christ's-thorn tree, which in legend had the misfortune of being used for Christ's crown of thorns, it is unlikely. Was it the lotus as described by Herodotus? 'The lotus fruit is of the bigness of a mastich berry; it has a sweet taste like the fruit of a date palm,' he says. 'The lotus-eaters not only eat it but make wine of it.'[35] Or was it in fact the date palm? Perhaps that is the most likely, since the tree grows readily here in Little Sirte. The date palm is very much at home on Djerba and in the Gafsa oasis in the interior of Tunisia, the once legendary 'oasis by the sea' of Gabés (increasingly endangered now by massive industrialization and population growth, which call for large supplies of water). But do we need to assume that some mind-altering substance is the plausible explanation for the episode of the three Greek sailors who gave themselves up to pleasure? Do we have to imagine a circle of male Lotus-Eaters taking drugs? Surely the circumstances – a meeting with obviously peaceful and hospitable people in pleasant surroundings, the enjoyment of exotic fruits after much physical stress and deprivation in many years as soldiers – were enough to make the three men's failure to return understandable? However that may be, they were allowed only a few hours of idleness on their *dolce far niente* trip. The dream of the three dropouts was soon over, for Odysseus sternly ordered his men to continue their voyage.

> From there we sailed on, our spirits now at a low ebb …
>
> (O, F 9, 118).

THE ISLAND OF GOATS. With divine aid they now sailed through the night under cloudy skies, and made landfall before they could see, in the early morning light, that they had come to an island …

> and reached the land of the high and mighty Cyclops,
> lawless brutes, who trust so to the everlasting gods
> they never plant with their own hands or plough the soil.
>
> (O, F 9, 119).

Perhaps we may conclude from the brevity of this account that they did not have far to go to reach the land of the Cyclops. What island could it have been? The Wolfs calculate as follows: a journey time of some nine to sixteen hours, at an average speed of some four knots, means a voyage of roughly thirty-five to sixty-five sea miles.[36] If we also take into account the prevailing current of the sea off Little Sirte – coming from the north-east and drifting to the west off Djerba to spread out in the Gulf of Gabés – and if we also consult the map, then within the maximum radius of sixty-five sea miles around Sirte, only the Kerkennah Islands on the same latitude as Sfax qualify. The classical scholar Ulrich von Wilamowitz-Moellendorf did make other suggestions, placing the Lotus-Eaters on Sirte and the Cyclops on the same coast, since we may take it that the voyage between the two was quite a short one. He assumed that Odysseus was sailing west.[37]

After a good hour the ferry, full of weekend visitors coming from Sfax, approaches the harbour of Sidi Youssef on Gharbi, the finest of the five Kerkennah Islands. A small hotel on the beautiful Sidi Frej beach is quickly found, and the island waits to be explored.

An essential quality of the Kerkennah Islands, if they were the model for the Homeric 'Island of Goats', is mentioned in the first line describing it: they are flat. *Now a level island stretches flat across the harbour* (O, F 9, 129.) Almost entirely flat, flat as a pancake with only a few slight rises. And so is the surrounding sea: it is shallow for a long way around the islands, with sandbanks here and there, areas that hardly know whether they are sea or land, lagoons or just ground that is sometimes flooded and lies shining silver when the floodwater drains off again, leaving a fine crust of salt. The useful aspect of these shallow waters is obvious even as you come into Sidi Yousef harbour. On both sides of the navigation channel, the surface of the water is marked by V-shaped zigzag networks like an arrow pattern, woven of palm fronds set close to each other on the bottom of the sea, like mysterious abstract symbols. However, they fulfil a very practical purpose: they are one-way streets along which the fish are driven at high tide into an enclosed space which they cannot escape.

Palm fronds – another clue to help us relate the place to the *Odyssey*. Woods grew on the island where the Achaeans landed. The tree most typical of the two main Kerkennah Islands, Gharbi and Chergui, is the date palm. The palms grow at some distance from each other, and only occasionally, when dwarf palms join their larger relations, does the impression become rather denser, almost like a forest.

If you see a flock of sheep moving in such a place, accompanied by an old shepherd wearing a thick, well-worn jacket and a scarf in spite of the great heat, we almost have our third clue – except that these are sheep, not goats. However, there will be goats to be seen elsewhere, perhaps in an attractive graveyard among palms by the sea, where they graze and keep the weeds down.

Large numbers of wild goats populated the island on which Odysseus landed, and they were a welcome catch for his men when they first explored it after waking early. They reached for bows and spears, and wished one another good hunting. Many arrows were shot, many spears thrown, and in the end nine goats had been killed for each of the twelve ships. The leader, reasonably enough, allotted his own vessel an extra goat. Then they began feasting where they had landed in the dark of night, under divine guidance, in a safe harbour.

CHERGUI. With divine help they had indeed made landfall by night, but safely, where there was ...

> no need for mooring-gear, no anchor-stones to heave,
> no cables to make fast. Just beach your keels ...
>
> (0, F 9, 151).

Flat, sandy beaches where boats and small ships can simply run in, or be pushed ashore by a few strong hands, are found in many places on Chergui, particularly on the south-east coast of the island facing the Gulf of Gabés. The difference in level is so slight that the dividing line between land and sea quickly changes. The coastline itself consists of sand, seaweed, and tough amphibian organisms that, if collected, smell of seawater for weeks. An addition to the coastal structure is the flotsam and jetsam of the modern consumer society that gets washed up there.

A man lives here by the sea, far from the nearest villages. It is difficult to guess his age. A lined, weather-beaten face with a cheerful, mischievous look, a big moustache, thick woolly cap pulled down over his ears, another sweater under his jacket, a length of cloth wrapped around his buttocks and thighs – he sits in an oriental pose on a mat under an airy awning made from pieces of driftwood with a couple of blankets thrown over them, crowing out loud in his hoarse voice, words coming swiftly from his toothless mouth as he expresses his pleasure in the preparation of a festive meal. Two men have brought him a piece of meat, and now it is being cooked in a battered pot with chopped vegetables. The hearth consists of three stones surrounding some charcoal; he is self-sufficient in fuel. He runs a small charcoal-burning business here on the beach. A few metres from the hearth is his kiln, with smoke rising from it. The raw material is visible in the background: as if they were the last remains of some ruined temple, palm trunks with their branches stripped away rise like columns from the flat ground, all that is left of what was once a little wood of palm trees. The old man uses their timber in his modest business. He does not seem to be particularly keen on tidiness and good order. Plastic bags, buckets, rags, empty sacks, tin plates – all his things are scattered around him, and he himself, in the centre of this little chaos, seems very much amused. His real home stands nearby, a hut barely the height of a man with a flat roof of corrugated iron and pieces of wood, held down by stones, the walls made of reed matting, blankets and sackcloth, all tied together with rope. His meal is more frugal than the feast eaten by the Achaeans, and as a devout Muslim he has no sweet red wine from Ismarus, but a canister of water to drink. And if days pass before anyone brings him meat again, perhaps to be bartered for charcoal, he will feed himself in the interim on what the fish trap brings him. For the rest he will murmur or crow – depending on his mood – *mektub*, 'it is written', with his toothless, twisted mouth. He has got by with that magic word to the present day.

Homer really speaks of a 'harbour' where the Achaean ships landed without any difficulty. But on an uninhabited island the word may also designate a bay. At all events, it was a place that was suitable for one of the low-built Homeric ships to run in to the beach.

In the harbour of El Attaya in the north of the island of Chergui, the eye is caught by tens of thousands of earthenware jars, all alike, shaped like amphorae and with pointed ends, tied together by cords as if on a chain and fitted into one another in piles of ten or fifteen at a time, so that they made a tent-shaped wall of vessels, ochre in front of the deep blue sea, a hundred metres long from one end of the quay wall to the other – a striking sculptural arrangement. However, they were not intended as a work of art. Until recently the people of the Kerkennah Islands lived mainly by fishing, and to this day one of their favourite methods is to put out these jars in the evening. Being hollow, they entice octopus and squid to go into them by night, and the fish can be taken out with a hook next morning. Using a creature's natural instinct to kill it more easily next day sounds almost like a trick worthy of the wily Odysseus himself. But back to that harbour or bay:

> And last, at the harbour's head
> there's a spring that rushes fresh from beneath a cave
> and black poplars flourish round its mouth.

(O, F 9, 154).

This passage does present difficulties, for there is nothing like a spring on the Kerkennah Islands. Without such springs of fresh water, they have to make do with what has seemed practical and useful: the *fsakia,* a large, slightly slanting surface, made of earthenware in the past, of concrete today, on which the rare and valuable water from any rainfall is caught and led to a cistern. Had anyone thought up this good idea in Homeric times? Presumably so, for the problem of a lack of springs of fresh water has always been present, and the archipelago was inhabited in times of antiquity.

Attractive remains are found on the beach of Sidi Frej, where the island has its closest thing to Mount Everest – a rocky rise a breathtaking thirteen metres high, crowned with the Spanish fort of El Hassar. From here the main island of Chergui shows its most attractive side, with gently curving bays where the spotlessly white cubes and domes of some small villas and hotels stand in groves of palm trees. And directly below the fortress, where the land falls gently to the sea, are the ruins of Punic and above all Roman buildings, with mosaic floors showing through under a layer of dust. However, any attempt to clear them of some of the dust to get a better view arouses the displeasure of a guard sitting on the wall of the fort and dangling his legs. But the total impression is enough for me to imagine that the former inhabitants tried to make up for their isolated life, far from busy cities, by living in beautiful villas with a wonderful position on the beach.

The Kerkennah Islands were a Phoenician base, the place to which Hannibal retreated after losing the battle of Zama against Publius Cornelius Scipio in 202 BC. Since Roman times the archipelago has been a place of exile, but also, because of its position as an outpost, it has been desired and fought for as a strategically important place. Which means that there was always a shortage of water, there were no springs, so some way of surmounting the problem had to be found, hence the *fsakia*. And with a certain willingness to overlook details, and a little narrowing of the eyes, one can look at the opening in the curved cistern, towering above the smooth surface of the *fsakia* like half a barrel, and transform it poetically into the pretty natural surroundings of a spring bubbling out of a grotto.

THE LAND OF THE CYCLOPS. When Odysseus and his companions were sitting beside the sea, feasting, they saw smoke rising from the land of the Cyclops across the water, and even heard the bleating of sheep and goats. How was that possible, in view of a line in Book 9 of the *Odyssey* telling us that the country of the Cyclops was not close? But one should quote accurately: a reservation is implied in the 'neither ... nor' construction of the original Greek (using *oute*, a word still found in modern Greek).

> A level island stretches flat across the harbour
> not close inshore to the Cyclops' coast, not too far out.
>
> (O, F 9, 129).

So it is difficult to decide just how close it is, until a deciding factor makes the pendulum come down on the likelihood of its being not too far away. First the men land on the beach to sleep. Next morning, after Odysseus has held a meeting to discuss the situation, he decides to cross to the land of the Cyclops with a few men and find out who lives here. While the others stay behind with the ships, he and his party set off.

> As soon as we reached the shore I mentioned – no long trip –
> we spied a cavern just at the shore, gaping above the surf,
> towering, overgrown with laurel.
>
> (O, F 9, 201).

This suggests that the land of the Cyclops must be close to the Island of Goats, though it may seem an exaggeration to say that Odysseus and his men could actually hear the bleating of goats and sheep. But assuming that a distance of some twenty kilometres between the furthest point of the island and the mainland at Sfax does not exceed the suggestion implied by 'not too far out', then we still have to locate the cave of Polyphemus on that stretch of coast in the country of the Cyclops – at least if we demand reality and the text of the epic to reflect each other perfectly. Then we would have trouble with the Wolfs' theory that cave dwellings of the Berbers living in the mountainous Matmata region may be seen as the models for the cave of Polyphemus. It is about 150 kilometres from the coast at Sfax to Matmata in the south, and moreover the site in the northern Dahar mountain chain is almost forty kilometres from the sea as the crow flies. So we should be wary of immediately identifying the home of the Cyclops with any of the cave dwellings of the Matmata Berbers; on the other hand, the Wolfs point out that in prehistoric times the settlement area of the Berbers and thus the terrain occupied by their caves was considerably larger than today.

If you want to keep the relationship between factual and literary reality in mind, you have to look further afield. Demanding everything to be in tune, like Beckmesser in Wagner's *Die Meistersinger* would be to deny the sovereign power of the poet. Denial of the connection between the *Iliad* and the *Odyssey* themselves by the German scholar Karl Lachman, who founded his argument on topographical and psychological inconsistencies between the two epics, would be, as another German writer, Egon Friedell, sensibly remarked, 'to suppose that it was a poet's first duty to avoid such inconsistencies, and the prime concern of an epic poem was to present its background as a reliable tourist guide.'[38] We can feel sure that Homer himself never went to North Africa. But can we be equally sure that no account coming from the Phoenician and Punic seaports, and bearing at least some relation to reality, ever reached him in his poet's ivory tower?

MATMATA AND THE CAVE OF POLYPHEMUS. It is easy to reach the shore mentioned by Odysseus on the ferry from Sfax. But you will not spot *a cavern just at the shore, gaping above the surf*, and you will have difficulty in locating the *mountain peaks* where the Cyclops *live in arching caverns* (O, F 9, 126). You will have to travel further through a monotonous landscape, to Gabés, and then take the C107 road into the increasingly attractive Matmata region, almost like a desert but with many ravines, precipitous ridges, and terraced fields laboriously won back from their stern natural surroundings. Olive and almond trees stand proudly on these fields, often in isolation. There are pomegranate and fig trees as well, a palm here and there, perhaps a small crop of grain is grown. A high pass, and then you

lance falls on Matmata itself, spreading over several hills. It is the
est-known surviving example of a village with underground dwell-
igs, today 'a tourist centre of the mountains', with all that modern
purism brings. When we stood here in 1968, metaphors spontane-
usly suggested themselves for the picture we saw before us: it was
 lunar landscape sprinkled with craters, or perhaps a hole punched
to the earth, without vegetation, as if a meteorite shower had fallen
ere. The colour white was still rare, but marked out a few stone
uildings standing above ground and looking rather like marabouts.
oday, many white buildings spread over the sand-coloured hills,
ost of the cave-dwellers have moved out of their caves and into
ouses above ground, the place has a tourist information office, a
ost office, cafés, a courthouse, even a theatre. And young women go
bout in jeans and T-shirts with pop idols printed on them, instead
f wearing brightly coloured traditional robes and tribal marks on
heir skin. Matmata is now chic, bright with pennants, cleaned up
nd tamed for the tourist trade, and it has about ten hotels. A bus
rings tourists from Djerba.

However, I am not revisiting Matmata to give myself an oppor-
unity for cheap cultural criticism, but on account of the Cyclops.
he many caves dug into the hills are typical of the Matmata region,
lthough most of them are now uninhabited. A Matmata cave has a
entral shaft, usually circular, dropping vertically about ten metres
own; this was once the hub of domestic life for the extended family.
t the bottom of the shaft, the courtyard living area is open to the
ky, with other living-rooms and bedrooms for individual families
rouped around it, as well as storerooms and stables. You reach the
ave dwelling along a tunnel dug into the lower slope of a hill and
losed by a wooden door – or even more securely by the Cyclopean
1ethod.

> And next he drove his sleek flocks into the open vault,
> all he'd milk at least, but he left the males outside,
> rams and billy goats out in the high-walled yard.
> Then to close his door he hoisted overhead
> a tremendous, massive slab.

(O, F 9, 268).

Earlier, Odysseus and his twelve bravest companions had gone to
he cave of Polyphemus, leaving the others on the shore with their

ship. As a good herdsman, however, Polyphemus had already taken his flocks out to pasture. The men were amazed: there were baskets in the cave full of cheeses, pails and buckets brimming with whey and separate pens for lambs and kids. Odysseus' companions urged him to take some of the cheeses, drive the lambs and kids down to their ship, and put out to sea at once. But they underestimated their leader's curiosity, and even more so the instincts of a born gambler which impelled him to let an adventure go its full length, even at the risk of his life and – which should have mattered more to a responsible leader – the lives of his men.

> But I would not give way –
> and how much better it would have been –
> not till I saw him, saw what gifts he'd give.
> But he proved no lovely sight to my companions.

(O, F 9, 256).

Yet worse was to come, as they soon discovered. Their foolhardy mood turned to outright hubris as they helped themselves to some of the cheeses and waited for the Cyclops to return,

> Herding his flocks home, and lugging a huge load
> of good dry logs to fuel his fire at supper.
> He flung them down in the cave – a jolting crash –
> we scuttled in panic into the deepest dark recess.

(O, F 9, 264).

It is easy to imagine the crashing and splintering when someone arrives with a load of wood and, perhaps to save himself the trouble of carrying it, throws the timber ten metres down a shaft instead of carrying it along the tunnel and into the yard in the normal way. We can imagine our heroes there in the cave scattering in panic, taking refuge in the most distant corner, angry with their own lack of caution.

Now the Cyclops drove the goats and sheep in and put the heavy stone over the entrance. After that he went about his business as herdsman, caring tenderly for the sheep, the goats and their young. Finally he lit a fire and fell into conversation with the Greeks, who had obviously ventured a little way out again, asking who and what they were and where they came from. Next we hear Odysseus' answer, both true and false. Two of his companions were soon killed, and two more the next morning; this was a very difficult situation, and all the skills of the wily Odysseus were called for. Here we see the inventive and ingenious character admired by so many, Odysseus *polymech-anos*. When the Cyclops went out next morning:

> He left me there, the heart inside me brooding on revenge:
> how could I pay him back? Would Athena give me glory?
> Here was the plan that struck my mind as best ...
>
> (O, F 9, 355).

Through the intricately spun network of arguments, all the pros and cons, the mind of Odysseus, working fast and keenly under the threat of death, came up with the idea of getting the Cyclops drunk on the wine he had taken from the Cicones and then, while he was intoxicated, putting out his eye with his own club sharpened to a point. He would only blind him; to kill him would have been suicidal, since the Achaeans would have been left in a deadly trap of their own making with the stone over the mouth of the cave. That evening, after the return of Polyphemus from his pastures and when he had tended the animals, and then devoured two more men, the survivors put the plan into practice.

The following passages, up to the end of Book 9, are a high point in the hero's wanderings and indeed in the entire *Odyssey*. There is great dramatic tension in the account given by Odysseus as first-person narrator, and the dialogue between him and the Cyclops, while all the stages of the sometimes primeval and barbaric, sometimes coldly calculated horrors are depicted vividly and with shocking realism. We hear of Odysseus' tricks and deceptions, and at the same time our hearts are touched by the emotions of the injured, lonely Cyclops. Odysseus, coolly sarcastic in view of the situation, suggests that after enjoying a meal of human flesh the Cyclops should enhance his pleasure by washing it down with good wine; we witness the hero's ingenious deception when he gives his name as 'Nobody', a trick which will protect him from the other Cyclops; we hear the merciless account of the blinding, expressed in a simile (*As a blacksmith plunges a glowing axe or adze ...*) which brought in at this point will cynically heighten the description of the dreadful deed; and barbaric as the nature of the Cyclops may be, the blinded monster's speech to the lead ram of his flock is a deeply moving and heart-rending lament. Finally, we witness the ingenuity of Odysseus culminating in hubris as he flings insults at the injured Cyclops while he gives his alleged name of 'Nobody', but finally boasts of his own real name.

It is not surprising that of all the adventures of Odysseus in his wanderings, the dramatic tale of Polyphemus was the one with the greatest appeal to visual artists. As an idea, it was 'so impressive and new that the Greek vase painters eagerly made use of the subject.'[39] The blinding of Polyphemus was a favourite theme, and representations of it have been found in various parts of the Greek world dating from the time when the *Odyssey* first became widely known. The earliest preserved example, a proto-Attic amphora found in Eleusis and dating from 680 BC, shows the iconographic features typical of the archaic period: the stake used in the blinding is not, as described in the text, driven into it like a drill but thrust in like a spear because artists of the time had not found out how to show movement. The Cyclops is depicted half rising, and both the offering of wine and the blinding are shown, although the latter must of course have come after the former.

In the classical era, artists almost entirely stopped depicting the various aspects of the Polyphemus story, although it had been shown so many times in the archaic period. Perhaps they could not make much of such folk-tale themes in the enlightened period of intellectual development. It was not until the Hellenistic and Roman period that the offer of wine to the Cyclops and the monster's blinding became artistic subjects again, this time as part of large-scale cycles of figures serving political and ideological purposes, for instance the Polyphemus gable at Ephesus, the group showing the giving of wine to the Cyclops in the imperial nymphaeum of Baiae on the Gulf of Naples, and – finest of them all – the Polyphemus group at Sperlonga in Latium, part of an '*Odyssey* in marble'.

Although Matmata has been taken over by tourism, there are still indications that the caves are in use. Here you may see a washing line with blankets on it hanging right across a courtyard, there a baking tin lies on the floor, a few pitchers stand in the shade of the high wall of a shaft. Up at the top there is a TV aerial, a satellite dish, a cable running down the wall. Today the family that would once have inhabited this cave probably live in the whitewashed stone house beside it, and use it only as a storeroom, to dry washing – and as a TV room, cool in summer, holding the warmth in winter. As I stand on the edge of the shaft of a particularly deep cave, my shadow falls into the yard below, extended to a length of ten or twelve metres.

– Cyclopean measurements. Polyphemus roared in pain, tore the stake out of his bleeding eye, *and mad with pain he bellowed out for help from his neighbour Cyclops, living round about in caves on wind-swept crags* (O, F 9, 446).

It does not seem too far-fetched to picture the Cyclops as inhabitants of caves not unlike the cave dwellings of the Berbers of Matmata. During the history of its settlement, southern Tunisia as a whole has found a fascinating variety of impressive architectural solutions to the problems posed by the landscape, the climate, and various conditions and requirements. In the south of the Dahar mountain range there are towering dwellings like fortresses, linked to storerooms with barrel vaults built like honeycombs several storeys high; in the central part of the region caves with terraced forecourts have been dug horizontally into the slopes; and here in the northern part of the area around Matmata we see whole complexes of dwellings of the shaft cave type, which are an ingenious response to climatic conditions, offering shelter from summer heat and protection from winter cold. They also suit the nature of the soil, which is loam and easily dug. The original Berber inhabitants withdrew to the Dahar mountains and the island of Djerba, leaving behind the more extensive areas which they had previously settled and the cave dwellings created, presumably, by prehistoric cultures. But might not information about them have come to the ears of the seafaring and trading peoples of early antiquity, the Phoenicians who settled the north African coast and who could have passed them on to Greeks?

TOUJANE. A trip from Matmata over the eastern mountainous country provides a vivid panorama of the landscape of southern Tunisia. The situation and architecture of Toujane make it a particularly impressive Berber village. It offers plenty of material for Cyclopean fantasies. The road runs over a high, hilly plateau scored with deep ravines that look like scars at the eastern end of the Dahar mountains. Several hundred metres below is a broad valley, sprinkled here and there with the white cubes of houses and green palm fronds, like pins with coloured heads stuck into a sand-coloured drawing board. On the other side of the valley there are more chains of hills with mauve and pale blue shadows on their steep eastern slopes. The last of the hills dropping to the Djeffara plain resemble the folds of a long dress falling to lie on the ground. The plain itself, in hazy tones of pale beige and light ochre, ends in a narrow strip of distant blue where the sea forms the horizon.

There are a few cave dwellings beside the road, one of them embellished for presentation to visitors as a troglodyte house, the others abandoned. The villagers now live nearby, in stone houses. An old Berber woman is busy about a hearth on the cement-hard earth of a hilltop that forms the unfenced yard of a small property. Her bracelets jingle as she hides her face with her hands. No, I reassure her, I wasn't about to take her photograph; there is more jingling as she lowers her arms again. Baksheesh, however, is welcome. In return she shouts something in the ear of her husband, who is hard of hearing, whereupon he stands to attention, a walking stick beside him like a gun. Is he remembering the days of glory when Europeans brought their own conflicts to Tunisia, and Tunisian soldiers had the honour of fighting on the Mareth Line? He adopts this martial stance a little clumsily. He probably hasn't had much practice recently – *al hama ullilah*, thanks be to God. The walls of the shaft of the nearby cave dwelling, once smooth, are now furrowed for lack of maintenance, like the mountainous landscape around the village. An entrance to the cave has just been closed by masses of loam that have slipped. Anyone down there? calls the man. Nobody replies – and there is indeed no one there. Soon the land of the Cyclops will be gone for ever.

At a sharp right bend, the plateau reaches a terrace high above the ravine and dividing the village of Toujane, which lies on two steep mountainsides beneath a dramatically cleft precipice. There is hardly a tree here, and no bushes; a few palms grow down below on the dry valley floor and on the outskirts of the village, otherwise there are only rocks and scree slopes. In this inhospitable, stony world, almost devoid of plant life, the cube-shaped houses are made of the material to be found all around them. It is only because their stone has been used before that they differ from their surroundings, where the natural shape of the rocks is not so regular and they do not cast such angular shadows, or glow with such a uniform caramel hue in the sunlight. There is another row of cave dwellings on the steep slopes, obviously no longer in use and falling into decay. These are not caves of the shaft type, but are dug horizontally into the slope and have large terraced yards outside, surrounded by walls and outbuildings. This type too resulted from local conditions: a steep hillside site, and soil consisting of firm limestone interspersed with layers of softer clay. The clay was removed, leaving layers of limestone to form floors and ceilings; masonry framed the doors and shored up the slope where the caves had been dug itself. The masonry itself was also intended to be aesthetic and imposing, as we can see from the attractive work around the cave doors and further tall stonework structures making additional rooms around the courtyard, which itself consisted of the trodden spoil from the digging – and there you had a fine house that made the most of local conditions, with plenty of room for a large extended family.

It would also have been enough for *a man-mountain rearing head and shoulders over the world* (O, F 9, 213). We can imagine Polyphemus in Toujane as easily as in Matmata: the shape of the caves here corresponds in many particulars with what the *Odyssey* says about the home of the Cyclops. Toujane, with its cave dwellings on steep slopes, the forbidding rocks above, cliffs and ravines on the edge of the high plateau, would have been just the place for the final confrontation between the two leading characters in the savage story: Odysseus risking everything yet again, after escaping from the threat of death by using his cold intelligence, and his wounded, humiliated barbarian opponent. What a spectacle: we stand on the terrace at the edge of the precipice, and see the Cyclops on the other side hurling great rocks down on Odysseus as he shouts insults, and on his surviving companions. Polyphemus only just misses the ship. Nothing makes life as real and vivid as a potentially deadly challenge, so once again bitter insults are hurled, and Odysseus only just escapes. Yes, the sea is far away; we see only its delicate fringe. Here the rocks would have fallen somewhere among the palms, rolling away where the mountain slopes fall to the plain, which is now bathed in the golden light of the evening sun. All the same, the sea is in sight, and perhaps in the past the coast lay much closer to the foot of this mountain range. It seems that this hilly country was once fertile, with fields, woods and pastures, like the land of the Cyclops. In the poet's mind, features that once went together might have merged, or have been seen as merging. Thanks to the imagination, possibilities became poetic truth.

Several groups of men sit beside the road running through Toujane, on the ground or on the steps of a house. Heads are bent over a board game. There are lively gestures, loud conversation. Silence and contemplation. A large fig tree stands in the yard of one. Its green leaves are beautiful in such a stony landscape. Its shade feels good. A whole family is lying down to rest in that shade.

Splendid Houses

Island of Aeolus – *Malta*

THE AEOLIAN ISLAND. It is not very far from Tunisia to Malta, from Tunis to La Valletta, from the Kerkennah Islands to Marsaxlokk Bay – and not very far from the island of goats to the island of Aeolus. Odysseus describes the voyage of the survivors of the adventure with the Cyclops briefly: *We reached the Aeolian island next, the home of Aeolus* (O, F 10, 1). He does not say how long it took them, what kind of wind they had or what way they were sailing. If we look at a sea chart for help, we find the following clues: the current of the sea in the Gulf of Gabés runs north at first, parallel to the coastline, but then the central current of the Mediterranean running east predominates. Even if a ship were only drifting, the current would take it into Levantine waters. And if the captain of such a ship was making for one of the Ionian islands, say Ithaca, then he would have been glad to put in at a safe harbour on the way, and Malta – almost directly on his route – would have offered one.

As you approach by sea the rocky coastline towers up, and an observer who expressed that impression as a gigantic wall would be choosing a good metaphor, for the same comparison was made by a famous poet long before him:

> A great floating island it was, and round it all
> huge ramparts rise of indestructible bronze
> and sheer rock cliffs shoot up from sea to sky.

(O, F 10, 3).

These forbidding coasts were not suitable areas for human settlements. Those lie inland and on the eastern and northern coasts, where deep inlets are excellent natural harbours. The communities around the capital of Valletta, once separate, have now merged into a single metropolis, with heavy traffic making its way through the streets. This, with the drastic reduction of green areas, creates serious ecological problems. However, anyone setting out from the fine Renaissance city to explore the island cannot expect to cover the short distances involved in a correspondingly short time. His car will be only one of the three hundred thousand permitted on the roads.

DINGLI. In the more sparsely inhabited west and south of the island the landscape, now domesticated, has terraced fields with stone walls to keep the precious soil in place and provide shelter from the wind. In some places, mainly on rocky hilltops, parallel grooves are deeply scored in the bare rock. Known as cart-ruts, they are a prehistoric mystery. But they too probably express human determination to cultivate the land, and perhaps the prosaic explanation is that they were used for the transport of salt and agricultural produce in the Bronze Age. Very close to one of these areas, in the village of Dingli – nicknamed Clapham Junction after the tangle of rails at the London railway station – we come upon wild and apparently untamed nature: huge cliffs shining in the afternoon with the bright golden yellow of the local limestone, which has been the building material used throughout the island for over five thousand years. Sheer stone walls, with a roughly textured surface showing hundreds of horizontal lines, rise from the sea to a height of up to 200 metres, curving forward and back – the interior of the earth turned inside out, and without any vegetation to cover it. The local flora is found only as sparse growths of low-growing *macchia* where the upper edge of the rock deviates from the vertical. Homer could have been speaking of formations like the gigantic rock walls of Dingli, covering many kilometres, when he mentioned the *ramparts of indestructible bronze* – meaning that they were impenetrable – surrounding the island where *sheer rock cliffs shoot up from sea to sky* (O, F 10, 4). Such walls of rock may well have seemed not just sheer but also smooth to seamen keeping a respectful distance from the mighty cliffs as they looked for anchorage. If they were, say, coming from the Kerkennah Islands and steering south past the Maltese archipelago, they would also be confronted by similarly huge and forbidding rocks on the island of Gozo.

GOZO. The section of coastline around the bay of Dwejra in the west of Gozo has few parallels for its monumental, bizarre appearance. Sharp-ridged cliffs jut into the sea, facing a rock that divided off from the main island in ancient times to form a monolithic islet, Fungus Rock. The bay looks as if it had been punched into the rock massif. The spectacular Azure Window, where a rectangle of sea is framed by an approximately semi-circular arch in a rocky headland around which the water laps, is not so much a window as a monumental gateway, or even better an arch in front of the dwelling of the god who, according to legend, lived in the blue, green and silvery element of water. His name was Poseidon, and Odysseus, having blinded and insulted the god's son Polyphemus, had to reckon with his vengeance until he finally reached Ithaca and home.

MARSAXLOKK. Homer sends his hero sailing past such coasts to meet the good spirit of the island of Aeolia, *Aeolus, Hippotas' son, beloved by the gods who never die* (O, F 10, 1). First he had to find a safe harbour. But where was it, if the home of Aeolus lay in the Maltese archipelago, and the high walls of rock on Gozo and Malta kept Odysseus from landing on the south-west coasts? Most likely on the very varied east coast of Malta, which really consists only of bays and headlands, but in the south-east adjoins the largest bay in the island. Did he make for Marsaxlokk Bay? It name means 'harbour in the south-east' in the Maltese language. Large and safe as it is and was, it is used today by large container ships as well as many small fishing boats, which in Catholic Malta still bear the eyes of Osiris painted on them to show that they are protected by the Egyptian god of the dead. In the year 1565 it was used by the Turkish armada carrying 40,000 soldiers for the Great Siege of Malta, which ultimately withstood the Turks, and in 1798 Napoleon stopped there with a fleet and 54,000 men on his way to Egypt, taking the opportunity of occupying the island at the same time. Two years later the British took it from him, and remained its masters – with considerably greater success – until 1964. Many centuries and many millennia before them, settlers and tradesmen came here, particularly the Phoenicians, as well as conquerors, merchants, shipwrecked sailors and wanderers. They were all able to cast anchor in the bay, finding protection from the rigours of nature there – or even drawing their vessels up on land if, like the Achaeans, they navigated in shallow boats without keels which could be beached.

The bay could certainly offer suitable beaches outside the village of Birzebbuga, in the places known as Pretty Bay and St George's Bay. We know that sea-going vessels landed here in ancient times, for only 500 metres from the beach of St George's Bay there is a huge cave that produced some remarkable finds during excavations in 1933 to 1937: over 17,000 animal bones from Ice Age fauna, mainly hippopotamus, elephants, stags, bears, wolves and foxes. These Pleistocene specimens can be seen in the museum of the Ghar Dalam cave, put together by experts and displayed in glass cases, but still in full possession of their skeletal beauty and shown in the wild in large paintings on the walls, looking as if they were depicted in the landscape just outside the museum door. A shallow valley sinks gently to St George's Bay, and the 'cave of darkness', Ghar Dalam, on which much light has been thrown by palaeontology and anthropology, is in the eastern hills. Displays in the cave show, with stratigraphic precision, that above the old limestone stratum, some 25 million years old, and the hippopotamus stratum, only 180,000 years old, there is a so-called cultural layer, 74 centimetres deep but going back 7,200 years, a vanishingly small length of time. Vanishingly small, that is, by palaeogeoraphical criteria, but remarkable by human standards. The wealth of pottery shards found in this stratum, the oldest ceramics of Malta, are evidence that human beings have lived here since 5200 BC. They were presumably the first generation of settlers in the archipelago, daring seafarers who reached Malta from Sicily by raft, carrying domesticated animals, seed corn, pottery, and tools on their small-scale arks. The last inhabitants of the cave left it in 1911.

BORG IN-NADUR. Closer to the bay, on the slope on the other side of the valley, lies the excavation site of Borg in-Nadur, only ten minutes away from Ghar Dalam, but more than 3000 years distant in terms of human history. By then cave-dwelling had been given up and people had settled in villages instead, the unique temple culture of the archipelago had come to its full flowering and died away again. Two waves of immigrants – coming presumably from Sicily, but perhaps also from Calabria and the mainland of Greece – had taken possession of the islands and brought with them a crucial innovation: the use of bronze to make weapons. These Bronze Age settlers were obviously no longer concerned with building megalithic temples in easily accessible places at a time of peace, without threat from outside; they wanted to secure their settlements by building defensive walls several metres high. Where could danger threaten? Only from the sea, now made navigable to shipping, mainly Phoenician. The largest village dating from the Bronze Age is Borg in-Nadur (period II, 1500 to 750 BC). Earlier there was a clear view of Marsaxlokk Bay from its slightly raised position on the hills running down from inland. Today we catch only a glimpse of the sea here and there between the houses of Birzebbuga, a patch of the white chalk cliffs on the other side of the bay, and a battery of oil tanks. The huge cranes of the container port raise their burdens through the air above the rooftops as if they were toys.

Borg in-Nadur is considered the best preserved of all the Bronze Age sites here, a classification that is only relative for the laymen among us, since compared to the monumental temple complexes the remains are not spectacular. So let us give the imagination freedom to roam, take the stones lying around in some disarray, although some are monoliths up to four metres long, fit them together into a handsome wall, and build houses behind the wall that deserve such epithets as 'splendid' and 'famous'. For that is how Odysseus described the halls of the lord of the winds, Aeolus.

It is here, in an environment with a Bronze Age past and strategically well situated near a secure harbour, that the Wolfs situate the city of Aeolus.[40] And anyone who ruled this area would have made a good choice. Such a bay, like the unique natural harbour of Valletta and other bays on the north coast of Malta, would presumably have given the Phoenicians, when they made this island a particularly important base for their extensive voyages, a plausible reason to call it Malta, place of refuge. We may assume that it was also a place of refuge and a safe harbour to many other seamen, blown off course by contrary winds or on a voyage of exploration themselves. Should we see the landing of Odysseus on the island of Aeolia as a fictional account, enriched by folktale, of contact made by Greek seamen with a Phoenician merchant lord on Malta? A man who knew the Mediterranean inside out, had all the contemporary nautical and geographical knowledge of the area, and could tell the Achaeans the way to reach home, advising them to wait here for four weeks until the right wind blew from the west? Can we also assume that there was some self-interested calculation behind the kindness of Aeolus in sending a potential future rival on his way, and was that why the reception he gave the Achaeans on their involuntary return was so rate and hostile, quite unlike his first welcome to them?

Odysseus and his companions, then, had found a place to land on the island of Aeolus, defended as it was by high rocky walls.

> To this city of theirs we came, their splendid palace,
> and Aeolus hosted me one entire month, he pressed me for news
> of Troy and the Argive ships and how we sailed for home (...)
> He gave me a sack, the skin of a full-grown ox,
> binding inside the winds that howl from every quarter (...)
> Aeolus stowed the sack inside my holds, lashed so fast
> With a burnished silver cord
> not even a slight puff could slip past that knot.
> Yet he set the West Wind free to blow us on our way,
> and waft our squadron home.
>
> (O, F 10, 16).

Aeolus gave Odysseus a gift of great value to take him home: Zephyrus, the wind of homecoming, was the only one left free, while all the countering winds were trapped inside the leather bag: a wonderful poetic idea that will continue to enchant readers through the ages. But its purpose, as Odysseus laconically remarked, was ruined by *our own reckless folly* (O, F 10, 31). As Ithaca came into sight after nine days and nights continuously at sea, and the ship was so close to home that the fires on shore could be seen, disaster struck. Odysseus, who had been steering the ship himself the whole time, was overcome by weariness. His suspicious companions opened the bag expecting to find gold and silver. Then the winds escaped, letting loose a squall that drove the ships all the way back to the island of Aeolus. Begging and pleading was useless; the Achaeans were clearly out of divine favour now, and Aeolus drove them away again at once. It was a bitter taste of Poseidon's revenge.

The island was left behind; Homer sketches few details of its features, but those few are worth noting. We hear of incestuous marriage between the children of Aeolus, his six lovely daughters and six sons *in the lusty prime of youth*, which could indicate Egyptian influence; the cultural standard is high on the island, the diet is varied, there are musical performances and elegant interior design, for instance of the bedroom in *Aeolus' famous halls* (O, F 10, 66).

HAGAR QIM AND MNAJDRA. The most famous buildings of the area, above all the monumental temple precincts of Ggantija on Gozo and Hagar Qim, Mnajdra and Tarxien on Malta,[41] had already been standing for one to two thousand years at the time of the Bronze Age culture of Borg in-Nadur. Cut off on an island and safe there, they were presumably the creation of the indigenous population who, with these unique examples of a highly developed prehistoric art – also including the magnificent necropolis of the Hypogaeum on Malta and the many sculptures of the great divine mother, the Magna Mater – have their place in the annals of human culture.

On a bare plateau on the south coast are Hagar Qim, the 'standing stones'. These vast structures, with outer walls or porches and ceilings made of rectangular and square stones fitted together with mathematical precision into facades and porches, surround a labyrinth of sacred rooms, altars and oracular chambers – perhaps built with some memory of the cave-dwelling days of the past in mind? The axes are in line with astral constellations, the main porch faces the rising sun and the full moon. The 'Venus of Malta' was found in the inner courtyard. In her realistically powerful physical structure, with voluptuous breasts, she is a credible recipient of the prayers for fertility that must have been made to her, despite her small stature of only thirteen centimetres. The Neolithic people represented Death as a reassuring figure in the shape of the small but famous 'sleeping lady', lying on her side with her limbs relaxed, her upper arms and thighs plump, her hips wide under the skirt she wears, as if death were eternal sleep that cannot impair the voluptuous body. An enchanting idea; this beautiful little figure has a room to herself in the National Museum of Archaeology in Valetta.

Only a few hundred metres below Hagar Qim are the temple precincts of Mnajdra. On a hill to one side, several large oval openings indicate the sites of cisterns carved into the rock, probably to provide the two large temple complexes with water in prehistoric times. All around lies rocky land, with a stone guardroom building, and around it small stone tables with metal rods protruding from them. Cages for decoy birds are fixed to the rods in spring and autumn, or tiles that may look to birds like a comfortable place to land. Mjnadra stands in a bird-catching area. Pale stone between tufts and cushions of dusty green vegetation that dries to ochre brown in summer, bordered without transition by the blue of the sea with a filigree of crests of foam forming a backdrop to the work of human hands in stone: these re the walls, gates and ramparts of Mnajdra. And beyond, on the horizon where sea and sky meet, the angular rocky island of Fifla stands like a container ship. The mighty outer walls of Mnajdra, consisting of three gigantic stones, and the trilithic entrance to Temple I, incomparable in its monumental simplicity, the passage between the two main chambers of Temple III, flanked by mighty orthostats and with a view of the sea through the (rudimentary) porthole slab of the entrance; niches with mysterious outlines covered with dotted décor like a honeycomb, altars, oracular chambers – all this leaves the impression of a strong creative will finding expression for its intellectual and spiritual ideas in the structure of monumental forms, while the ornamentation of round holes covering the surface in their hundreds shows a camouflage element softening the monolithic weight.

TARXIEN. The megalithic architecture and its decorative components come to their finest flowering in the temple complex of Tarxien, in the middle of the village of the same name near Valletta. There is an inspired variety of spiral motifs, as well as animal depictions adoring altars and walls in delicate *bas relief*. Artistic skill enhances the sculptural constructions, for instance in large stone vessels each carved from a monolith and perfectly worked, decorated coffins, and above all – although they are not found here alone – statues of the Magna Mater, developing organically from full, curved forms. These are figures of surprising modernity, reminding one, for instance, of the voluptuous figures of Botero. They are all fertility idols, like the figure also found in Tarxien, originally some 2.5 metres tall, with a pleated skirt and thick thighs, and thought to be the oldest colossal statue in the world.

GGANTIJA. And to cite another superlative, the oldest of the great megalithic temple buildings in the Maltese archipelago is also the oldest free-standing structure of buildings in the world. It is found on the little island of Gozo, and was built between 3600 and 3000 BC, in a slightly rising landscape contoured by the play of lines of the stone walls. The domes of the parish churches, which are like cathedral domes in size, compete with the temple remains for supremacy. The never-ending history of the building of temples, churches, palaces, administrative buildings begins not hesitantly but as if with a mighty drum roll: the temple walls are eight metres high, with gigantic slabs of rock weighing up to fifty tonnes and almost six metres in length, once enclosing two temples of an estimated height of sixteen metres. Enough figures. The temple complex of Ggantija, Maltese for 'tower of giants', which from a distance looks like an impregnable fortress, speaks for itself. But just as it does no harm to know that the *Iliad* and *Odyssey* consist of 16,000 lines and 12,000 lines respectively, it hurts no one to know a few of the dates and measurements of the Ggantija temple, which is a seminal work of architecture with the status of a cultural heritage site. In fact, the experience of seeing it can be even more rewarding if the visual impression is reinforced by some figures.

Did the ancient peoples of the Mediterranean know about these mighty buildings? The Phoenicians are most likely to have done so, for they included the Maltese archipelago in their far-flung network of nautical bases and trading posts, and thus ventured into its isolation. Did the Greeks also know of it? The Phoenicians passed on to them astronomical knowledge, such as the first use of the Pole Star for navigation. Did Greek sailors perhaps have contact with Maltese architecture themselves, and could they speak of buildings built from stones of Cyclopean size, such as we find in Homer in *King Aeolus' famous halls*?

CALYPSO'S CAVE. And then there is the old story, leaving a trail still followed in some modern travel guides and a name that even appears officially on maps: Calypso's Cave on Gozo, just two kilometres north-east of Ggantija and above the Bay of Ramla. The Hellenistic scholar and poet Callimachus, born in Cyrene in Libya in 305 BC, was the first to suggest Gozo as the island of the divine nymph, and presumably because of his reputation this idea has come down through the centuries. Because Gozo was regarded as the island of Calypso, it was included in the places for young British aristocrats to visit on the Grand Tour of the eighteenth century. Goethe meant to go there from Syracuse for the same reason, but dropped the plan. After the Second World War the English naval officer Ernle Bradford, following in the tracks of Odysseus in a sailing boat on the Mediterranean, supported the idea that Calypso's Cave was in the Maltese archipelago, although he preferred the steep west coast of Malta as its site.

Calypso's Cave, then, is hidden away among rocks at the far end f a slope overgrown with reeds and Indian fig above the sandy bay f Ramla. Today, pleasingly, it has a visitor in the shape of a young eauty who has come up from the beach. She has velvety skin in a hade of hazelnut brown, she picks up her skirts and steps carefully ɪ her light sandals over the uneven space in front of it – and she has wealth of hair worthy of the nymph herself: *the nymph with lovely raids* (O, F 5, 63). But her laughing mouth contradicts another pithet, *dangerous*, also applied to Calypso, which in a strange combination with another description of her hair – *the seductive nymph ʋith lovely braids – a danger too* (O, F 7, 284) – can arouse wonder nd surprise, alarming fascination. No, this young woman's appearance is of a different, lighter sort, like a brief refreshment. Annoyed y wasps that come swirling out at the narrow entrance of the cave, he quickly retreats to the beach, past 'Ulysses' Lodge' half way up he slope. Calypso's Cave is a rather cramped, musty, dark cave in suroundings that have little in common with *the spacious cave where the ʋmph had made her home* (O, F 5, 62) or the delightful atmosphere f the poet's tavern. Goethe would have had little reason to regret his hange of plan in retrospect. His mistake, rather, was in deciding not o visit Syracuse.

And our heroes – what adventure faces then now, and where will ɪ take them?

King Cannibal's Realm

Land of the Laestrygonians – *Trapani and its surroundings*

APHRODITE AND MOUNT ERYX. As you approach the seaport of Trapani on the west coast of Sicily, the eye keeps turning to mountain dominating this part of the coastline like a gigantic monument: Mount Eryx. It 'rises alone, like an island, and is shaped like pyramid. I think it the positive ideal of a mountain, a masterpiece of Nature in her mountain-building,' wrote the cultural historian Ferdinand Gregorovius[42] enthusiastically when he was visiting Sicily in the year 1886.

If you happen to see Mount Eryx at a sunny moment, the view is breathtaking. But you need to wait patiently for that moment to come, for the meteorological conditions on this huge crag have their own quirks. When the land and sea all around are sunlit, the peak of the mountain and the town of Erice are often shrouded in clouds or veiled in mists that look as if invisible strings held them there.

This is the evening of the third day of our stay in Valderice, east of Erice, and not so much as a wisp of cotton wool hovers above the mountain. A grey Norman castle stands on a rocky ledge above steep slopes falling hundreds of metres, with the masonry and the natural rock united in a single work made of stone and defying wind and weather. But now the evening sun makes the grey stone shine like the wide land all around: the massive walls of the fortress, the dome and pinnacles of San Giovanni and the castle of Pepoli, the flourishing green belt below the built-up slope on which Erice stands, the vertical precipices of rock with the hills lavishly patterned with fields around them, in the south-west the Trapani salt works glittering dull silver, in the north the rocks of Monte Cofano and Monte Monaco standing out sharply against the horizon of sea and sky like gigantic sculptures.

In Valderice two days ago the sky was cloudy, it was windy, with grey sea and white crests of foam on the Golfo di Bonagio. Monte Cofano, dull anthracite, seemed to be propping up a bank of cloud of the same colour, the two of them balancing each other. On the way to Erice, only a few kilometres further on, a violent wind rose. Suddenly there was dense fog, allowing a view of only a few metres ahead as we walk. But are we to let the fog deter us from visiting legendary Mount Eryx, ruled in ancient times by a goddess who showed her favour to seafarers by keeping Eryx free of mists, while her anger was visible when vapours climbed the mountain? How angry is the goddess this evening? At last the first walls emerge, a street lamp with its hazy light shining, muted, on the paved road. We turn into a street with houses visible only vaguely to left and right and a neon sign announcing safety: the Café Venus.

> Then, on the crest of Eryx, a shrine, nigh to the stars, is founded to
>   Venus of Idalia, and to Anchises' tomb is assigned a priest with
>   breadth of hallowed grove.
>
> (*Aeneid* 5, 759).

Only a Roman could speak in these terms: Virgil who lived in the first century BC.[43] In the mythical period in which his epic *The Aeneid* and its characters are set, there was no Venus yet. To Theocritus, a poet born about 300 BC in Syracuse, the goddess of the temple on the peak was still called Aphrodite.

> O Queen that lovest Golgi, and Idalium, and the steep of Eryx, O
>   Aphrodite that playest with gold![44]

The name Venus appears for the first time in the fourth century BC on a bronze mirror from ancient Praeneste, today Palestrina. The images engraved on it tell the touching story of Venos – as she is spelt there – first weeping hot tears over the lovely Adonis, later to be her youthful lover. The boy lies in a basket between Venos and Proserpina, to whom Venos has given the enchanting boy for safe keeping after his birth in the basket, away from other greedy eyes, never guessing that the goddess of the underworld herself would fall passionately in love with the beautiful Adonis at first sight. They quarrel, Jupiter must settle the dispute, and finds a compromise that satisfies Proserpina but not Aphrodite. She wants Adonis all to herself. There are tears at the beginning of the story and tears at its end, when Adonis is killed by a boar while out hunting. His blood flows away, with red anemones springing from it, to mingle with the water of a river in the Lebanon.

The Lebanese river of Nahr Ibrahim was once known as the river Adonis. High in the mountains east of Byblos, it pours from the mighty Afqa grotto on the slope of a high escarpment, flowing out into the daylight and tumbling in cascades down the steep slopes of Lebanon, through a great ravine, and so to the ancient city by the sea. Oil lamps are still lit in the grotto in honour of the 'lady' who haunts this spot, Zahra, who for Shi'ites and Christians alike is the image of Venus and her ancestresses transported to the present.

It is spring, the water of the river is red with the blood of Adonis pouring into the sea and tingeing it too with red. The secret rites begin in the temple of Baalat and commemorate the death of the young lord: 'He is dead, Adonis the beautiful is dead.' After a week of ceremonies death turns to resurrection: 'He is risen again, Adonis is risen again,' comes the cry from the throats of thousands of devotees, and in trance-like ecstasy they see Adonis up on the rocky spring returning from the grave to radiant light and beauty.

In the Semitic home of Adonis, his lover was called not Venus but Astarte. And in the Greek texts that told the story of this myth she appears as Aphrodite, while her rival for the favour of Adonis is not Proserpina but Persephone, the Greek goddess of the under world. The Semitic cult of Adonis reached the Greeks in the sixth century BC, no doubt by way of Cyprus, where the oldest and most important shrines of Aphrodite lay. The great love goddess also had close neighbours in the east, where she was worshipped as Ishtar or Ashtoreth, a name converted by the Greeks into Astarte.

Astarte, Aphrodite, Venus – changing names for the oldest goddess in the Mediterranean, the great goddess of love, full of desire herself and bringing lust. She is more prominent in writing, sculpture and pictorial art than any other divine or human figure, fascinating to the present day, when great art exhibitions pay tribute to her. Sumerian Inanna, Akkadian Ishtar, Syrian Astarte, the divinities Anat and Atargatis – they are all names and personifications of the same great goddess of love.

One of the epithets of Greek Aphrodite is 'the heavenly one', or to create a link between love and heaven her name was heavenly love Urania.[45] Urania was 'the heavenly one' but born of the sea, at least in the theogeny of Hesiod, who tells the ancient tale of the god of heaven Uranus. As he made love to Gaia, the earth, his own son cut off his penis with a sharp-toothed sickle of grey steel. It fell into the sea, drifted here and there, white foam formed, *aphros*, and the sea foam gave birth to the fairest of the fair – Aphrodite, the foam-born. As Venus Anadyomene, 'emerging from the sea', the masculine imagination has shown her in many fascinating forms, from the Hellenist painter Apelles to Botticelli, Ingres, Cabanel and all the way to Böcklin.

As the goddess born of the sea, and so closely linked to it, Aphrodite Urania was worshipped by seafarers. Sappho offers a *propemptikon* to Aphrodite, a prayer for a fortunate voyage, asking the goddess to let her brother come back safely – *Now bring him safely homeward, Cypris!/Keep storms away, protect him/on his journey home.*[46] Similarly, seamen approaching the most westerly point of Sicily or passing through the straits between Drepanon, the port of Erice, and Carthage, begged for the protection of the goddess in her temple high on Eryx, were anxious when the peak was shrouded in mists, full of hope when visibility was good. By night their eyes were guided there by the red light of an eternal fire burning in the sacred precincts. The seafaring Phoenicians probably spread the cult of Urania when they set up trading posts along the shores of the Mediterranean. And so the rocks of Eryx themselves became a shrine to Astarte or Aphrodite, and the goddess of Mount Eryx was given another epithet referring to the locality: Erucina or Erycina. Another Aphrodite, no less revered by the seamen, and not by them alone. With all the trappings of Phoenician luxury, her predecessor Astarte conquered the coast of the great ocean with the seafaring Phoenicians. She was surrounded by incense, fine robes, intoxicatingly scented ointments and oils, shining jewellery with gold and precious stones, elaborate ivory work, like an aura to arouse the senses and prepare them for the epiphany of the naked goddess, offering her breasts cupped in her own hands, giving life and sexual pleasure, as Astarte is shown on a clay plaque found in a tomb at Tharros on Sardinia. Astarte was followed by Aphrodite and Venus.

The Museo Nazionale in Rome has a colossal head of Aphrodite-Venus from a Phoenician/West Greek shrine to Aphrodite, possibly from the temple on Mount Eryx, the work of a Greek sculptor in Phoenician service. The face, constructed from simple forms, radiates peace, confidence and self-possession. This is the goddess of whose favour seamen could be sure if they looked up to the peak and saw it standing out clearly against the sky. Go on your way, I will protect you. But at the corners of the mouth, and only there, or perhaps also on the rather expectant full lips, hovers the suggestion of a smile. Expressing the majesty of the goddess? Or perhaps faint contempt for the human race that is so ready to trust her? Her goodwill could suddenly turn to anger for unknown reasons. Then her smooth brow was clouded, and mist surrounded Mount Eryx and the likeness of Aphrodite Erycina. Scylla and Charybdis were omnipresent at such times, and vessels escaped shipwreck only with difficulty, or not at all.

For some time the shrine of Erycina on Mount Eryx was the Mediterranean centre of the worship of the goddess of love, so it is not surprising that the hierodule system was particularly prominent here. Hierodules were servants of the temple who belonged to the goddess in all the shrines of Astarte and Aphrodite; they lived in the temple precincts where they exercised their profession of sacred prostitution. Throngs of pilgrims came by land and sea, helping to fill the coffers of the temple treasury. The many aspects of the cult of the love goddess however, could not be more clearly evident than in the surprising fact that the goddess was honoured in this way not only by the temple servants of Aphrodite (or Venus), but by many representatives of the female sex who, as respectable people would now see it, were their precise opposite, married women who venerated the goddess of love. The double aspect is illustrated in two wonderful figures; one woman sits on her marriage bed, heavily veiled, a bride making an offering of incense, and the other is a naked hetaira, her legs casually crossed, playing music and depicted on the Ludovisi Throne of 460 BC now in the Museo Nazionale in Rome.

The hierodules were famous for their beauty; the temple precincts of Venus were not just a place of pilgrimage, but one where seamen could rest and recover from the rigours of a voyage. 'Even today the women who live in the little town of San Giuliano, within the walls of the old temple, are thought the most beautiful in all Sicily,' remarked Rudolf Alexander Schröder, German translator of the *Aeneid*.[47] Would they have been potential candidates for the profession of hierodule if they had lived earlier? When Gerd Gaiser, writing about Sicily in 1959, visited the rocky haunt of Venus, he did not like to find that the figure of the goddess had such a bad reputation. He speaks of whistling winds, mists, pouring rain on Mount Eryx and hen, suddenly, 'Sun, the heavens clear and biting cold (...). Considering the air, the salty, rainy air, the bitter scent of laurels and pines in it, the faint remaining trace of the storm's sulphur and ice crystals, then this did not seem a place for the lasciviousness of which the goddess was accused. This was not the air of sultry intrigues: a stern mistress seemed more at home than a debauched one in this radiant, stormy brightness.'[48] But the two female figures on the Ludovisi Throne do show that dual aspect: love in light-hearted sensuous pleasure, and love as part of a marriage relationship.

AENEAS AND SICILY. The western coastal area of Sicily is an important setting in the *Aeneid*. Virgil gives his Trojan hero Aeneas experiences similar to those that plagued Odysseus. Like Odysseus, he and his men wander, pursued by the anger of a god. Raging storms attack them; Polyphemus, blinded by Odysseus, as well as Charybdis and Scylla (located by Virgil on Etna and in the straits of Messina) threaten destruction. Sailing along the south coast of Sicily, they are received at last by *the harbour of Drepanum and its joyless shore* (*Aeneid* 3, 707). Anchises, Aeneas's old father, dies here in the seaport of Drepanum, later Trapani, worn out by the stress of the long and dangerous voyage. He is buried here.

A year later, when Aeneas, after his Carthaginian adventure and love affair with Queen Dido, is forced off the route to his real destination of Italy by a storm, he once again comes to *the fateful shores of Eryx and the Sicilian ports*, and is sighted *afar off, on a high hill-top* (*Aeneid* 5, 35) by King Acestes. He holds great funeral games on the first anniversary of his father's death. Virgil allows the reader to take part in a varied programme of competitive games, covering fourteen pages of Book 5 of the *Aeneid*, beginning with rowing races between four ships named Sea-Dragon, Chimaera, Centaur and Scylla, and going on to footraces, boxing, archery and spear-throwing, and ending with mounted jousting.

The race between the ships is described very vividly, as if by an eloquent sports reporter of antiquity presenting the suspense of the event with great poetic power. The point at which the course of the race turns is a rocky reef:

Far out at sea, over against the foaming shores likes a rock which at times the swollen waves beat and overwhelm, when stormy North-

westers hide the stars; in time of calm it is voiceless, and rises from the
placid wave a level surface, and a welcome haunt for sun-loving gulls.

(*Aeneid* 5, 124 ff.)

This rock has been identified as tiny Isola Asinelli west of Piz-
zolungo, easily visible from the peak of Eryx, like the gulf off Piz-
zolungo itself, where the ships could have raced.[49] And the track
for the footraces, with rising tiers of seats arranged like an amphitheatre, can easily be imagined in the meadows between the nearby
sea and the foot of Mount Eryx. There is some reason to suppose
that Virgil was familiar with the topographical conditions around
Mount Eryx, and set the account of the funeral games against the
realistic background of an ancient landscape relating to mythology
and a great past.

MOZIA. If we follow the Wolfs, we may see Mount Eryx as the site of
the craggy fort of Lamos, which Odysseus reached after he had been
driven away from the island of Aeolia.

Six whole days we rowed, six nights, non-stop.
On the seventh day, we raised the Laestrygonian land,
Telepylus heights where the craggy fort of Lamos rises.

(O, F 10, 88).

It is at Mount Eryx, a landmark visible from afar, that the 'real wanderings of Odysseus' would first have come close to Sicily, and voyaging
around it was to be at the centre of the hero's subsequent adventures.
A factor that appears particularly significant to the Wolfs is the proximity in time of the Greek colonization of Italy to the west, and the
presence in both the *Iliad* and the *Odyssey* of elements that might be
described as travel writing. Many other scholars before them had seen
geographical knowledge acquired from Greek trading ventures westward during the 9th and 8th centuries reflected in the *Odyssey*.[50] The
Wolfs now turned to finding firmer ground for the already plausible
idea that the epic referred to the experiences of colonizers going west,
and looked for it in a real geographical system which could be seen
to agree in every point with Homer's navigational data. In a general
sense Hölscher too saw the *Odyssey*, in its graphic account of contemporary life, reflecting 'the century of the second colonization, when

Greek culture forced its way into the Mediterranean, newly restless and dangerous as it was.'[51]

In that version of events the Homeric heroes, driven from the island of Aeolus and rowing until they were exhausted because their sails had been ripped to pieces by the storm, would have set out from Malta, reached Sicily, and then, off the Isola delle Correnti at the southern tip of the island, they would have been driven off course and westward, until on a cloudless day they saw Telepylos, the proud fortress of Lamos on Mount Eryx that dominates the land around – or perhaps, at night, they would have seen the sacred fire of Astarte, as sailors today by night can see the electric lighting of Erice from very far away.

After six days of fear, deprivation and exhaustion, they wanted to find a harbour with waters sheltered from the violence of the sea. Exactly such a harbour, offering a haven to ships that have just rounded the outermost western point of Sicily at Capo Lilibeo, is the sound of the Stagnone di Marsala, a bay to the north of the city of Marsala, almost enclosed by the Isola Grande to form a horseshoe-shaped natural harbour. Since the northernmost point of the island was very probably linked to the mainland in antiquity, the bay would have had access only from Capo Lilibeo to the south. Odysseus and his companions come into such waters, protected from the open sea:

> We entered a fine harbour there, all walled around
> by a great unbroken sweep of sky-scraping cliff
> and two steep headlands, fronting each other, close
> around the mouth so the passage in is cramped.
> (O, F 10, 96).

In the opinion of the Wolfs, this was the harbour of the Phoenician colony of Motye.

It is about fifteen kilometres from Trapani to the moorings for the boats that transfer visitors to the tiny island of San Pantaleo in the Stagnone di Marsala, otherwise Mozia, the Phoenician Motye. For us, it is a beautiful spring day, but Mount Eryx cannot be persuaded to stop sulking, and although a cloudless sky surrounds it, it keeps its cloud-cap on until early in the afternoon.

On the right, the road follows a semi-circle around the bay where the saltworks lie south of Trapani: shallow water where long-legged birds – storks, ibis, flamingos – pick their way around, rise briefly in the air and come down again in the brine, pecking with their pointed beaks for anything edible. The first windmills appear, marks on the flat landscape from which, as ever, Mount Eryx rises to the north. After going for a short way overland you reach the saltworks outside Mozia, shallow basins of water surrounded by low walls and exposed to the sun. The wonderful white crystals are freed from the brackish liquid; stacked on embankments beside the waterways, the salt is built into regularly shaped, tall piles, gleaming white where they are not covered with hipped roofs of ochre and red-brown tiles. The boat makes its way along the straight channels of water towards the island of Mozia, which is notable for its geometrical and stereometrical regularity. The landscape around the salt pans, which themselves are indifferent to the seasons, is one of lavish growth in spring – yellow and red seas of flowers are shaded by parasol pines and surrounded by the changing blue and green of the sea.

But for thousands of years Mozia has been no Garden of Eden untouched by human hand. It is a land with an ancient tradition of civilization, first established by the Phoenicians as a trading base, and the name of a nymph – Motye – bestowed on the island shows that they had no warlike intentions. The mother cities of Byblos and Tyros owed their prosperity not least to the legendary skill of the Phoenicians in making and dying fine woollen fabrics. As well as textiles – particularly the purple fabrics so highly prized in the ancient world – Phoenician craftsmen were masters of making metal vessels, glass, and ivory carvings. Motye flourished, and became one of the richest Phoenician colonies in the Mediterranean. It was chosen in line with the strategic aims of Phoenician colonial policy: they founded their settlements either on a cape projecting into the sea or – and even preferably – on an island in a sheltered lagoon, with secure anchorage for ships that had a shallow draft. Motye went through all the phases typical of human settlements: their rise, their prime, their fall and destruction (in this case by the Greek ruler Dionysius I of Syracuse). It then slumbered like the Sleeping Beauty for centuries before it was finally woken again in the 19th century.

From the 18th century onwards, a wine industry had developed in Marsala only a few kilometres further south – like Mozia, a very early Phoenician trading post – with the idea of breaking the port monopoly of Portugal with its own dessert wine. In the 19th century the English wine merchant Joseph Whitaker bought the island of

Mozia on which to plant the grape varieties used in making Marsala. He was not only a successful wine merchant, but also an enthusiastic student of the ancient world. A visit to Mozia by his friend Heinrich Schliemann gave both men the idea of searching beneath the Arcadian and agricultural surface of the sleeping island for a Sicilian Troy. And as soon as a small corner of the island had been investigated, the remains of a civilization that had ruled the Mediterranean coasts for centuries came to light. The longer the digging went on, the more impressive became the picture of an urban settlement, the Motye of antiquity, embracing the whole island. The German writer Martin Mosebach, in an essay on the most famous find from Mozia, an extraordinarily fine life-size male figure, paid tribute to that altruistic patron of archaeology Whitaker: 'The remains of Phoenician walls, a wild garden, and olive and vine plantations surround the modest but attractive little buildings, the lapidarium, a chapel, dwelling houses; an idyll that might come from the pages of Adalbert Stifter, in which a wise landowner with humanist ideals combines agriculture with scientific research.'[52]

Positively tropical flora greets visitors to the island as they reach the landing stage, and they are guided past a magnificent hedge of red-flowering aloes a metre high to the Museo Whitaker. The Ephebe of Mozia, as the slightly larger than life-size marble statue is called, was probably created by a Greek sculptor for a Phoenician patron in the 5th century BC, and stands alone in a room with cool stone walls, a suitable lodging for this delightful male statue. The pleated robe dropping from his shoulders to his feet is beautifully depicted, clinging to the young man's well-shaped body with many finely modelled straight pleats. His nakedness is only apparently veiled, for it shows under the second skin of the robe to good effect. The arms are missing, but the hand preserved where it is thrust into the garment over the left hip strikes a challenging note in presenting the impressive physicality of the figure, proudly erect yet shown casually turning, a note unmistakably emphasizing the genitals swelling under the delicate robe, the strongly muscular buttocks, and the powerfully modelled right leg, which is free of the robe. They become a triumphant expression of erotic charisma and self-confident masculine power.

Beyond the museum we go along a beaten track through a field of tall yellow daisies that seems to be running right into the sea. The path leads along the bank, beneath the remains of the ancient city wall that once surrounded the entire island and was almost 2400 metres

long, and to the northern gateway, the two lateral bastions of which
are preserved. The tracks of cartwheels, still visible in the paving of
the ancient road, stimulate the mind to imagine life in Motye at the
time: one can visualize horse-drawn vehicles driving down the main
street of the city and out of this northern gate, to reach the mainland
over one of the embankments crossing the lagoon with their wheels
still dry (which would be impossible today), carrying their funereal
burden to the later cemetery laid out in the 6th century once the old
necropolis outside the wall, to the left of the north gate, could take
no more dead. At the beginning of the 20th century donkey-carts
could still drive along this road, but it has been covered by seawater
for many years now; the west coast of Sicily is sinking all the time. So
now the road ends on the shores of the island, and only the gaze can
cross to the land north of the lagoon with its low-built white houses.
Above them, on the horizon, the distant mountain of Aphrodite
almost hovers above the slight mist on the plain, like an airy figure,
sister to Morgan le Fay .

The magic of spring does not care whether bustling life or the
burden of death once reigned on this or that part of the island. It is
covered with flowers and grasses in vivid colours such as Emil Nolde
might have used, lush growth that can be kept only by main force
from the dead in their necropolis, or the Tophet, the dreadful place
where the remains of children and adults burned alive were buried –
sacrifices offered in the utmost reverence to Baal-Hammon and Tanit
when it seemed that, in some circumstances, animal sacrifices had
not been enough to satisfy the gods. Carthage was not far away, and
Moloch's hunger for human sacrifice was still insatiable.

IN THE LAND OF THE LAESTRYGONIANS. On the side of the
island opposite the north gate lies one of its most remarkable ancient
remains. It is called the Cothon, and is the artificial Phoenician
harbour basin, with a channel running through the southern outlet
to the sea. This channel could be closed off by a barrier. The basin
was cut out of the rock, and its walls faced with stone slabs. There
is still water in it, although increasing amounts of sand have made
it a shallow pool, now surrounded by vigorous springtime growth
where, when it was still in use, paved quays and harbour buildings
must once have stood.

Standing slightly raised on the stones of the harbour exit to the

outh, you can see Cape Lilibeo with the city of Marsala, Phoeni-
ian and Roman Lilybaeum, only a few kilometres away across the
ea to the south. In front of you is a harbour which probably has no
qual anywhere for its design, a shape reminiscent of a wineskin with
narrow channel linking the sea and the harbour basis. Eryx is visible
utlined on the northern horizon.

> Six whole days we rowed, six nights, non-stop.
> On the seventh day, we raised the Laestrygonian land,
> Telepylus heights where the craggy fort of Lamos rises (...)
> We entered a fine harbour there, all walled around
> by a great unbroken sweep of sky-scraping cliff
> and two steep headlands, fronting each other, close
> around the mouth so the passage in is cramped.
>
> (O, F 10, 88).

And now disaster struck.

Odysseus, that wily and farsighted man, is the only captain not
o take his ship into the harbour. He ties her up to a rock outside it
nstead. Then he climbs the rock for a view: no sign of humans or
nimals. Next he sends men out to gather information about the land
nd its people. They meet a young woman drawing water, who directs
hem to the house of her father King Antiphates. He, as his name
uggests, is a murderer and cannibal. He immediately seizes one of
he men and eats him. We are in the land of the Laestrygonians. They
ome in crowds when called by their king, who is already devouring
uman flesh, and hurl boulders down on the ships.

> A ghastly shattering din rose up from all the ships –
> men in their death-cries, hulls smashed to splinters –
> They speared the crews like fish
> and whisked them home to make their grisly meal.
>
> (O, F 10, 135).

Only Odysseus and the crew of his ship manage to escape.

Different translators use slightly different terms in describing
Homer's Laestrygonian harbour. Not too surprisingly, perhaps, it has
ometimes been suggested that the rock formations make Scandina-
ian fjords the scene of the cannibal story. We do not have to allow
he imagination to roam quite so far afield. But Homer certainly

speaks of rocks on both sides of the harbour. There are no such rocks however, on the flat island of Mozia. The present terrain around the ancient harbour basin is only slightly above the level of the water, and even earlier the quays will have been laid out at most a few metres above sea level. The Wolfs resort to suggesting that the description of a 'sky-scraping cliff' and 'steep headlands' is not to be understood as the height of rocks but instead represents 'the steep gradient'. In that way we can imagine the Cothon surrounded by stone slabs that were set at a steep angle where they met the quay, to make it easier for ships to tie up and the crews to climb out, That would have been a help in disposing of Odysseus' comrades, for however strong and muscular the Laestrygonians were, how could they have speared the Greeks 'like fish' from the top of a high cliff? The use of spears certainly presupposes close combat – and such combat would have been perfectly possible from quays on about the same level as the ships in the harbour.

(In one English translation, the passage runs:

> Here we found an excellent harbour, closed in on all sides by an
> unbroken ring of precipitous cliffs, with two jutting headlands
> facing each other at the mouth so as to leave only a narrow channel
> in between.

(O. R 10, 87). [Translator's note])

If we accept the Wolfs' explanation, and replace the idea of natural rocks – precipitous cliffs – with that of stone slabs ('An excellent harbour, closed in on all sides by an unbroken ring of stone slabs') the Homeric account does bear some resemblance to the appearance of the Cothon. So they cannot be accused of being illogical when they add, 'But anyone coming into this harbour, unique in Sicily, was regarded as an enemy by those living around it and had fallen into a trap. The intruders could be pelted on all sides with stones and spears thrown from above, just as Homer describes it.'[53]

Surprisingly, the artists of antiquity very seldom appear to have made use of this episode, which seems to cry out for pictorial description. According to Bernard Andreae only a single example survives. It is in the best-preserved cycle showing the wanderings of Odysseus, probably created in a Roman villa on the Esquiline Hill as a fresco around 30 BC, and now, except for a fragment in the Palazzo Massimo alle Terme, in the Sala Aldobrandini of the Vatican Library

ts landscape paintings are among the oldest in European art. It is true
hat huge rocks tower up on both sides of the bay in the four frescos
howing scenes from the Laestrygonian episode. But the rocks from
which the Laestrygonians, hurrying up, throw boulders on the ships
re no more than three times the height of a man above the water,
nd some of the giants have even jumped into the sea, are standing
n its bed and tipping ships over, in an elaborate spatial landscape
f rocks, sea and sky artistically designed with an eye to the effect
f depth. The representation of the Laestrygonians attacking from
ow rocks and the shore backs up the Wolfs' idea that the Cothon
f Motye could have been the model for the Laestrygonian harbour.

Their ideas are also borne out by the situation of the Laestrygo-
ian city in the west of Sicily. After being turned away by King Aeolus
Odysseus could credibly have reached it, given the wind conditions
nd the time his ships took to row to land: six whole days and nights.
By modern calculations of rowing speed, that would mean a voyage
f about 200 sea miles, from Malta to the area around Marsala and
Trapani.

Mount Eryx, with its settlement thousands of years old, could
otentially be a real model for a mountain fortress. But for a ship
oming from the south, the mountain rises about 20 kilometres
eyond the island of Mozia, whereas Odysseus and his men see
amos first, and only then reach the harbour. That might mean
hat the little fleet could first have reached the bay of the salt works
utside Trapani, not far from the foot of Eryx, but then found the
lace unsuitable – the description of the harbour in the *Odyssey* does
ot fit it – and sailed back to the apparently safe harbour of Motye.

Before the companions of Odysseus were slaughtered, three of
hem had gone on a scouting expedition.

> They disembarked, and set out on a beaten trail
> the wagons used for hauling timber down to town
> from the mountain heights above ...
> and before the walls they met a girl, drawing water,
> Antiphates' strapping daughter – king of the Laestrygonians.
> She'd come down to a clear running spring, Artacia,
> where the local people came to fill their pails.
>
> (O, F 10, 113).

By 'town' the harbour town is obviously meant, and 'the wagons used for hauling timber' come to it. The spring of Artacia, where the daughter of Antiphates was drawing water, would have been outside the town, a little way inland. So the men would have been on their way along a level path to a town by the sea and met the girl outside it, at the spring. It is easy to imagine the forested slopes of Eryx and 'the mountain heights above'. So how do we picture the situation of the fortress of Lamus called Telepylus? The text is ambiguous here. If we accept the Wolfs' identification, we have to assume that Eryx and Mozia, a good 15 kilometres apart, have been brought closer to each other by poetic licence.

There is another fundamental problem with the Wolfs' theory: the Cothon was not built until the end of the 6th century, well after the Homeric period. It may, however, be suggested that there could have been a natural basin capable of acting as a harbour in early Phoenician times.

Perhaps, in view of a text that is not easy to interpret, and the basic problem of finding realistic geographical references for an epic 2700 years old, there is no totally satisfactory solution of all the contradictions to be found. It may be enough to imagine that Homer had not been to these places, but had heard of the major Phoenician colony, and Mount Eryx, which would surely have remained in any seaman's memory, and fitted them together in a kind of collage where the fortress of Lamus and its good harbour can co-exist happily in the context of an epic.

An Island of Indulgence

great haste, with the terrible sight of the men speared like fishes
fore their eyes, Odysseus and his remaining companions rowed
hard as they could, and only just escaped from the scene of the
saster.

They rowed until they made landfall again. Exhausted, they disem-
arked from their sole remaining ship, collapsed, and lay where they
ere for two days and two nights. Then, pulling himself together,
dysseus set out to discover more about the place where they had
ome ashore. He saw rising ground ahead of him, climbed it, and
alized that they were on an island:

> I scaled a commanding crag and from that height
> surveyed an entire island
> ringed like a crown by endless wastes of sea.

(O, F 10, 212).

ater all around, and the jagged Sicilian coastline can be made out
ly on a clear day. Ustica, a small island 50 kilometres north of the
orth-west coast of Sicily, covers an area of 8.6 square kilometres. As
u come closer, its outlines become more distinct, and you see a plot
land in the sea, patterned in ochre and green with a sprinkling of
ghter colours, with houses, a lighthouse, and a white globe on the
ghest point of the island, which the map identifies as a meteoro-
gical station.

The white, yellow, and pink-washed houses of the little town of
stica rise in tiers, like an amphitheatre, among the dense green of
e trees that cover the nearby hills on both sides of it. Not many
ssengers leave the ferry at the landing stage in the little harbour this

November day, which is almost like late summer. The season is ove
and the island, which is considered a paradise for divers, is returne
to its inhabitants for six months. Fortunately one hotel is open all th
year round. Soon after our arrival on Ustica, then, we are ready f
a walk. The island bus takes us to our first destination on the opp
site, south-west side of Ustica, the Punta dello Spalmatore, a jagge
promontory of sharp-ridged lava stone. Two north-facing headlan
surround a small natural harbour into which a narrow quay has bee
built. In the past, boats bringing the mail tied up here. And who can
even further back in the past?

After the catastrophic encounter with the Laestrygonians, Ody
seus tells us, of the survivors:

> In terror of death they ripped the swells – all as one –
> and what a joy as we darted out toward open sea,
> clear of those beetling cliffs ... my ship alone.
> But the rest went down en masse. Our squadron sank.
> From there we sailed on, glad to escape our death
> yet sick at heart for the dear companions we had lost.
> We reached the Aeaean island next, the home of Circe
> the nymph with lovely braids, an awesome power too
> who can speak with human voice.
>
> (O, F 10, 142).

Here again, the extremely laconic account of the voyage between th
two places may indicate that Homer imagined Circe's island lyi
not very far from Telepylus. Where was it? The Wolfs think th
Odysseus could have reached Aeaea only by going north-east.[54] Th
would correspond to the north-easterly direction of the current fro
the westernmost point of Sicily, which the sea chart shows wou
carry a vessel to the little island of Ustica north of Palermo.

Almost the entire island stands on a plinth of steep cliffs 50 to
metres high. The exception is where we now are in the south-we
between the Punta dello Spalmatore and the Punta Cavazzi, whe
you can walk over the solidified lava right down to the sea. Tw
mountains rise in the middle of Ustica, with a col between the
to the west are the Guardia del Turco and the Guardiola, to the e
the Guardia Grande, with the white globe of the meteorologi
station visible from afar. To the north-east, the island rises again li
the keel of a boat from the fertile plain known as the Tramontar

orming a small pyramid-shaped peak above the harbour of the little
own. The south-east is full of fields, gardens and meadows, while the
oastal strip in the west between the Punta dello Spalmatore and the
Guardia del Turco is bleak, barren land.

Fleeing from the Laestrygonians, then, keeping a safe distance
rom the land to starboard with the mighty rocks on its coast rising
ke Cyclops – were they really modelled on Monte Erice, Monte
Cofanoa and Monte Monaco? – and going with the north-easterly
urrent, Odysseus and his companions were aware only of endless sea
head of them. But suddenly they thought they saw something in the
istance besides sea-water, sky and clouds, perhaps an illusion con-
ured up by their overtaxed senses, but then taking on more distinct
hape until they were sure of it: there was land ahead.

> We brought our ship to port without a sound
> as a god eased her into a harbour safe and snug,
> and for two days and two nights we lay by there,
> eating our hearts out, bent with pain and bone-tired.
> When Dawn with her lovely locks brought in the third day,
> at last I took my spear and my sharp sword again,
> rushed up from the sea to find a lookout point,
> hoping to glimpse some sight of human labour,
> catch some human voices.

(O, F 10, 154).

If we are to accept the Wolfs' thesis that Ustica could have been
Circe's island, it is only logical to bring Odysseus and his companions
shore where the course they were following would first have carried
hem to the island, besides giving them an opportunity to land: in
he south-west, where the coast lies lower and there are several small
ays like the one at the Punta dello Spalmatore. The place could well
e described as *a harbour safe and snug*, enclosed by rocks on three
des and open only to the north. It would not have been comfortable
o lie on the sharp, jagged rock of the cliffs, eroded by wind, weather
nd salt water, so one imagines the men disembarking from their
hip, going up to the nearby meadows and lying down under their
oaks (O, F 10, 197) or *rugs* (O, R 10, 179), to recover their strength
nly two days and two nights later. When the sun rose on the third
ay, Odysseus saw rising land before him and climbed it, hoping to
e signs of cultivation or hear men's voices (O, R 10, 147).

On the other side of the little bay the forested mountain ridge of the Guardia del Turco and Guardiola rises from the bare meadow. Going round by road, first along the precipitous red-brown coastline then turning inland and passing a few holiday homes and small properties surrounded by tall hedges of Indian fig or thickets of reeds, you can climb the Guardiola quite comfortably apart from the last and steepest part – unlike Odysseus, who reached his lookout quickly and by the direct route, since he was in a hurry to discover what the locality was like. If this were the place, he would have chosen well. The panoramic view would have told him that he had reached a small island surrounded by the wide sea, as he told his companions when he returned from this scouting expedition. But first he made another important discovery: he saw smoke rising among the dense scrub and the trees, and he knew at once that this was Circe's dwelling.

Odysseus also said that the island was flat, without rising land. That would be difficult to reconcile with the morphology of Ustica, since almost the whole central part of the island lies inside the mountain chain. And opposite the Guardiola rises the even higher Guardia Grande, blocking out the view of the Cala Santa Maria, the harbour of the village of Ustica. But we do not have to take Homer quite so literally; we can merge the three high points of the mountain ridge in a single lookout post; seen from that vantage point, almost everything would look like flat land; the rectangular meadows surrounded by low hedges beyond the south-west part of the coast, with the Punta dello Spalmatore – perhaps Odysseus waved his shirt to give a sign to a sharp-eyed man down by the ship – and the handkerchief-shaped fields, meadows and gardens in the north and south-east, fertile with volcanic soil. In fact Circe's home is described as being in a valley and Odysseus reaches it by passing through several valleys but also crossing forested hills.

In Homeric times, and even earlier, the dense forest that still grows on the north-west flanks of the Guardia Grande and the Guardia del Turco would have covered the whole island. And smoke could certainly have risen somewhere, for instance from the huts of a Middle Bronze Age village like the Villaggio Preistorico in the north of the island. The site of Circe's palace? If we place it in the col between the Guardia Grande and Fortezza Falconiera, to which the more modern part of the village of Ustica has now spread from its cramped hillside location on the Tramontana plain, imagine this rising land covered by forest and picture a palatial building of *dressed stone* (O, F 10, 23

- and the houses, roads and walls in much of Ustica are still built of
dressed stone, black, grey or ochre in colour – then from the *cleared
rise of land* (O, F 10, 230) we can see the view of the sea to the west
and east that corresponds to the view today. So let us now allow the
magic wand of fantasy to take over, and listen to the lines of the fairy-
tale singing of the enchantress Circe's dwelling, her nature and the
magic she works:

> Deep in the wooded glens they came on Circe's palace
> built of dressed stone on a cleared rise of land (...)
> she opened her gleaming doors at once and stepped forth,
> inviting them all in, and in they went, all innocence.
> Only Eurylochus stayed behind – he sensed a trap.
> She ushered them in to sit on high-backed chairs,
> then she mixed them a potion – cheese, barley
> and pale honey mulled in Pramnian wine –
> but into the brew she stirred her wicked drugs
> to wipe from their memories any thought of home.
> Once they'd drained the bowls she filled, suddenly
> she struck them with her wand, drove them into her pigsties,
> all of them bristling like swine – with grunts,
> snouts, even their bodies, yes, and only
> the men's minds stayed steadfast as before.

(O, F 10, 229)

Dense woods of pine and cypress trees grow on Guardia del Turco,
and the ground is covered with a thick layer of needles, providing
a springy surface to walk on. It is sprinkled with the white, violet-
striped flowers of orchids and their leaves, still green in November.
All around, the sea appears between the branches like a transparency,
tinged with dull pink against the sun in the south that makes the
tree-trunks stand out from the twilit woods like columns of light,
their other sides glowing in many shades of blue. The wind rushing
through the treetops and the sound of the distant breakers comple-
ment each other, playing the music of the spheres, and it is tempting
to lie among the orchids and abandon yourself to the seductive and
enchanting effect. Looking through a gap among the trees down to
the Punta dello Spalmatore, it is easy to imagine wanderers landing
here, waiting for their leader to return from his scouting expedition
with the depressing report:

Listen to me, my comrades, brothers in hardship,
we can't tell east from west, the dawn from the dusk,
nor where the sun that lights our lives goes under earth
nor where it rises.

(O, F 10, 207).

Here they had reached the limit of their wanderings, they had lost all
sense of direction, and least of all did they have any idea what way to
travel on. Despair spread, and *they burst into cries, wailing, streaming live tears* (O, F 10, 220). But Odysseus, who seems to have taken
the danger and difficulty of any situation as a positive challenge,
first making a judicious analysis and then coming to his decision,
remarked of his companions' outburst only, *That gained us nothing
– what good can come of grief?* (O, F 10, 220). He gave orders for the
next steps to be taken; after casting lots, he himself stayed beside the
ship with some of the men, while Eurylochus set off with the others
to search for Circe's dwelling.

The men of the scouting party marched up to Circe's house and
called to her. Only Eurylochus hung back, and thus escaped his companions' fate. Back at the ship – our point of view switches several
times between Punta dello Spalmatore and the Tramontana – at first
he could not get a word out, he was still so terrified by his experiences, but at last he was able to tell Odysseus how his foolish comrades had accepted the invitation of a *goddess or woman*, and none of
them had come out of her house again. At this Odysseus himself set
out to solve the mystery. Just before reaching Circe's palace he met
the god Hermes, who gave him the herb moly to protect him, along
with precise instructions for outwitting the divine enchantress and
her wiles.

The magical herb moly is a fairy-tale motif in the Circe episode.
Its root is black and its flower white as milk (O, F 10, 338), drawing
magical powers from the dark earth to change above ground into the
white of their healing effect. It protected Odysseus from the magic
potion of the goddess that would have turned him into an addict
in the shape of that unclean animal, the pig. Drawing his sword, he
tamed the beautiful and proud hetaira, threatening to kill her, and
she submitted to him, clasping his knees, flattering him and promis-
ing that if he shared her bed *we'll breed deep trust between us* (O, F
10, 372).

But after they had made love, Odysseus refused to touch the

festive banquet she served until his companions had been turned back into human form. Circe, now abandoning her old magic deceptions and full of goodwill, thereupon recommended her lover to go back to his ship, draw it up on land, and come back with the rest of his companions. And so he did.

For a year the men lived in luxury, and Circe's bed was not deserted. Uvo Hölscher has prettily described this episode as an indulgence, while he gives the term 'captivity' to the much longer time spent by the hero later with Calypso. Odysseus' companions had to remind him to think of his fatherland and set off for home again at last (incidentally, there is no mention of Penelope here).

The fragment of a pitcher found on Ithaca, with a male figure holding a plant at the end of his outstretched arm like a priest with a monstrance, presumably dates from the time before the creation of the *Odyssey*, which would indicate the great age, pre-dating Homer, of the legend of Circe. In front of him stands a woman, raising her arm before her face in a defensive gesture of alarm: Odysseus is imperiously showing Circe the magic herb moly, aware that he has the upper hand, and the enchantress seems to understand the situation – hers is a gesture of submission to be seen, says the social philosopher Theodor Adorno, as 'female self-estrangement in the patriarchal world.' [55] The magical story of Circe on Aeaea will be one of the folk themes that the poet of the *Odyssey* found in the stock of traditional material available to him. The island of Aeaea features, not least, in the tale of Jason and the Golden Fleece.

A much later red-figure pitcher of around 450 BC, now in the Metropolitan Museum in New York, depicts the dramatic first meeting of Odysseus and Circe with what may be described as classic equilibrium. It shows a warrior who, as Homer says, has just drawn his *sharp sword sheathed at [his] hip* to attack the enchantress, who herself holds her magic wand in one hand and in the other the golden bowl of poison, which Odysseus has just drained without being turned into an animal. Her arms reach out to both sides, her body is turned away in self-defence and a spontaneous impulse to flee, with her head turned away from the attacker. Her mouth is closed, but she is about to open it to ask:

Who are you? where are you from? your city? your parents?
I'm wonderstruck – you drank my drugs, you're not bewitched!

(O. F 10, 361)

Artists of antiquity used the transformation of Odysseus's companions into pigs and other animals as a subject more often than this one as a fairy-tale scene to stimulate their imagination. It was a theme they intended to exploit to the full.

We cross the fields past the Guardia Grande, walking over *macchia* and coarse grass, until we reach a cattle track that leads us to the garden of a farm near the ring road on which we return to the village of Ustica. The gardens and fields along the way are often enclosed by massive, sometimes almost Cyclopean walls of lava stone, and houses are built of the same material. You do not have to spend much time searching for it. The paths, roads and squares are solidly built of stones that look as if they would endure for ever. However, while the local people are happy to use the material, they do not want to have black or grey façades in front of them all the time. Most of the village houses are plastered and then painted in an assortment of pastel colours, a suitable background for the frescos adorning many of the walls.

The village goes to bed early. There is still a bar open, presumably the only one on the island. A few men are sitting on the steps outside the bar, smoking – they have to sit outside because of the notice 'Vietato fumare' inside the place. And the no-smoking rule is strictly observed, here as in Palermo, in the bakery and supermarket alike, in the delicatessen and the restaurant. Amazing, but those are the facts in Sicily and Ustica.

One of the many lights that cast a pleasant yellow glow over the Piazza Umberto I and the narrow streets and alleys is the moon. It shines unrivalled when you sit under the tall bay trees by the war memorial, looking up at the sky and out to sea, where the waves are illuminated by its trembling light all the way to the little harbour of Cala Santa Maria. No doubt this place was often frequented by the men whose picture we saw at noon in a little bakery here, although the photograph says nothing of their subsequent history. Men of about thirty or forty, with angular, almost ascetic faces, smiling even though they were political prisoners deported by Mussolini to live in exile here. One would like to know more about the fate of these men; did they, like Odysseus, find a Circe to be a good fairy to them?

> But I will set you a course and chart each seamark,
> so neither on sea nor land will some new trap
> ensnare you in trouble, make you suffer more.

(O. F 12, 29).

VILLAGGIO PREISTORICO. There is a delightful walk to the site of
the earliest settlement on the island, along the narrow roads out of
Ustica, where many flowers and plants in containers stand outside
the houses, and hibiscus and bougainvillea, sometimes in overpower-
ing abundance, hang over the walls. The way now leads up the steep
hill crowned by the Fortezza Falconiera to the Roman necropolis of
dark caverns in red-tinged stone, then down to another and entirely
different necropolis, its buildings white and lavishly adorned with
flowers. This is the local graveyard, separated from the sea only by
the road, on the edge of the Costa del Camposanto. There could be
nowhere more beautiful in which to lay the dead to rest and hope for
their happiness. I feel sure that this would be a good place to speak
to the departed, with the constant *ostinato* of the rushing sea in your
ears while your eyes enjoy the endless view over it.

The road goes on along the steep coastline to the northernmost
tip of the island and the Villaggio Preistorico, where a Middle
Bronze Age village has been excavated. Cultures that had already
made trading contacts as far as the Aegean around 1400–1300 BC
flourished for thousands of years on Sicily and the Liparian Islands,
as Mycenean ceramics show. Ustica too was inhabited at this time,
probably by settlers from Sicily. Is it impossible that Mycenean ships,
engaged in bartering goods with Lipari, Panarea and Filicudi, made
their way to Ustica, that Mycenean seamen knew about this distant
islands, passed on their knowledge, and their tales flowed one day
into the stream of heroic songs of the aöides and rhapsodists, elabo-
rated and intermingled with sailors' yarns and the world of fairy tale,
as if entwined by rambling plants and water lilies?

The rectangular foundations of the Bronze Age huts reach almost
to the rocky coast. We see a few stones lying around, about 50 cm in
size, with smooth hollows in their upper surface. Stones for washing
or for sacrifice? At present they are useful as stone seats, and sitting
there we can let the imagination roam, seeing huts and houses standing in dense woods all the way to the hills, with smoke emerging from
their straw thatch, betraying the presence of human beings to any
observer standing on the peak. We can imagine the poor pigs shut
up in a sty, trying to forget their troubles in eating acorns, beechnuts,
and the fruit of the wild cherry.

A year of indulgence came to an end. The men had spent it *feasting
on lavish quantities of meat and mellow wine* (O, R 10, 466), and now
they were urging Odysseus to set out. They wanted to go home at last.

Odysseus begged Circe to let them leave, and the divine enchantress agreed at once. In addition, she told them about the particular way they must go home, and how they must first visit the realm of the shades, to speak to the old Theban seer Tiresias in Hades:

> He will tell you the way to go, the stages of your voyage,
> how you can cross the swarming sea and reach home at last.
>
> (O, F 10, 594).

To Odysseus' anxious question – how were they to reach the realm of Hades? – the goddess (as Circe is referred to at this point) returns a clear and reassuring answer, not the usual ambiguous statement made by oracles:

> Royal son of Laertes, Odysseus, born for exploits,
> let no lack of a pilot at the helm concern you, no,
> just step your mast and spread your white sail wide –
> sit back, and the North Wind will speed you on your way.
>
> (O, F 10, 553)

City in the Mist

The Halls of Hades – *Himera, Enna*

IMERA. It was early morning when Odysseus woke his companions. Circe had given him sensible clothing for his voyage, *sea-cloak and shirt*, while she herself appeared magnificently robed for their farewells. Soon the ship was made ready to leave, and Circe

> (...) sent us a hardy shipmate,
> yes, a fresh following wind ruffling up in our wake.
>
> (O, F 11, 8).

It was a north wind, and hoisting their sail they voyaged all day long, or in prosaic terms probably for some twelve to fifteen hours. At an average speed of four knots they could have covered fifty to sixty sea miles by sunset. Where would a ship be then if it had set out from the island of Ustica in the morning, and stayed roughly on a southerly course depending on the wind? It would have reached the north coast of a land mass that, if we consult a map, can only be Sicily. According to the Wolfs, the location can be narrowed down even further if we remember the directions given to Odysseus by Circe:

> But once your vessel has cut across the Ocean River
> you will raise a desolate coast and Persephone's Grove,
> her tall black poplars, willows whose fruit dies young.
> Beach your vessel hard by the Ocean's churning shore
> and make your own way down to the mouldering House of Death.
> And there into Acheron, the Flood of Grief, two rivers flow,
> the torrent River of Fire, the wailing River of Tears
> that branches off from Styx, the Stream of Hate.
>
> (O, F 10, 558).

If, like the Wolfs, we take this passage to mean that two rivers flow into the sea here, the whole description of a flat, tree-grown shore with two river mouths suggests the Imera area, between Termini Imerese and Cefalù. Approaching this coastline from the sea, you see a long beach with broad, flat banks beyond it, and mountains coming down on both sides, the foothills of the Monte San Calogero and the Monte d'Oro. Roughly in the middle of the plain, a kilometre from the sea, a table mountain rises, reaching out south and falling steeply to the north. In front of it there are fields almost all the way to the sea, with a motorway running through them. To the left and right the eye is caught by the wide ravines of the valleys of the rivers Torto and Grande.

Where there are now fields, meadows and orchards, the lower part of the town and the necropoles of ancient Himera stood in antiquity. If you climb the steep mountain to the plateau on top, your first impression is that you are standing on a particularly large lookout platform with an impressive all-round view: over the fields and orchards to the sea, up to the mountain peaks cutting off the coastal plain on both sides like gigantic pylons, on to the mountainous country further away, where the river courses of the Fiume Grande and Fiume Torte wind for some way through narrow fields. But an informative notice soon tells you what you have beneath your feet. The place looks at first as if it were nothing but land sparsely grown with grass and littered with stones, but this is the Upper Town of ancient Himera.

Like Zankle (Messina) and Syracuse, it was founded near the Phoenician sphere of influence, and developed into the largest and most important Greek settlement on the Tyrrhenian coast, passing into the annals of history mainly for the battle fought here between the Greeks and the Carthaginians in 480 BC. The Greeks' victory made them masters of the Mediterranean. Well aware of that, they did not hesitate to build three monumental temples of victory, the Doric temple in Syracuse, the Olympic temple in Akragas (Agrigent) and the Doric temple of Himera, erected in the Lower Town. The little that is left of it – the base of the temple, some stumps of columns, a few walls – lies at the foot of the hill where the city stood, between the road and the railway line, even further removed from any look of liveliness by a wire fence.

The Greeks had only six decades in which to thank the gods for their great victory. Then their fortunes changed: in 409 BC the

emple was destroyed by the Carthaginians and the Upper Town
razed to the ground. It was never rebuilt – luckily for the archaeologists of Palermo University, who have periodically carried out excavations here since 1983, for it means they do not have to work their
way down through later layers to reach the remains of the city of
the fifth century BC. At present there seems to be a pause in excavation. We two visitors are alone on the extensive terrain of what was
once the walled part of Himera, covering the entire plateau. We pass
the foundation walls of residential areas, go down the main street of
the Hippodamian grid plan, and find it easy to imagine the people
of Himera in its prime, walking around their city with the sense of
superiority that was part of the Greek position of pre-eminence, and
could withstand the trials of everyday life.

What connection could there be between this city on its mountain, which must be bathed in bright sunlight on many days of the
year, and too hot for comfort in high summer, and the place where,
it was thought, access could be gained to the underworld? The place
where, as Homer says,

> Cimmerian people have their homes – their realm and city
> shrouded in mist and cloud. The eye of the Sun can never
> flash his rays through the dark and bring them light,
> not when he climbs the starry skies or when he wheels
> back down from the heights to touch the earth once more –
> an endless, deadly night overhangs those wretched men.
>
> (O, F 11, 16).

Supporters of the theory that the place where Homer sent his hero
Odysseus down into the underworld is located here, in the country
behind ancient Himera, have put forward several arguments. As
well as the meteorological and geographical factors mentioned by
the Wolfs, they point to the similarity of name between Himera and
the Cimmerians; both are non-Greek names that the Greek settlers
could have found when they came here. Hölscher, on the other hand,
does not think the Cimmerians of the *Odyssey* ever had any existence
in history, only in their mythological home on the River Ocean. It
is difficult, he says, to reconcile the account of their living 'shrouded
in mist and cloud' with the real Cimmerians, a tribe of equestrian
nomads who originally lived in southern Russia on the same latitude
as Venice. Around 700 BC they came south to the Ionian coastal

towns, spreading terror, and destroyed the Phrygian realm. But the Cimmerians of the *Odyssey*, says Hölscher, 'living enveloped in mist and clouds, in a place where no ray of sun can come, are a mythical people on the borders of the underworld.'[56]

Homer's account of the underworld river network, the Wolfs think, could reflect the widespread opinion in antiquity that the northern river of Himera (the Fiume Grande or Imera Settentrionale) and the southern river of Himera (the Fiume Salso or Imera Meridionale) sprang from the same source. In fact their sources, although not far apart, are separate, and lie in the mountainous country about thirty kilometres south-east of Imera.

Legendary and ancient Enna also lies in the area of the Fiume Salso river, towering on a mighty plateau standing high above its surroundings, and often shrouded in mist. Here, on a rocky promontory, stood the shrine of the earth mother Demeter, who ripened the harvest and bestowed rich gifts. And not far below Enna, in a valley by Lake Pergus, Persephone was abducted by Hades and carried off to the underworld, to the great grief of Demeter her mother. It was a long time before Demeter could take her beloved daughter in her arms again. In the version of the Roman poet Ovid, mother and daughter bear the Latin names of Ceres and Proserpina:

> Not far from Henna's walls there is a deep pool of water, Pergus by name. Not Cayster on its gliding waters hears more songs of swans than does this pool. A wood crowns the heights around its waters on every side, and with its foliage as with an awning keeps off the sun's hot rays. The branches afford a pleasing coolness, and the well-watered ground bears bright-coloured flowers. There spring is everlasting. Within this grove Proserpina was playing, and gathering violets or white lilies.[57]

Tourists are shown a grotto on the Lago di Pergusa, the scene of this incident; it is supposed to have been the entrance to the underworld.

So the mists that often rise around the rock city of Enna, shutting out the sun, and the close connection of the place and the nearby Lago di Pergusa with the cycle of myths about Demeter, Hades and Persephone, are arguments that help to support the Wolfs' theory when they locate the country of the Cimmerians and the realm of Hades in the landscape between the town of Himera, close to the sea and providing access from the north, and Enna itself.

The motorway to Enna and Catania is an easy journey at first, and after leaving the coastal plain at Imera it runs a little way along the Fiume Grande through flat country where vegetables are grown. The upper course of the river to the north bends sharply east at Scillato. Its source lies higher up, in an almost inaccessible fold of the mountains in the Monte dei Cervie, part of the Madonia conservation area, and here the rivulet springing from the rocks bears the very appropriate name of the Fosso Inferno, the trench of the underworld.[58] We are on the right track. In all Italy and Sicily, only here is the river name of Fosso Inferno found! The sky is still serene and blue above the sea and the coast, but thick mists are rising from the flanks of the mountain range. Steep slopes where groves of olives grow alternate with pastures and occasionally huge fields, extending over hills and the lower areas between them, brown after crops have been harvested or bright green with new sowings. Later, the southern Imera river, the Imera Meridionale, runs down from the mountains and, a little further south, joins the Fiume Salso into the river that runs right through the island and into the sea at Licata. It is not a torrential river, but a waterway that flows gently along, flanked by eucalyptus trees, shining as it passes below and beside the motorway, which runs on overpasses here for long stretches. It does not seem to have a cheerful sparkle to its waters, and why would it, with the many tons of cement that have spread over the river valley? It may look different in spring, when melting snows from the Madonia and spring rains swell the rivers. 'Wet weather had set in, making travelling very uncomfortable, since we had to ford several greatly swollen water-courses,' wrote Goethe on 29 April 1787, when he was on his way to Enna. 'At the Fiume also, where you may look around in vain for a bridge, a remarkable institution surprised us. Strong men were waiting; two by two they picked took up the mules and their riders and packs by the middle, and so took them through a deep part of the current to a large gravel bank, and in this way we also passed over the second arm of the river.'[9] It is easier today, so one should not criticize civilization too severely. You can sit in the bus and be taken comfortably and quickly to Enna on its rocky plateau, 1000 metres above sea level.

ENNA. The sky is grey, the view of the Piazza Coloianni over Enna Bassa, spreading as if organically out below, is rather bleak. We return to the bus station along dismal streets. We wonder whether to go to the Lago di Pergusa, which we can vaguely see from the nearby cemetery, down in the valley below. An underworld site that we really ought not to miss on a Homeric journey through Sicily. On a map of ancient Sicily, drawn in 1595, it is shown as a lake represented by a small ellipsis, surrounded by a ring of tall trees, and described as *Pergus lacus. Hic Proserpinam a Plutone raptam ferunt.* And the lake appears in a picture of 1819 nestling in a wildly romantic landscape with vapours rising from Etna in the background, while there is a group of people in the foreground on the banks of the lake, dark silhouettes against the light of early morning reflected in the water.

The next bus to Pergusa does not leave until after dark, and no taxi can be found although there is a cab rank nearby. Anyway, a modern photograph shows a stretch of water that leaves no room for mythological illusion. Presumably to increase tourist interest in the rather uninteresting interior of Sicily, a motor-racing circuit has been laid out around Lake Pergusa, which now resembles a huge swimming pool. The race-track is fenced in with wire a metre high and surrounded by a slightly raised area, planted with low-growing shrubs that are kept short and allow a free view, like the stands of a large stadium. Nature tamed, that is the impression conveyed by this postcard. Where are the forests surrounding the lake like a garland, their foliage so dense that the rays of Phoebus cannot shine in; where are the songs of swans on the gliding waters? And there is not even an Etna towering above the hilly horizon, in spite of the cloudless blue sky in the photo.

We leave our bags at the bus station and go back along the gloomy streets, past people already wearing thick jackets, while down in the coastal towns late summer still reigns.

In a café on the Via Roma that runs through the Old Town, Alban Nikolai Herbst[60] helps us to forget our dismal mood with his dithyrambic eulogy of the young people of the city, especially the young women – 'Enna vibrates,' he says. Herbst took part in the evening *corso*, the ceremonial walk with its ritual encounters between the young of both sexes in their prime – and it led him to write a vibrant work of literature which may be better than the reality. Today, at least, the whispering girls and strutting boys seem reluctant to put in a public appearance.

We go on along the Via Roma, past churches and palazzi, up to the massive Castello di Lombardia. Suddenly a pale grey, airy cloud of something rises behind the great corner tower of the fortress. Perhaps smoke from a campfire somewhere? But within seconds it is

illowing up from the southern slope and wrapping the towers as if
in cotton wool. The mists are upon us. I run to the Rocca di Cerere,
oping at least to get a view of the Great Mother's rock in reason-
ble light, although for want of a taxi we mythologically interested
visitors must miss seeing her daughter's lake. But I am almost too
 late – the Rock of Demeter itself, the great lookout post of Sicily,
which offers such famous views in clear weather, is already under
attack. Without a sound, the mist rises up the great plinth of rock on
which the temple of Demeter once stood, adorned at the entrance
with statues of the mother goddess, her daughter Persephone, and
Triptolemos, the man who told the mother what had happened to
her daughter and was rewarded with corn that he distributed among
mankind. The eye just has time to look far down from the outermost
part of the temple, where traces of the foundations can still be seen,
and into the valley below, before that too is instantly veiled in mist.
From the depths, where all sense of place is lost, a note rises, an all-
pervasive humming note, the monotonous sound of the cars crawling
round the bends on the rock of Enna. You see nothing of them, no
lights, you only hear their common note humming up through the
mist to the heights of Da-mater, Da-mater, the earth-mother of primeval times, now vanished for ever.

Apparently the people of Enna claim that these heights are surrounded by mist for nine months of the year, and now we have
found how it can rise within minutes on a clear day, swallowing up a
city and a landscape. It has always been like that, it is a natural phenomenon that may have inspired the creation of myth and fairy tale
in early times. *Their realm and city* are *shrouded in mist and cloud*
(D, F 11, 16). Yellow street lights are now on in the city. The cars
move at snail's pace with their own lights on. Swathes of mist creep
through the streets, making the compact forms of the cathedral,
the churches, the palazzi into vague structures with their contours
merging. In the evening, the bus to Palermo gropes its way through
the mist surrounding the city on its plateau and down to the valley
and suddenly the landscape is free of mist, it widens out again, and
a glance back at the mighty rock where Enna stands offers a picture
like something out of a fairy tale: patches of mist, glowing white in
the illumination of the headlamps of cars, hover over the dark slopes,
and above them stars sparkle in the gaps between the ragged mist as
it disperses. The mist disperses as silently as it came, gathering only
above the buildings, while it has already left the chain of lights along

the edge of the rock free. Then there is another last and spectacular special effect: deep black clouds, delicately lighter at their edges, have come up against the iridescent cap of mist on one side. They swiftly change shape, and there she is, the shining disc, as if drawn up from behind a black curtain: Pandia, the 'very bright', the brightness of a night of full moon born when Selene does not shrink from the advances of the father god. Night has to fall before there is light in the land of the Cimmerians.

There are many sulphur mines in the country beyond the two Himera rivers, and they have been worked since antiquity. Perhaps, Wolf & Wolf suggest, we could also think of the workers at the mine face as realistic models for the Cimnmerians 'shrouded in mist and cloud', toiling underground for many hours to find that it was night when they finally came up from the mines, and the sun had set – *the eye of the Sun can never flash his rays through the dark and bring them light* (O, F 11, 17). In the story by the Nobel prize-winner Luigi Pirandello, *The Smoke*,[61] there is a passage describing exactly this fate for workers in sulphur mines. 'And each of them thought, on going home, that a hundred, two hundred metres underground, beneath these slopes illuminated by the pale moonlight, people were still scraping and toiling – the poor face-workers, who did not care whether it was day or night up above, since for them it was always night.' While we may think any possibility that Homer knew about the work and living conditions of Sicilian workers in the sulphur mines very speculative, the Wolfs have put forward that idea, and cannot be dismissed out of hand, for there are accounts in antiquity of the inhuman fate of miners to whom the sun was a distant heavenly body, known to them almost entirely from hearsay.

RETURN TO USTICA. After Odysseus had seen the ghosts of the famous dead in the underground realm of Hades, and those of tens of thousands of unknown people too, he felt a sudden fear that Persephone might regard him as an intruder into her kingdom and send the Gorgon's monstrous head with its dreadful fangs to attack him. Knowing that anyone who saw Medusa's terrible face would stop breathing and be turned to stone at once, he hurried back to his ship as his companions were already preparing to move away. First rowing, then sailing with a favouring wind, they soon came back to land on Aeaea.

From the flowing waters of the River of Ocean my ship passed into the
wide spaces of the open sea; and so reached the island of Aeaea, where,
ever-fresh, Dawn has her home and her dancing-lawns, and where the
Sun rises. Here we beached the ship on the sands and climbed out on
to the shore.

(O, R 12, 1).

ack to Aeaea meant back to Circe's island, and thus a return from
ne north coast of Sicily to Ustica. At least, that is how the Wolfs
aterpret this passage. And they also have a theory of where the
anding took place: at the main harbour of the Cala Santa Maria in
ne north-east of Ustica. In terms of navigation there is something to
e said for the theory that a ship coming from the south-east, that is
o say from the north-east coast of Sicily at Imera, could have taken
uch a course. Moreover, the fact that Odysseus and his men come
shore on that part of the island where *Dawn has her home and her*
ancing-lawns, and where the Sun rises is understood by the Wolfs
s a poetically phrased clue to an eastern landing-place on Circe's
land, i.e. 'where the Sun rises'. That again, one may add, would have
seant a voyage of some twelve hours. Within twenty-four hours,
om one dawn to the next – from the coming of Dawn, enthroned
a gold, to her next appearance newborn – they would have gone
om Circe's island to the limits of the Ocean River, thought to sur-
ound the world, to the land and city of the Cimmerians, and back
gain across the river and over the sea to Aeaea.

A round trip from Ustica to Imera/Enna and back again? Here
Jvo Hölscher issues a warning. We should not allow ourselves, he
ays, to think in terms of such models as realistic geographical ideas.
'hat would be to misinterpret the mythological language employed
ere in the account of the nocturnal journey across the Ocean, which
a parallel to the path traced by the sun at night.[62] Yet it is easy to
magine the vivid scene of the meeting between Circe and the men
s she tells them the way to go after their return to her island, and
sere could hardly be a more beautiful place for the feast to which
he nymph's serving maids brought *trays of bread and meats galore*
nd glinting ruddy wine (O, F 12, 18) than the benches in the shade of
ll laurel trees near the Piazza Umberto I in Ustica. With a telescope,
lthough not quite with the naked eye, the visitor can even get an
lea of where Odysseus's next adventure was waiting, at bird-headed
Capo Peloro on the north-east point of Sicily.

Back again from the realms of night and on Circe's island, Odysseus and his companions buried the youngest of the men, Elpenor who had accidentally broken his neck in Circe's palace after drinking through the night before they set off for Hades. After that Circe tells the men the course they should set, and warns them of all the dangers of their voyage back to Ithaca: the island of the Sirens, the straits between Scylla and Charybdis, Thrinacia the island of Helios. Ustica was Circe's island, and the land and city of the Cimmerians as well as the House of Hades were to be found just beyond the ancient city of Himera, then the way home, the *nostos,* must lead them east along the north coast of Sicily, until they had passed through the Straits of Messina between Scylla and Charybdis, thus reaching the Ionian Sea and home waters. But the two Sirens were lying in wait for passing seamen even before they reached Scylla and Charybdis.

The Perilous Magic of Music

Island of the Sirens – *Cape Peloro/north-east Sicily*

Sirens in the physical sense are easily encountered on land or water – although it is less easy to find the zoological species, the manatee or sea-cow, and you would have to go to the coasts of the American continent, Africa or India to do so – but such sirens are not at the centre of our interest here as we track down the Homeric clues to the course of the *Odyssey*. The Sirens to be feared there were mythical beings, often with such enchanting names as 'she whose voice awakens longing' or 'she of the beautiful voice', or are simply described as 'enchanting', 'intoxicating', or 'the white goddess'. These sirens were bird-shaped but had human heads, and often female breasts and arms. They were particularly associated with music, played the lyre and the double lute, and sang with clear and lovely voices that aroused longing. On Ionian and Attic funerary monuments, they were shown as seabirds accompanying and mourning the dead, or receiving them into the underworld with song, music played on stringed instruments, and the sound of flutes to make their fate more bearable. No greater compliment can be paid to any art than to believe that it can alleviate the bitterness of death.

Certainly the best known are the murderous Sirens of the *Odyssey*. On the surface, the epic sounds positively Philistine in its attitude to music, at least in the Sirens episode. Odysseus stopped the ears of his companions with softened wax as the ship passed, so that they would not hear the Sirens' song. At a closer reading, however, you realize that a deep respect for the enticing power of music lies behind his approach to the subject. The tale in Book 12 of the passage past the flowery meadow, which can have taken hardly more than a few minutes, is told no less than three times: first in Circe's prophecy of the way and its dangers; then in the captain's instructions to his crew

after they have put out to sea from Circe's island, which are brief but
indicate the potentially mortal danger; finally in the more extensive
account by Odysseus of their encounter with the bird-women and
the soft song of the Sirens, which was seductive but deadly if you had
no wise adviser like Circe.

> Race straight past that coast! Soften some beeswax
> and stop your shipmates' ears so none can hear,
> none of the crew, but if you are bent on hearing,
> have them tie you hand and foot in the swift ship,
> erect at the mast-block, lashed by ropes to the mast
> so you can hear the Sirens' song to your heart's content.
> But if you plead, commanding your men to set you free,
> then they must lash you faster, rope by rope.
>
> (O, F 12, 53).

Odysseus gave his companions similar instructions, and thus fore-
armed they embarked upon the venture, well aware of their fate if
they did not follow Circe's advice:

> Whoever draws too close,
> off guard, and catches the Sirens' voices in the air –
> no sailing home for him, no wife rising to meet him,
> no happy children beaming up at their father's face.
> The high, thrilling song of the Sirens will transfix him,
> lolling there in their meadow, round them heaps of corpses
> rotting away, rags of skin shrivelling on their bones.
>
> (O, F 12, 46).

The moment has come. The Sirens have sighted the ship passing by
within hearing distance. Enchanting song rings out across the water,
and not only is the sweetness of the melody enticing and seductive,
so are the promises of the words:

> Come closer, famous Odysseus – Achaea's pride and glory –
> moor your ship on our coast so you can hear our song!
> Never has any sailor passed our shores in his black craft
> until he had heard the honeyed voices pouring from our lips,
> and once he hears to his heart's content sails on, a wiser man.
> We know all the pains that the Greeks and Trojans once endured

on the spreading plain of Troy when the gods willed it so –
all that comes to pass on the fertile earth, we know it all!

(O, F 12, 200)

One can understand that only radical measures were enough to protect the men from such temptation, raised to its highest degree – the power of the musical notes made potent by the promise of god-like omniscience. Their ears must be stopped. But Odysseus, torn between grim earnest and play, between inexorable fate and self-determination, between reason and a gambler's instincts, between myth and enlightenment', had himself tied to the mast in line with the dictates of reason, but with his ears open, for his *heart was filled with such a longing to listen* (O, R 12, 194). Horkheimer and Adorno have drawn some extremely illuminating ideas from the wonderful passage in the *Odyssey* describing the Sirens' song: 'It is impossible,' they write, 'to hear the Sirens and not succumb to them; they cannot be defied. Yet defiance and infatuation are as one, and those who defy them are lost to the myth that they oppose. Cunning, however, is defiance made reasonable. Odysseus does not try to find some route that will help him to avoid the Sirens' island. Nor does he try to assert his own superior knowledge and listen freely to the temptresses, imagining that his independent mind is sufficient protection. He is humble; the ship takes its predestined and fateful course, and he realizes that, however deliberately he distances himself from nature, as he listens he will be seduced. Momentarily abandoning the terms of his thraldom, he struggles to free himself from his bonds and rush into the arms of the Sirens who would destroy him (...) Odysseus, technically an enlightened man, recognizes the archaic power of song by having himself tied to the mast. He bows to the song of desire and thwarts it, as he thwarts death. Hearing it, although bound, he longs to go to the Sirens like any other man. But he has organized matters so that, although he has succumbed to their song, he does not succumb to them.'[63]

Temptresses, destroyers – that is how the Sirens appear in the *Odyssey*, where they are not described in any detail. In particular, there is no mention of their appearance, which was somewhere between bird and woman. They are shown thus, however, in many works of pictorial art, the earliest dating from about a hundred years after the composition of the epic. It is on a Corinthian aryballos, a bulbous oil flask from the Ludwig Collection in the Museum of Antiquities in

Basle. There are later depictions on oil and wine jars, storage vessels
for wine, pitchers, bowls, engraved gems, pottery lamps, urns and sarcophagus lids, on a Pompeiian fresco, on top of a pediment, and as
freestanding statues of bird-women, while several Etruscan urns with
relief decoration show the Sirens in purely human form, as women
musicians playing the lyre, syrinx and flute. Particularly vivid and dramatic is the encounter of Odysseus and the Sirens, showing him still
bound to the mast but desiring them with all his heart, on two wine
pitchers in the Berlin Collection of Antiquities, one black-figure on
an orange background, one red-figure on a black background, both
of about 360 BC. Also impressive is a red-figure wine storage jar of
470 BC, in the British Museum in London; its stark contrast of red
and black is very dramatic. Bernard Andreae offers an enlightening
explanation for the representation of the Sirens as bird-women in
pictorial art although the literary text does not describe them in that
form: 'The Sirens of the *Odyssey* are shown as half-birds in order to
give graphic visual form to their sweet song.'[64]

Such hybrid beings had reached Greek art through the tradition
of the ancient East and Egypt. But in addition 'the Sirens of the
Odyssey must themselves contain a poetic memory of the bird-men
in ancient Eastern and Egyptian funerary art.'

But where, we may ask as we look for the trail of Odysseus after
all our deviations from it above, where was the flowery meadow in
which the bird-maidens sang so sweetly? In pictorial representations,
the Sirens are almost always shown sitting on cliffs or rocks. But we
hear only of a meadow in the *Odyssey*, a *flowery meadow* (O, R 12, 159)
at that, and it lies on *the isle of the two Sirens* (O, M 12, 167). From
antiquity to the twentieth century, it has been thought that the Bay
of Naples, with Capri and the little Galli islands at the entrance to
Sorrento Bay, were the home of the Sirens.

The Wolfs have their eye on another location as the place where, in
Homer's account, Odysseus escaped the song of the Sirens, although
sore at heart. In their view it is more likely to be the dune running out
from land in the form of a bird's beak to the extreme north-east of
Sicily, which with Capo Peloro forms the north-western limit of the
famous or infamous Stretto di Messina, the Strait of Messina. Once a
small island, today the map shows it as a peninsula, but divided from
Sicily itself by two lagoons that are becoming increasingly silted up
with sand. The smaller, Pantano Piccolo, has long lines of wooden
poles and floating canisters in it, making the slightly rippling water

with its blurred contours look, in the evening twilight, like a large scarf covered with appliqué work and incrustations. Men stand beside their boats in the shallow water at the edge of the lagoon, letting out ropes and tying canisters and wire baskets to them. What exactly is their mysterious activity? They are simply farming mussels.

If you came across the Tyrrhenian Sea from the west from the island of Ustica, from Palermo, Cefalù, passing needle-like Capo Rasocolmo – as Odysseus would have done in the theory proposed by the Wolfs – you would see the coastline running out to the low-lying end of Capo Peloro, which had a lighthouse on it in later centuries, Torre Faro.

The water close to shore here is pale green, changing further out to greenish blue, then blue-green, until off the Calabrian coast there is a strip of ultramarine blue water surrounded to left and right by mountains, some shadowed with blue, some with light green. The pale walls of the houses of Scilla are there before you, and the famous rock itself is visible to the naked eye.

The flat, sandy shore off Torre Faro extends around Capo Peloro to the north, and continues into a strip of coastline many kilometres long, past the sandy dune of Capo Rasocolmo, which is over-grown with vegetation, to the Milazzo refineries which manufacture their own cloudy sky. Little fishing villages promise no more than a bathing beach and modest summer pleasures.

A chain of hills follow the flat coast to Torre Faro, with fields and meadows interspersed by a few houses. Imagine them gone, as well as the abundance of modern rubbish lying around, and you could picture flowery meadows with women musicians sitting on them, as they did on the island of Anthemoessa, 'rich in flowers', given to the Sirens, according to Hesiod, by Zeus.

But why, in Homer's account, must the Sirens bring destruction as they sing and play, piling rotting corpses and shrivelling scraps of human skin up around them? Had the poet heard of the dangers of navigating too close to Capo Peloro, where changes of depth are a threat? Modern sea charts and handbooks to the Mediterranean still issue warnings. 'Keep *at least 1000 m* clear of Capo Peloro (...). Ships approaching from the north-west must (...) avoid the shallows between Capo Rasocolmo and Capo Peloro.'[65] Homer lived at the time of the great Greek colonization of the lands to its west. Could this have been a case of using ancient legends – which perhaps reflected real facts – and new information as raw material for the poetic imagination to make a highly dramatic, gripping scene from what may at first have been a harmless tale of Sirens mingling with seafarers' reports of particular dangers here? Had Greek seamen spoken of the perilous attractions of a coast that seemed to invite them to land on it, although constantly changing shallows made it dangerous to do so? Perhaps they had seen a beach with people waving and even audibly calling to them, just before they had to navigate the notoriously difficult Strait of Messina on their way from the Tyrrhenian into the Ionian Sea?

On one hand, since time immemorial the Strait of Messina has been considered the site of the rocks of Scylla and Charybdis, making it a kind of fixed point in our idea of Homeric geography; on the other Odysseus, leaving the island of the Sirens, tells us, *We had no sooner put this island behind us than I saw a cloud of spume ahead and a raging surf, and heard the thunder of the breakers* (O, R 12, 201) – the first signs of the turbulence associated with Scylla and Charybdis. The Wolfs therefore assume that the island of the Sirens was not far from the place where the sea monsters lived, on the dune of Faro close to Capo Peloro and at the entrance to the Strait of Messina.

Myth Made from Reality

Scylla and Charybdis/The Clashing Rocks – *Straits of Messina/ Stromboli*

SCYLLA. And now disaster follows disaster. Odysseus and his men have only just escaped the enticing song of the Sirens and the fate of other seafarers – to be added to that great pile of bodies rotting on the flowery meadow, or perish with the skin shrivelling on their bones – when the next catastrophe threatens them. *We had no sooner put this island behind us than I saw a cloud of spume ahead and a raging surf, and heard the thunder of the breakers* (O, R 12, 201). The violence of Nature heralds danger: a cloud of spray, raging surf and huge breakers, a low and thunderous droning sound. The men are paralysed and let their oars drop; the ship comes to a halt. But Odysseus, undaunted, has another great scene to play. He addresses his crew:

> Friends, we're hardly strangers at meeting danger –
> and this danger is no worse than what we faced
> when Cyclops penned us up in his vaulted cave
> with crushing force! But even from there my courage,
> my presence of mind and tactics saved us all,
> and we will live to remember this some day,
> I have no doubt.

> (O, F 12, 227).

Undaunted Odysseus may be, but he is also chilled to the heart: he gives the steersmen and crew short, clear orders. He does not tell them what Circe has revealed to him: they are in a dilemma, and now they must decide between the dreadful alternatives Scylla and

Charybdis. Circe has warned him that Charybdis was even worse than Scylla. Charybdis 'gulps the dark water down,' and then:

> Three times a day she vomits it up, three times she gulps it down,
> that terror! Don't be there when the whirlpool swallows down –
> not even the earthquake god could save you from disaster.
> No, hug Scylla's crag – sail on past her – top speed!
> Better by far to lose six men and keep your ship
> than lose your entire crew.'

(O, F 12, 116).

One of the pleasures of studying ancient writers is suddenly finding echoes of them in the present day, for instance, when you find that in modern Greek the word *glykipikros*, first found in Sappho ('bittersweet', like the wound inflicted on the poet herself by Eros) still exists 2,700 years later. Or when, in Messina, you board the ferry to the Villa Giovanni on the Calabrian side of the straits and in your mind's eye you see a rock that you have just glimpsed from Torre Faro, some kilometres along the coastal road from the Villa San Giovanni. The rock appears before you as you round a bend on the Capo Pasci, rising steep and rugged from the sea, flat on top, with a fortress on it. Then a col leads on into the coastal range of hills, where houses stand crowded side by side. You are approaching the entrance to the village. And there, on the white sign with its narrow black rim, is the name of the village in simple lettering: SCILLA.

Scilla! It is no coincidence that the name given to the village, the rock with the fortress, even the rocky coast from here to the Punta del Pezzo, sounds so like the name of the monster in the *Odyssey*. According to a generally accepted tradition dating from antiquity, this is the place supposed to have been haunted by the horrific figures of Scylla and Charybdis. Thucydides, our oldest source for the story, gave this interpretation of the Scylla and Charybdis episode in the *Odyssey*, which presumably derived from an old seafaring yarn, in a factual geographical description with a reasonable explanation of the nautical difficulties: 'Now the strait is that arm of the sea between Rhegium and Messene, at the point where Sicily is nearest the mainland; and it is the Charybdis, so-called, through which Odysseus is said to have sailed. On account of its narrowness and because the water falls into it from two great seas, the Etruscan and the Sicilian, and is full of currents, it has naturally been considered dangerous.' [66]

Obviously the historian, who lived in Athens around 460 BC and is regarded as the father of modern historical writing, saw a natural phenomenon behind the fairy tale of Scylla and Charybdis, for to him reason was the absolute prerequisite for the understanding of history. His way of putting it – 'the Charybdis, so-called, through which Odysseus is said to have sailed' – makes it clear that he is distancing himself from the poetic narrative of the *Odyssey*.

The view when you approach Scilla from the opposite side along the autostrada is equally spectacular: green slopes falling to the sea from Aspromonte, until you can see the rock with the fortress on it, and the houses built close together up the mountainside and along the bay. Up in Scilla, on the green terrace by the main square, a handsome spur of rock overhanging the Lower Town, you feel inclined to populate the rocks of Scilla, the strait, Capo Peloro on the other side and Stromboli in the distance with the men, monsters, hybrid beings and scenes of the *Odyssey*.

If you picture the geographical and topographical conditions in the region of the north-east point of Sicily, with Calabria and the Liparian Islands lying opposite, then the thesis, first proposed in antiquity, that you are particularly close to the trail of events in the *Odyssey* seems plausible even to those who know little of the subject. The outstanding scenic feature is undoubtedly the Strait of Messina, which presents seafaring problems that have certainly been known since navigation in these waters first began. And such a striking, impressive and terrifying natural phenomenon as the volcano of Stromboli, rising over 900 metres above sea level and almost constantly spewing out lava, stone and ash, deserved mention in a work of literature that had any relation to reality.

CIRCE'S DESCRIPTION OF THE ROUTE. If we are following the traditional interpretation of the text of Book 12 of the epic, the difficulty is not so much whether we can assume links between this region and the *Odyssey* as how to reconcile the text with the geographical facts. Circe had described the course that Odysseus must take after passing the island of the Sirens as follows:

> But once your crew has rowed you past the Sirens
> a choice of routes is yours. I cannot advise you
> which to take, or lead you through it all –

you must decide for yourself –
but I can tell you the ways of either course.

(O, F 12, 62).

I cannot lead you through it all … but I can tell you the ways of either course. Is Circe slightly confused, is this a small lapse in concentration? She usually expresses herself so clearly and precisely. Did the poet lose the thread of his ideas for a moment? This is a contradictory textual passage, and it has led to much controversy.

As the following lines show, Circe is generous with her information, giving a further detailed description of the route. Here there are difficulties of interpretation in the passage speaking of two rocks:

On the other side loom two enormous crags …
One thrusts into the vaulting sky its jagged peak,
hooded round with a dark cloud that never leaves –
no clear bright air can ever bathe its crown,
Not even in summer's heat or harvest-time.
No man on earth could scale it, mount its crest,
not even with twenty hands and twenty feet for climbing,
the rock's so smooth, like dressed and burnished stone.
And halfway up that cliffside stands a fog-bound cavern
gaping west toward Erebus, realm of death and darkness –
pass it, great Odysseus, you should steer your ship.
No rugged young archer could hit that yawning cave
with a winged arrow shot from off the decks.

(O, F 12, 82).

(…)
The other crag is lower – you will see, Odysseus.

(O, F 12, 112).

There is a widely held view that the two rocks indicate the limits of the straits, with the higher foothills on the Calabrian coast representing Scylla, and the flatter Sicilian side being Charybdis. However, it would be hard to reconcile this interpretation with the geological facts. The alleged Charybdis side is a positive pinnacle of rock, not at all flat even on top, and the rock of Scylla is certainly a massive one but no more than 100 metres high. The buildings climbing up the slope soon rise above it, and it is far from thrusting its peak – which cannot be called jagged – into the sky.

But where can a geological formation to fit the text be found n the topographical area of the Lipari Islands with Stromboli and he Straits of Messina? It has to be a particularly striking natural ohenomenon. And the eye falls on Stromboli! Of course it could oe Stromboli, with its head reaching to the sky and the dark cloud constantly emerging from its fumarole! Such a thesis could also be reconciled with the previous passage about the rocks known to the gods as the *Wandering Rocks* (O, R 12, 61), or *Clashing Rocks* (O, F 12, 68), a threat to all seamen. In other words, the Clashing or Wandering Rocks and the tall, pointed peak belonged together as a poetic version of an imposing natural feature, unmistakably indicating one of the two directions between which Odysseus must choose.

But for everything to fit together as briefly outlined here, we have to rearrange some of the lines in the text of the *Odyssey* Book 12, lines 55–110, as it has come down to us, assuming that at some time mistakes crept into the original order. This is Armin Wolf's basic thesis, with the position of line 56. 'The puzzle is solved if we recognize that the position of this line is absurd. The line (*I cannot give you precise advice – you must choose for yourself* [O, R 12, 56]) does not make sense at the beginning of the description of a route, but at its end.' [57] The rearrangement of several lines as suggested above gives us a sequence that does indeed allow us to trace the route taken by Odysseus, reduced to the lowest common denominator, as follows: after passing the island of the Sirens, there are two possible ways for him to voyage on, either northward past the landmark of Stromboli, or southward into the nearby Strait of Messina.

STROMBOLI. Let us look at this possibility in more detail, taking up the story again at the point where Circe tells Odysseus that she will point out two ways he might take, but leaves the choice between them open. Then she gives a detailed description of the way to the Clashing Rocks. If we follow the rearrangement suggested by Wolf – reading lines 73 to 84 directly after lines 57 and 58, and then lines 59 to 72 – we have a sharp peak of rock reaching to the sky and surrounded by a dark cloud that never disperses. Armin Wolf sees these lines as a good description of the volcanic island of Stromboli with its permanent crown of smoke, the fumarole. The impossibility of climbing the gigantic peak or even setting foot on it is easily explained if we imagine the vertiginously steep lava field of the Sciara del Fuoco, the 'stream of fire', leading from the crater to the sea. And the hollow grotto, so far away from ships passing by below that even a strong young man could not shoot an arrow up to it, could be the crater of the volcano itself. Stromboli is always active, flinging up lava, red-hot stones and ash every ten to twenty minutes to race down to the sea over the Sciara del Fuoco. Was Homer describing this vast natural spectacle in lines 59 ff? In English, Rieu's version runs:

> One [route] leads to those sheer cliffs which the blessed gods know
> as the Wandering Rocks. Here blue-eyed Amphitrite sends her great
> breakers thundering in.

If modified by Wolf's theory, this would read something like:

> From there rocks [fall] sheer, and blue-eyed Amphitrite sends her great
> breakers thundering in. The blessed gods call these [i.e. the stones flung
> hither and thither] the Wandering Rocks.

To continue with the standard arrangement:

> The very birds cannot fly by in safety, even the shy doves that bring
> ambrosia to Father Zeus (...). For any sailors who bring their ship to
> the spot, there is no escape whatever. They end as flotsam on the sea,
> timbers and corpses tossed in confusion by the waves or licked up by
> tempestuous and destroying flames.
>
> (O, R 12, 61 ff.)

Wolf would replace the idea of flames licking up by outbreaks of flame. Stones are flung from the crater on the island, he suggests in his comments on these lines, and the outbreaks of flame denote the red-hot lava flowing to the sea. In general, he sees this passage as a description of the volcanic activity of Stromboli, even if he considers the regular destruction of all passing ships as 'the exaggeration of a sailor's yarn'.

We decide against taking an *aliscafo* from Panarea to Stromboli for the sake of leaving at a better time or reaching our destination faster, at least on our first visit. These hydrofoils offer almost nothing one wants from a crossing apart from speed, which must of course be important to the islanders in everyday life. A trip on an *aliscafo* means a bone-shaking voyage in a kind of bus skimming he water, with acoustic accompaniment from a rasping TV that ives only distorted images, while the pictures outside can hardly e seen through the milky, scratched panes. When going from the ttle Lipari island of Panarea to Stromboli this first time, of course e prefer to take an ordinary ferry with a deck, and freedom to 1ove about and look at the view. Three of us travellers have all the enches on deck to ourselves; the islanders know what the scenery 2oks like and either shelter from the wind in a corner or go into he cabin below.

We, however, never tire of the views: back to Panarea, with the hite houses of San Pietro and Ditella set in the semi-circle of rocks s if in an amphitheatre; ahead to the scattered crowd of little islands nd cliffs of the Basiluzzo group with their bold, bizarre rock for-1ations – in many places looking almost like Gothic tracery, or the lamboyant style, or wedding-cake style, created in the workshops f nature with Manueline exuberance – beyond which the great, alm, regular mass of Stromboli seems to look casually at the merry scapades of the Scoglio Spanazzola, Panarelli, Bottaro and Co. We lance back again past Panarea to the delicate pastels of the more istant islands of Filicudi, Salina, Lipari and Vulcano, which appear lmost immaterial; then ahead, where only Stromboli draws the eye 2 itself. It is not so regular as we come closer but gains in volume, ructure and individuality, until we see before us a mountain with variety of formations, with sharp ridges, deep valleys and ravines, ast ashfields. Again and again, at fairly regular intervals, grey smoke ses from the peak, quickly forming a mushroom shape, an umbrella ine, piled cloud that soon disperses as the smoke blows away – from distance, it is as if the mountain were quietly puffing at a pipe, and 1ere is no sense of a forceful volcanic eruption. The houses of the illage of Ginostra in the west of the island, a place with a population f thirty souls and accessible only by boat, are white, so are the houses f the harbour village of Scari in the north-east, while the lava sand n the beaches in front of those villages is black.

We go into Scari, walking up a slight rise to the churchyard of the an Vincenzo part of the village. Here there is a bar that goes by the 2od old Italian name of 'Ingrid' and has a picture-book view. 'Ingrid' for summer visitors only, its club is closed, the panorama magnifi-ent, the place empty. A man comes up and asks if we are looking 2r accommodation for the night. His boarding-house is not far off, few metres from the house where Ingrid Bergmann stayed during

the shooting of the film *Stromboli, Terra di Dio*, now the Ingrid Berg
mann House. The boarding-house is very simple, very quiet, and as i
only to be expected on the Liparian Islands expensive, even if there
are few tourists here.

Sunlight over the sea and the volcano, cloud only above its peak
– cloud produced by the mountain itself, merely a feather in its huge
hat. The weather forecast for tomorrow does not promise such good
conditions as we have today. That means I must make the most of i
and see how far up towards the crater I can get. The ascent begins a
I leave the Piscita area at the north-west end of the village of Strom
boli. It has been made quite an easy walk for hikers at first, with a
paved road of black lava stone that runs uphill along the northern
flank of the island for a while and into extensive beds of tall reeds
which come as a surprise to anyone expecting the typical *macchia* o
Mediterranean mountains. The only particle to show on the endles
surface of the sea is Strombolicchio, the tiny volcanic island a kilome
tre and a half north of Scari. Its massive, vertical cliff is the visible par
of a stone column going deep into the sea; all that is left of the lav
inside a volcanic chimney obliterated by the patient work of destruc
tion of the waves.

The paved road, by now only a narrow track, ends at the Filo de
Fuoco, a small clearing at the edge of an abrupt precipice. Looking
across it, I see opening up before me for the first time the breathtak
ing view of the Sciara del Fuoco, the huge ashfield of the volcano
falling from the opening of the crater 150 metres below the peak t
the sea. It is about 750 metres long and 1000 metres wide. Now it i
afternoon, and the Sciara del Fuoco and the steep slopes beyond i
to the south are dark mountain massifs, back-lit, with the sunligh
forming a dazzlingly bright track on the slightly rippling sea betwee
the pale pink of the islands of Salina and Filicudi silhouetted on th
horizon.

The path now become very straight and steep, passing throug
macchia and loose, stony soil. The Sciara del Fuoco is out of sigh
now, but clouds like mushrooms and umbrella pines above the dar
outlines of the crater guide us on our way. And then there is an inci
dent – no, not red-hot lava pouring over my feet, not rocks flyin
dangerously close. Two mountain wardens come towards me, tellin
me to turn back; visitors are allowed only as far as the Filo del Fuoc
Rather reluctantly, I follow them back there. Soon a third mountai
warden emerges from below – by now the other two have move

way – and offers to let me climb with him. His destination is a man-
made platform covered with a metal grating at about 400 metres up,
a small helicopter landing pad by the very edge of a precipice. The
man is observing the activity of the volcano from here.

He leaves me to admire the wonderful panorama. Above, I can
clearly see the notched rim of the crater opening with a pale cloud
tinged with pink and yellow above it. The whole Sciara del Fuoco
down to the sea is now covered by layers of the finest ash-dust, swirled
up by the wind. It catches the path of light cast by the sun and unites
the colours of the sea, alternating between gold, pink and blue. There
is not a sound to be heard, not from the crater or the sea, no human
or animal voice.

The peak, enveloped in vapours, the smooth, almost impassably
steep gradient of the mountain, the opening of the crater to the west;
the waves that break high at the foot of Stromboli in stormy weather;
the purely mineral Sciara de Fuoco, hostile to all life; finally, the jets
of fire cast up to a height of a hundred metres and more when there
is a eruption – all these phenomena display an astonishing likeness
to the Homeric description in Book 12 of the *Odyssey* with the text
readjusted as Wolf suggests.

The moon is already visible as twilight begins to fall; time to turn
round. As I stumble over *macchia* and lava stone, Stromboli finally
performs what the travel guides offer as a 'spectacle several times an
hour', although it had not yet put its show on for us: it spews fiery
lava that makes the Sciara del Fuoco, for the most part a stream of
ash, the 'stream of fire' for which it is named. Back at the Filo del
Fuoco, I see the lava falling down the steep ashen slope like a trail
of syrup. Reaching the sea, it turns the water to thick steam towering higher and higher up, until a huge bluish white mountain range
of cloud is created. The absolute majesty of this natural spectacle is
ensured by the subtle lighting provided by the setting sun, dissolving
sea and sky into an ephemeral ecstasy of colour.

A small correction here: the travel guide did not tell the truth.
Stromboli did not spew fire for me, and the description in the para-
graph above, I am afraid, is not my personal experience but comes
from coloured postcards and photographs of the volcano when
active. But on postcards you do see the mighty cloud of vapour, born
from the sea and touching the sky, and photographs show the orange
lava making its way down the black slope. However, you do not need
an eruption in order to appreciate the infinitely beautiful sunset with

the fiery plume of dust over the Sciara del Fuoco, which as the light leaves it finally turns, with fine nuances of colour, into a delicate veil of grey hovering over the mountainside like light and misty down, or the mountain, black as soot at last against the paean to light sung by the sun setting between the islands of Filicudi and Alicudi, or the sky when only the reflection of the sun kindles some strips of cloud to a bluish glow, like an abstract medieval altarpiece.

And there is even a magical nocturne when, as the visitor climbs on down, he can see red clouds glowing through the tall reeds on one side, the white moon shining on the other side, and a dark mushroom cloud standing high above the jagged black volcano and dispersing into the light blue sky.

A serenade of farewell to the Aeolian Islands. Early evening and warm light in the little harbour of the town of Lipari. We are sitting at the foot of the broad flight of steps of the Salita San Giuseppe leading to the church of the same name, at one of the tables of a small bar set out by the harbour basin outside. The Chitarra Bar. And that is not just its name; the proprietor is sitting on the quay wall with some guests who are friends of his. He has fetched a guitar, hands it to one of the men, who plucks a few chords, another man begins to sing softly, quietly, just for himself and his friends – and for us who happen by chance to be in the audience too. Twilight has fallen now, there is lamplight, the moon is full, the sea murmurs – perhaps I should be ashamed of such kitsch. Well, I am a little ashamed, but I listen, enchanted, to the beautiful songs, which are so full of feeling. The guitar is passed from hand to hand, everyone contributes another melody; now and then all the voices sing together, either in unison or in heart-wrenching thirds in two-part harmony. One man leaves; another strolls over to the group, humming along, and after a while takes the guitar himself and sings – very softly, with great care; it is amazing to hear such delicate notes come from his stout massive body. A schoolgirl runs up, bangs her satchel down on a table. A young woman arrives, kisses the landlord and sits down. The music goes on. Suddenly the proprietor goes into his bar and soon reappears singing the note *a* at standard pitch (presumably he has checked it with a tuning fork) and still singing it – *la, la, la* – communicates it to the present guitarist, who re-tunes the instrument. Another melody, another song, hovering above the ostinato of the quiet murmur of the sea. Then the bells from the nearby church of San Giuseppe break into this fine filigree of notes and sounds. Their peal is shrill, deafening. The magic is broken, the magical hour over. *Il conto, prego.*

UNDERWATER EARTHQUAKE. Curiously enough, in spite of Circe's dire warnings as she describes the route, the Clashing or Wandering Rocks are never mentioned again once Odysseus and his men have left the island of the Sirens behind, when they ought to be deciding which way to go: past the Rocks or into the strait. But in any case Odysseus and his companions immediately find themselves threatened by the next peril, a wave of surf approaching with a mighty roar, foaming and towering high, even before they reach what Circe has warned may be the deathtrap of Scylla and Charybdis.

What exactly could this great wave (*mega kima*) and the raging surf mean? Ancient authors such as Thucydides, Strabo and Pseudo-Aristotle, oceanologists such as Petro Ribaud, sailing manuals and even stories in the modern media have spoken of the dangers peculiar to the Strait of Messina. There is a phenomenon here which is found hardly anywhere else in the Mediterranean: a tidal ebb and flow, which can be further accentuated by temperature differences between the Tyrrhenian and Ionian Seas. The currents can have a speed of up to 1.5 knots, presenting problems even to modern shipping. When the tide is high the main current runs north, when it ebbs it runs south. At the turn of the tide every twelve hours, when the northward current comes to an end and the southward current takes over, there can be violent convulsions of great masses of water, particularly turbulent in the eye of the needle between Torre Faro and Scilla, and waves which are often metres high can have small vessels in difficulty. Armin Wolf imagines that this phenomenon, known as the *taglio*, could be the model for the 'great wave' encountered by Odysseus.[68] But it is also possible for an underwater earthquake to begin with a huge wave, as in the case of the devastating earthquake of 1783 in Calabria, and the violence and fury of such waves, swallowing up human beings, could be seen as the monsters Scylla and Charybdis. On that occasion, fearing earthquake damage, the people of Scilla had fled to the beach and to their deaths: hundreds were swept away by a *mega kima*. (After the South-East Asian disaster of Christmas 2004 such a great wave has become known to everyone as a tsunami.) Armin Wolf thinks it possible that Scylla is a metaphor for the risk of earthquake on land or under water, in line with the fact that the area around Scilla is noted for particularly strong seismic activity. In his view, the Scylla episode in the *Odyssey* is to be seen as the first description of an underwater earthquake.

Odysseus has encouraged his men and told the helmsman to keep the ship well away from the huge breaking wave, and to follow Circe's advice by steering for the cliffs of Scylla while Charybdis wide berth.

> Now wailing in fear, we rowed on up those straits,
> Scylla to starboard, dreaded Charybdis off to port,
> her horrible whirlpool gulping the sea-surge down (...)
> But now, fearing death, all eyes fixed on Charybdis –
> now Scylla snatched six men from our hollow ship,
> the toughest, strongest hands I had, and glancing
> backward over the decks, searching for my crew
> I could see their hands and feet already hoisted,
> flailing, high, higher, over my head, look –
> wailing down at me, comrades riven in agony,
> shrieking out my name for one last time! (...)
> So now they writhed,
> gasping as Scylla swung them up her cliff and there
> at her cavern's mouth she bolted them down raw –
> screaming out, flinging their arms toward me,
> lost in that mortal struggle.
>
> (O, F 12, 253).

Although Odysseus knew in advance that Scylla would take six of his comrades, he had made the ship pass close to her cliff. Then he had to watch as the terrible monster snatched the men from the ship and swallowed them alive. Hardened as he was, the dreadful sight struck terror into him:

> Of all the pitiful things I've had to witness,
> *suffering, searching out the pathways of the sea,*
> *this wrenched my heart the most,*
>
> (O, F 12, 280).

THE DESCRIPTION OF SCYLLA. As well as the monster's terrifying appearance, Homer mentions the fearsome sound she makes: a high yelping bark, no louder than a puppy's but dreadful all the same. Could there be anything in Strait of Messina to explain this phenomenon? In the text of Book 12 of the *Odyssey*, lines 55–110 as traditionally arranged, Scylla lives in a cave in the taller of the two cliffs, the one with its peak surrounded by a cloud. This cave is a *murky cavern (...) coming down to Erebus* (O, R 12, 81), that is to say facing west, where the domain of Erebus, born of Chaos, lay. The rocks of Scylla are usually regarded as the monster's dwelling. There was a cave facing west here once, although it was destroyed in the earthquake of 1783. It was one of many caves on this rocky coastline. When the wind blows into them, making its way through narrow cracks, and the waves of the sea break on the rocks below, there is indeed a kind of yelping sound from the caves, as the stone howls and hums. And when the wind and water are high, threatening sailors, such yelping and howling may well seem terrible.

In Homer's account of Scylla, which is of course a literary description, the reader is introduced to a destructive nightmare of a monster: she has twelve feet with terrible claws, *six long scrawny necks* carrying six heads *with triple rows of fangs, set thick and close, and darkly menacing death* (O, R 12, 89).

Surprisingly, pictorial depictions of this myth do not follow Homer's literary model except for a single exception, and the exception is also the oldest pictorial representation of Scylla. It is on an ivory Etruscan pyx (a type of box) from Chiusi, entirely covered with decorative bands like a frieze, dating from the seventh century BC, and was carved barely two generations after the creation of the epic. We see only one man, rowing a boat with its sail reefed in, but he seems to be rowing as hard as he can, for his boat is obviously being pursued by a Hydra-like monster with three long necks each bearing the head of a dog. Scylla in person! It seems obvious to assume that the skilful ivory-carver was inspired by Homer's poem.[69]

All later works, up to and including a Carolingian fresco in Corvey Abbey, follow a different design. Its standard version is first found on a relief of around 460 BC from the island of Aegina, now in the British Museum. Here Scylla is shown as a triple hybrid with the torso of a naked woman, a fishtail for her lower body, and dogs' heads growing from her waist. If this Scylla wore a long skirt the viewer would be deluded at first sight into thinking her an inviting and beautiful woman, for her terrifying parts are hidden. But woe to the man who let the beautiful torso seduce him, for if Scylla loosened the belt of her skirt all his male power would be torn to pieces, and his flesh devoured. Almost 400 years later, Virgil makes literary mention of this deceptive hybrid:

> But Scylla a cavern confines in blind recesses, whence she thrusts
> forth her mouths and draws ships within her rocks. Above she is of
> human form, down to the waist a fair-bosomed maiden; below, she is a
> sea-dragon of monstrous frame, with dolphins' tails joined to a belly of
> wolves.[70]

And his colleague Ovid, twenty-three years his junior, tells in the *Metamorphoses* of the transformation of Scylla who *was herself once a virgin. Many suitors sought her,*[71] but who became a monster and murdered seamen. Scylla, in south Italy the daughter of Crataeis, scorned all men and even the sea god Glaucus. Furiously angry at his rejection, but even more maddened by love, he seeks out the enchantress Circe and asks for a spell or a magic herb to help him win the love of Scylla. Circe, instantly succumbing to the handsome Glaucus herself, tries to persuade him to forget the fickle girl and offers herself frankly to him. But Glaucus rejects Circe's offer, and the scorned enchantress brews a wicked potion. She does not give it to the god himself to drink, for she still loves him, but pours it into a small bay near Rhegium where Scylla, whom he prefers to her, goes to bathe.

Scylla comes and wades waist-deep into the water; when all at once she sees her

> loins disfigured with lurking monster-shapes (...). Scylla remained
> fixed in her place, and when first a chance was given to her to vent her
> hate on Circe, she robbed Ulysses of his companions. She also would
> have wrecked the Trojan ships had she not before their coming been
> changed into a rock which stands there to this day. The rock also is the
> sailors' dread.[72]

And let those who do not believe the story go to Scilla on the Calabrian coast, sit on the beach, and stare across at the rock, if necessary narrowing their eyes, until it undergoes a metamorphosis and turns back into the beautiful, terrible, murderous mermaid, with dogs' heads baring their fangs around her waist.

CHARYBDIS. Circe had warned the seamen against venturing too close to *dread Charybdis* who *sucks the dark waters down* (O, R 12, 104), advising them to keep close to Scylla's rock, and Odysseus passed that order on to his helmsman. It could have been Homer, equipped with knowledge of the peculiar dangers of these waters, who sent his hero along the coast to the point – the Punta del Pezzo – where it turns almost at a right angle and, with the Sicilian coast opposite, forms the shape of a funnel opening to the south. At this place, the narrowest between the mainland and the island, the rocky base on which the mainland stands thrusts out towards the Sicilian coast like a hurdle right across the current, constantly creating turbulence that, about an hour and a half after the tide turns, can lead to a second *taglio* with waves and swirling water even more violent than the first. Avoid Charybdis, take the ship past close to Scylla's rock – this Homeric advice, put into Circe's mouth, is followed to this day by shipping that passes through the Strait of Messina.

On returning from Scilla we look out towards Capo Peloro from a raised place on the Punta del Pezzo. The delicate shape of the lighthouse towers far above the horizon in the bright afternoon sky. Below us, the surface of the sea is calm, shimmering in silvery dove-grey; further towards Capo Peloro it looks almost as if there were not even any ripples on it, it seems so smooth. Or is the eye unable to see far enough to detect slight movement there? Could Charybdis be treacherously camouflaging her whirlpool with a surface as smooth as oil?

If Charybdis served Homer as a poetic figure of speech for the natural phenomena peculiar to the Stretto di Mare, we can say that they still exist today. Because of the particular geological and maritime conditions in the Strait of Messina, there can be gusts of wind in these parts of up to 220 km per hour, earthquakes and underwater earthquakes up to Force 7 on the Richter scale, and earth tremors anywhere. Many features come together here to cause effects – choppy seas, sudden tall waves, whirlpools, swirling currents – that were undoubtedly known to navigators in antiquity. They tried to overcome these dangers through traditional seafaring knowledge and skill, and by ascribing magical power to them in fairy tales. While the whirlpools, currents, waves and shallows off the Sicilian headland level with the villages of Ganzirri and Torre Faro can still be hazardous for small ships today, and demand respect even from the captains of the big ferries, it is easy to imagine the terror they inspired in seamen of Homeric times with their small craft. They will have reported experiences and told tales, adding more and more embel lishments and certainly exaggerating, until a tissue of seamen's yarns had been created to make a good sea story. It was all material for the great epic poet, and he conjured up powerful images. Was he working in the knowledge that there were real reasons behind the story, threads of reality running through the texture of the songs?

> Awesome Charybdis gulps the dark water down,
> Three times a day she vomits it up, three times she gulps it down,
> That terror!
>
> (O, F 12, 115).

Three times a day? How can that be reconciled with the division of the day by the tides into a two-part rhythm as the water ebbs and flows? The Wolfs explain this discrepancy by citing an ancient manner of counting which depends not on the duration of a peri odic phenomenon but on the point where it begins, so that if you plan to see someone in a week's time (seven days) you speak in some languages of doing so 'in eight days' time'.

Tidal currents up to 10 km/h, turbulence, whirlpools – we can see detect all this in the account of the terror aroused in Odysseus and his companions by the fearsome Charybdis. It is easy to imagine their sheer horror from the Homeric images.

Reality, however, lags a little behind the horror on a mild, sunny day in late spring with hardly a breath of wind. Back on the beach of Torre Faro, not far from the places that once could have conjured up the nightmare vision of Charybdis, we look out at a sea shining green and blue, full of colour in the light from the west that spread between the shores, shimmering, rather like the surface at the time of a *taglio*. But the breakwaters, ugly, shapeless modern concrete blocks, show that the whirlpool zone which now looks so calm and inno cent can spring a surprise, threatening the shore with high seas. Their bleak functionality, however, has its romantic side; here and there they provide privacy from prying eyes for lovers lying on the sandy beach at low tide.

Over there is the rock of Scylla, so far away as to look small and standing out from the Calabrian mountain chain only because of its stone, bare of vegetation and bright in the sunlight; from our vantage point on shore we cannot even guess at Charybdis, the goddess who swallows and then spews out water. Nothing alarming seems to have happened to Goethe, either, when he passed through the Strait on his way from Messina to Naples, although 'some movement in the water was pointed out to us, quite a long way off to our left, but on the right and rather closer we saw a rock projecting from the bank, the one, we were told, being Charybdis, the other Scylla.'[73] However, the poet obviously did not see an exciting or dramatic panorama, but only a wide view of the calm sea, with a slightly livelier brushstroke suggesting movement in just one place. From this he drew a surprising conclusion: ' On occasion, because the two naturally stand so far apart, but are brought so close by the poet, readers have complained of his narrative, forgetting that the human imagination, when it wishes to present objects as significant, is very much inclined to make them taller than they are broad, thus giving the picture more character, gravity and dignity.'[73] We need not stop to wonder how much dignity Goethe would have shown if he had passed through the strait in a strong wind at the turning of the tide, or *taglio*, but we can feel sure that his character and gravity would have been in evidence. And over the millennia seafarers were confronted again and again with the gravity of the situation in the Strait of Messina.

The Sole Survivor

Island of Helios – *Messina and its surroundings*

MESSINA. Where would a not very large ship of Homer's time, having just escaped the deadly danger of Scylla and Charybdis, first find safe harbour? The Wolfs think it would have been Messina, directly down the coastline of Sicily, with Scilla and Punto Pezzo on the other side of the Strait. The course leads along the Calabrian coast, and after passing Punto Pezzo would be maintained right into the harbour which offered shelter to vessels coming into the Strait of Messina from the Tyrrhenian Sea at ebb tide, as if spreading out its arms to them, arms now represented by the quay walls.

But that was not what Odysseus wanted. The blind seer Tiresias and Circe had warned him not to set foot on the island of Helios, Thrinacia.

> There you will make the island of Thrinacia ...
> where herds of the Sungod's cattle graze, and fat sheep
> and seven herds of oxen, as many sheepflocks, rich and woolly,
> fifty head in each (...)
> Leave the beasts unharmed, your mind set on home,
> and you all may still reach Ithaca – bent with hardship,
> true – but harm them in any way, and I can see it now:
> your ship destroyed, your men destroyed again.
>
> (O, F 12, 137).

With this warning in mind, Odysseus positively implored his companions, *Row straight past these shores – race our black ship on* He spoke to them *sick at heart*, presumably guessing how his men would react; very understandably, they rejected his plea. They were exhausted, both physically and mentally. They did not want to go on

nto the black night, which might bring some further calamity, some
unknown horror, maybe a whirlwind. Ahead of them they saw a bay
obviously offering good shelter, so close that from the ship they could
even *hear the lowing cattle driven home, the bleating sheep.* Odysseus
gave way, but insisted that his companions must swear an oath that
if

> '(...) we come on a herd of cattle or fine flock of sheep,
> not one man among us – blind in his reckless ways –
> will slaughter an ox or ram. Just eat in peace,
> content with the food immortal Circe gave us.'
> They quickly swore the oath that I required
> and once they had vowed they'd never harm the herds,
> they moored our sturdy ship in the deep narrow harbour.
>
> (O, F 12, 323).

Wolf & Wolf locate it in the natural harbour of Messina, the only one
for a long way around that fits this description, and the currents in
the Strait favour the way in through its northern opening.

The heights of the Monti Peloritani rise directly behind Messina.
From there, merely by half-turning your head, you can see the north-
east coast of Sicily, the Strait, and Calabria opposite. If we follow
Homeric geography as the Wolfs suggest, three of the scenes of Odysseus' adventures are visible from this vantage point: to the left in the
north-east, the filigree line of Capo Peloro with the dune of Faro,
the island of the Sirens; nearby the waters of Charybdis, lying inno-
cently like a smooth blue expanse incapable of capsizing a nutshell;
and opposite the blurred outline of the rocks of Scylla. To the right in
the south, beyond the roofs of Messina, you see the natural sea-wall
reaching far out, and the opening to the north welcomes vessels into
the bay. Those who come safely into this secure harbour need not fear
storms and tempests.

There are silvery clouds above the milky blue of the Calabrian
mountains. The land at their feet on the sea coast is an almost unbroken conglomeration of buildings from Villa San Giovanni to far
beyond Reggio di Calabria. Only the distance that the immaculate
gulf places between the two coasts prevents the impression, inescapa-
ble at close quarters, of their ugliness and the way they have destroyed
the beauty, famous among travellers, of the Calabrian coasts.

The mole forming a semi-circle is crescent-shaped, hence,

according to Thucydides, the first name of Messina: Zankle, the Sickle, given to it by the pre-Greek Sicels. In 730 BC the city was founded by settlers from Euboea; only later was it given the name of Messina, after the Greek home town of the tyrant Anaxilas of Rhegium on the other side of the Gulf, who had seized the neighbouring city. Perhaps in pre-Greek times the peninsula was an island, one of the sandbanks lying off the mainland, and it is possible that the Homeric name of Thrinacia, meaning 'triangle', related to this geographical structure. And indeed, today the mole with its three projections still suggests a huge triangle.

> There you will make the island of Thrinacia ...
> where herds of the Sungod's cattle graze, and fat sheep
> and seven herds of oxen, as many sheepflocks, rich and woolly,
> fifty head in each.
>
> (O, F 12, 137).

Whether we think of it as the island of Thrinacia or the Zankle peninsula, this geographical formation was sure to catch the eye. Word of it would have reached the motherland and could have come to the ears of the author of the *Odyssey*; he might even have seen a sketch of it. Or perhaps Homer himself saw Sicily and the waters around it, as by the famous late eighteenth-century Sicilian archaeologist Saverio Landolina assumed. The German travel writer Johann Gottfried Seume took advantage of his very competent guidance when he visited Syracuse at the turn of the eighteenth to nineteenth century: 'He also said that Homer, who to judge by the precision of his description must have been in Sicily, cannot have met with a very good reception in Sicily, since he takes every opportunity to express a rather uncomplimentary opinion of the island.'[75]

If Homer found the model for his Thrinacia in the island or peninsula of the dune off Messina, where fat, fine, strong cattle and sheep grazed, three hundred and fifty of each, he would have difficulty today in finding a single specimen of a cow or any small domestic livestock here. The days when ox-drawn carts brought wares to the harbour are past in Messina, as elsewhere. At most, you might find a sheep in a meadow behind the tall, wire-fenced walls of the Zona Militaria, spoilt and tended by the cookhouse staff to vary the monotonous barracks diet with sheep's milk cheese for special occasions. The harbour is no paradise for animals. Filling every corner, preading all over it, is a chaotic confusion of old buildings and rumbling walls, ships' cranes tower among them, and rusty pipes and huge black tubes like the tentacles of great primeval squid lie around. Discarded freight trucks stand abandoned on overgrown tracks; rubbish, rusty refrigerators and plastic debris are scattered everywhere. The Sunday anglers seem entirely unimpressed by this less than idyllic atmosphere. They have eyes only for their rods, which they have fastened to the bumpers of the cars they have driven up to the harbour wall. And if they do happen to raise their eyes, before them lies what from a distance is the attractive sight of their city, with the undulating chain of hills and mountains curving around behind it.

Brilliance and misery, riches and destitution, hubris and hesitancy - the fate of Messina and its population has always swung between these opposites. Over and over again the city has survived, or almost, wars, earthquakes, cholera, and finally the devastation of the Second World War, when no less than 27864 Allied bombs were dropped on Messina. In its days of glory it must have been a magnificent sight, particularly the imposing row of noblemen's palaces in a crescent known as the Palazzata, confidently parading the wealth of Messina before visitors arriving from the sea. 'The people of Messina were right,' notes Seume, 'in saying that there was nothing in the world as magnificent as their façade on the harbour, which they called for that reason the palace.'[76] Then came the terrible earthquake of 1783, and four years later Goethe found 'the sight of the so-called Palazzata very sad; it is a crescent-shaped row of real palaces, that now has many sad gaps in it, and is ruined, for the blue sky shines through almost all the windows.'

REGGIO DI CALABRIA. Today, because of the unattractive built-up area by the harbour, it is better to look at the city from the pier. Then, in the afternoon, you can take the ferry to Calabria, increasing the distance so that you see less and less of our modern inadequacies, and at sunset you will be able to stroll up and down the most beautiful kilometre in Italy. Or so at least said Gabriele d'Annunzio, speaking of the Corso Vittorio Emanuele in Reggio di Calabria: *il più bel chilometro d'Italia*. He must have meant when it is seen as a whole, and we can still get a good idea of the total effect: the two parallel roads, the Corso Giacomo Metteotti and the Corso Vittorio Emanuele, with a strip of beautiful botanical specimens between them, and accompanied to the city by a long row of white palazzi and villas dating from the end of the nineteenth century, like a graceful and rather haughty gesture of defiance in the face of the constant threat to this city, as to Messina, from the restless earth under it. On the side closest to the sea, the Corso is flanked by a broad promenade paved with beautiful natural stone, which would seem to go on for ever if it did not come up against the long, curved outline of the Sicilian mountains. Now the evening sun breaks through the clouds and transforms the Strait of Messina into countless golden glittering reflections, pouring its light over the mountains as their shapes seem to dissolve, reappearing only further north, at first as the faintest hint, then more clearly, until they are a strong, dark blue silhouette standing over Messina against the evening sky, which is shot through with light.

Reggio di Calabria, Rhegion or Rhegium in antiquity, was founded by settlers from the island of Chalchis around 725 BC, only a few years after Messina. Between them, and controlled by both of them, lay the most important sea route for trade and tourism between the motherland and the Greek settlements in Tyrrhenian Italy. Spellbound by the triumph of masculine beauty in the famous bronze statues now in the National Archaeological Museum of Reggio di Calabria – although both figures have the peculiarity of what is really a female type of pubic hair – the imagination has little difficulty in seeing the heroes of the *Odyssey* in the mind's as they looked when, suspecting nothing of what lay ahead, they joyfully set off from Troy. Perhaps, after feasting illicitly on *the Sungod's finest cattle* they once again looked as magnificent in the flesh as these bronze statues,.

For it turned out just as Odysseus had feared. Adverse winds from the south and the east kept the companions on the island for a month. The provisions they had brought were running out; they could not catch enough fish and birds to satisfy them, and *hunger racked their bellies* (O, F 12, 358). The situation was critical. Odysseus looked for a lonely place where he could pray to the gods to show him a way home. His men exploited his absence to round up the best of the cattle of Helios. If the angry god destroyed their ship on the way home because of their crime, they thought, they would rather be swallowed up by the waves than starve to death on the island. And before Odysseus, returning, could put a stop to it, the cattle had been slaughtered. Helios was furiously angry, and asked the assembled gods to punish the evil-doers severely. He backed up his emand with a threat that alarmed even the father of the gods, and made him quick to promise satisfaction. (It is not explicitly stated in the text, but is unmistakeably there to be read between the lines.) The sun-God threatened to withdraw light from the heavenly world and give it to the kingdom of shadows instead. That would be the end of the eternal bliss of the gods, living on and by light: the twilight of the gods indeed. An outrageous threat. Zeus understood, and acted. He immediately gave an assurance that punishment would be drastic.

> Stepping the mast at once, hoisting the white sail
> we boarded ship and launched her, made for open sea.
> But once we'd left that island in our wake –
> no land at all in sight, nothing but sea and sky –
> then Zeus the son of Cronus mounted a thunderhead
> above our hollow ship and the deep went black beneath it.
>
> (O, F 12, 432).

SHIPWRECKED. On the seventh day after the men began their hateful feasting, the wind that had so far prevented them from sailing on home died down. They sailed away, left the shelter of the bay behind and *made for open sea*. Does Homer mean the place where ship crosses the line between Capo Sant'Alessio and Capo dell' Armi, that is to say where Calabria ends, and the funnel-shaped narrowest part of the Stretto di Messina opens out on what looks like the infinite expanse of the Ionian Sea? The Wolfs think so, and see confirmation in the description of the *sombre cloud* (O, R 12, 405) passing above the ship. 'A sign of the southern opening of the funnel shape of the strait is the striking, dark or sometimes coloured plume of vapour from Etna, which is 3000 m high. (...) With the west wind mentioned by Homer, the plume of vapour would in fact have been driven towards the strait.'[78]

For a terrible west wind, Zephirus, now rose; raging like a hurricane and accompanied by thunder and lightning. It struck the ship and swept all the men to their death except Odysseus, who managed to escape. Lashing two pieces of the ship, the mast and keel, together with a cable to make a raft, he *made them one, riding my makeshift raft as the wretched galewinds bore me on and on* (O, F 12, 458). A laconic conclusion to the gripping description of a highly dramatic incident. The picture on the neck of an Attic wine jug of 750 BC, executed in

the naive silhouette style of the late geometric period that is remini
cent of children's art, shows a shipwreck: all the chaotic confusion c
a vessel smashed by hurricane winds and lightning is depicted, wit
the sailors still alive or already drifting dead in the water. This famou
example of a late geometric vase painting with a shipwreck as i
subject, now in the State Collection of Antiquities in Munich, seem
like a pictorial commentary on the epic incident in the *Odyssey*:
boat drifting keel upwards, with a man sitting on it, while the bodie
of other men drift among fish in the water all around. But the pitche
is older than the epic and is only one, if the most impressive, in
series of depictions of shipwrecks.[79] Such a nautical disaster has bee
part of the experience of seafaring in all times, and may not have bee
a rare occurrence in the era of early Greek colonisation, when man
vessels navigated strange and distant waters. These were subjects no
just for discussion but for depiction in painting and poetry.

> Then, then in the same breath Zeus hit the craft
> with a lightning-bolt and thunder. Round she spun
> reeling under the impact, filled with reeking brimstone,
> shipmates pitching out of her, bobbing round like seahawks
> swept along by the whitecaps past the trim black hull –
> and the god cut short their journey home for ever.
>
> (O, F 12, 447).

'At last, although the west wind died down,' is the sense here in
German translation by Wolfgang Schadewaldt, and he is right to ad
the 'although', absent from most translations – for if a west wind die
down, as we are now told, what use is that if a south wind rises? It woul
mean being driven back into the funnel of the Straits, all the way to th
zone of deadly danger that was the area around Scylla and Charybdi
This terrible thought occurred to Odysseus as soon as he noticed th
change of wind. The ship had set out from the island of Helios at day
break. Twenty-four hours later, Odysseus on his raft *reached the cra
of Scylla and dire Charybdis' vortex* (O, F 12, 464) – a period of tim
that the Wolfs can reconcile with a voyage from the mole in Messin
to the opening of the funnel and then, with the aid of a south wind an
a northerly tidal drift, back on the makeshift raft to the northern ex
from the Strait of Messina. It would not, then, be very outlandish t
suppose that Homer described the way through the Strait of Messin
twice, first going from north to south, then in reverse.

Odysseus survived the terrible Charybdis, who dragged the raft from under him, by grasping the branches of the fig-tree *that over-shadowed Charybdis*, and clung there, exhausted, for twelve hours, until the keel and mast emerged from the whirlpool again and he was able to drop on them. He succeeded in seating himself on the raft and *rowed hard with my hands*, having already foreseen *that I should have once more to retrace my course to the dread Charybdis*.

The Wolfs have given some interesting interpretations to the final passages of Book 12, lines 429 to 444 of the original. They think that, in the account of the whirlpool of Charybdis subsiding and then in the evening – at just the hour when a man *the day's work done, turns home for supper* – bringing up the mast and keel again can be taken as a poetic depiction of the tides ebbing and flowing. As mentioned before, the Mediterranean is tidal only in the Strait of Messina. Their interpretation of the fact that he obviously had to pass Scylla and Charybdis twice, in opposite directions, gives the clue to the further wanderings of Odysseus. We shall soon see what surprising results this has for locating the island of the Phaeacians. However, we must remember that the text does not actually mention it, saying only that Odysseus, once on his raft again, paddled back through the strait, which would imply that he went south into the Ionian Sea. In line 428 we have already heard that when the south wind rose Odysseus rightly feared he would have to *retrace his course to the dread Charybdis*. The German translator Schadewalt again translates in a manner suggesting that if the incident happened at the northern exit of the Strait of Messina, it can only mean that for the penultimate stage of his hero's adventures – his sojourn on Calypso's island of Ogygia – Homer was sending Odysseus north to the Tyrrhenian and not back to the Ionian Sea. Ogygia would then have to be located somewhere north of the Strait of Messina.

The dangerous nymph with glossy braids

Island of Calypso – *Panarea*

PANAREA. Where could it have lain, the island to which the gods brought the shipwrecked Odysseus, straight into the arms of the loving goddess? His journey from Charybdis to Calypso is described briefly, in just three lines in the original, without any mention of such data as the direction of the winds or the constellations of stars in the sky:

> I drifted along nine days. On the tenth, at night,
> The gods cast me up on Ogygia, Calypso's island,
> Home of the dangerous nymph with glossy braids
> Who speaks with human voice.

> (O, F 12, 484).

If we follow the Wolfs in assuming that after the shipwreck Odysseus passed through the strait going north, and had not been driven back into the Ionian Sea, then once he had escaped from the greedy jaws and clutches of Scylla and Charybdis he could have come to land only on the Calabrian mainland, or on one of the seven islands of the Aeolian (or Liparian) archipelago.

The archipelago owes both its names to its ancient human history as reflected in myth. The people of the main island, Lipari of course will not allow the group to be called anything but 'Liparian', the Isole Lipari, while officially and on the other six islands the term Isole Eolie, Aeolian Islands, is used. In the first case the name is said to derive from the legendary King Liparos who led the Ausonians coming from central Italy around 1250 BC; the second comes from the name of the lord of the winds, Aeolus, who according to many sources was married to the daughter of Liparos, and whom he colonial Greeks understandably claimed as their patron. Even in Thucydides we find the Liparians mentioned as the home of Aeolus, after whom the group of islands was, consequently, known (although the ever-sceptical Thucydides speaks of the archipelago only as 'the so-called Aeolian Islands'). This tradition was continued, by way of Petrarch, right into the 20th century in the Homeric geography proposed in the 1920s by the French classical scholar Victor Bérard, who identifies Stromboli as the home of Aeolus, king of the winds, and his numerous family.[80]

But back to the question of where Odysseus came ashore. Calabria can be ruled out, because Ogygia is expressly defined as an island. The Wolfs therefore assume that one of the Aeolian Islands was the home of the divine nymph Calypso.

Which of the seven pearls – *sette perle,* as they are called with some justification in Italian tourist guides – can claim to have served as the model for Calypso's island, with all its paradisal features? So far as human settlement is concerned, they all have a long enough pre-history to span the time-frame of the Trojan War, and the main island Lipari was settled much earlier. Obsidian and ceramic finds on the site of the rocky fortress that towers over the place go back to the early 4th millennium.

Where would a raft without any means of steering drift if it were driven from the mouth of the Stretto di Messina into the Tyrrhenian Sea? By the rules of physics and navigation, not to the Aeolian Islands, since the current of the sea here goes in exactly the opposite direction. Here the Wolfs express critical doubts of their own identification of Ogygia with one of the Aeolian Islands.

So now what?

A suggestion: allow the doubts, but put the question differently. Must Homer have known about such fine nautical points as a current in one tiny part of the great sea? The answer may well be no. But in collecting his material he may have heard of islands that came in sight if a sailor looked west after passing through the Strait of Messina, and had impressed them for ever on his memory because of the mighty landmark of Stromboli, spewing out fire and lava, both an alarming and a fascinating phenomenon. And which of the islands would most closely correspond to a poet's imagination when he wanted to give the lovely nymph Calypso, with all her charms, a home that, with its wealth of plants and birds, could offer an equivalent in terms of landscape to her feminine beauty?

It could well have been the smallest and, in many people's opinion, most beautiful of the Aeolian Islands: Panarea. Because of its many species of flora and fauna, it seems to the Wolfs a likely candidate for the island of Ogygia, with its flourishing plant life and many birds.

'You want to visit Panarea? You'll have the whole island to yourselves at this time of year,' says our American landlady in Lipari harbour as we wait for the boat to Panarea. And when we arrive it is soon clear how right she was. It is November, and people are in their own homes. The affluent visitors who populate the island in summer have gone back to the prosperous north of Italy, and the real inhabitants of Panarea remain, already settling into the quiet routine of the winter months. It is quite difficult to find accommodation, but to our delight we do, in a spacious room occupying the whole upper storey of a house with a large terrace, offering all we could wish for in the way of a view. Nearby there are well-tended, rectangular houses, whose spotless white is an attractive contrast to the southern tropical vegetation in the gardens; beyond them the view is of the tall rock massif rising behind the village of San Pietro, its reddish stone showing through the green *macchia*; and then across the sea, from which the curiously shaped little satellite islands of Dattila, Liscia Bianca and Basiluzzo rise close by, while in the background Stromboli rises majestically like a pyramid, greeting us with a mushroom of vapour sent up from the peak.

In terms of the geological history of the volcanic predecessor of the archipelago, Panarea can claim to take a prominent place, and in terms of human history too, for that goes back thousands of years here. Remains found on the Punta del Corvo – the highest point of the tiny island at 431 metres above sea level – indicate a place of worship dating from the third millennium. It must have been a magnificent location in which to honour divine spirituality, represented in these natural surroundings by incomparable beauty that opens the senses up to an aura of the numinous. Almost a thousand years younger, but still of venerable age, is the now famous village of huts on Capo Milazzese in the most south-easterly part of the island, dating from the Middle Bronze Age. An evening walk there towards the setting sun, as it sheds an endlessly rich play of light on the varied world of the island, has a special place among the many roads that can be trodden in search of Odysseus. He did not come here, and nor did Homer ever set foot on this island. But with Book 5 of the *Odyssey* in mind, one would like to think it was Panarea where the nymph with the glossy braids lived. And let us imagine Hermes landing on Calypso's island to bring the decision of the gods. The picture of the messenger of the gods hovering in over the *violet sea* is vividly evoked when, on the way to the Villaggio Preistorico, we pass a small landing pad for the helicopters that come down here in the high season, the contemporary equivalent of winged Hermes. And of course one of the many shades of colour in the sea is violet blue.

If you have come from the main village and the harbour of San Pietro to the neighbouring village of Dranto to the south, you have already sampled much of the magical beauty of the island. The low-built white houses are very much at home in the beautiful gardens, here there is a wealth of flowers even in November, and summer leaves are still on the trees. Soon you are facing a bay. The paved road ends, you walk over a sandy beach, climb a steep rise to a hilltop and look down at Capo Milazzese, winding away into the sea like a lizard shape, linked to the island only by a narrow rocky ridge flanked by the bays of Cala del Moro and Calo Junco.

This was the means of access to the Bronze Age village on Capo Milazzese, and it was certainly easy to barricade. An unusual situation: almost entirely surrounded by the sea, divided from it and thus from potential attackers by steep rock walls; linked to the rest of the island and its sources of nourishment, but easily isolated from them if danger threatened from that quarter – in fact, it was a natural fortress.

The second phase of the Aeolian Bronze Age, from 1400 to about 1270 BC, is called after this village in the hills. The remains of twenty-three stone huts with paved floors and thatched roofs have been excavated. So, most important of all, have many pottery items and everyday objects like pokers, mortars and millstones. They can be seen in the Museo Eoliano in Lipari Castle. It is not quite certain who destroyed this culture, probably brought to its flowering by Sicilian settlers, after it had been in existence for 130 years, but presumably it was the Ausonians from the mainland who burned the magnificent village and brought the culture of Milazzese to an end.

The only survivors, hidden in a cavern from the attack of the burning and raping conquerors, were a few women. Among them was an impressive figure repeatedly described later as 'glorious', or 'powerful', even 'terrible'. Can the alarming beauty of a female figure be described in such terms? At least everyone agrees on the glory and elaborate arrangement of her hair: she had flowing locks, lovely braids, and another outstanding quality too, the gift of eloquent language:

> The gods washed me up on the island of Ogygia, the home of Calypso
> of the braided tresses, that formidable goddess with a woman's voice,
> and she received me kindly and looked after me.
>
> (O, R 12, 447).

A wonderful and breathtaking passage, the goddess with beautiful tresses, her hair braided elaborately – and at the same made terrible by her beauty and by the words she spoke – perhaps in flattering tones? This goddess, with her beautiful hair and gift of human speech, was powerfully seductive.

Mycenaean ceramics have been found in large quantities on Capo Milazzese, and are on display in the Aeolian Museum on Lipari. There was also plenty of trading contact between the Aegean and the Aeolian islands. One day a ship could have come in as before, laden with products of the art of the Mycenean potters. But the merchants and seamen no longer met with their usual welcome from a delegation of the people of the settlement on the beach of the Cala Jugo or Cala del Moro. No one was there; they might have climbed the hill, wondering what had happened – to see only burnt earth where the many oval huts and the village chief's large, rectangular house had once stood. We can imagine a search party setting out to explore the island and I see the men suddenly stop with bated breath and eyes wide: before them a wide cavern opens out, and there they see a woman of enchanting beauty sitting behind a hearth where a great fire burns.

> Deep inside she sang, the goddess Calypso, lifting
> her breathtaking voice as she glided back and forth
> before her loom, her golden shuttle weaving.
> Thick, luxuriant woods grew round the cave,
> alders and black poplars, pungent cypress too,
> and there birds roosted, folding their long wings,
> owls and hawks and the spread-beaked ravens of the sea,
> black skimmers who make their living off the waves.
> And round the mouth of the cavern trailed a vine
> laden with clusters, bursting with ripe grapes.
>
> (O, F 5, 68).

Full of wonder they stand there, spellbound by this glorious apparition, surrounded by paradisal nature. And when they go home in their ship, perhaps they tell the story of the distant island in the western sea, where they met a feminine being whom they could describe only as a nymph if not a goddess. So the place, surrounded by such an aura, remains unvisited. *No one, god or mortal, dares approach her there* (o, F 5, 285), as Odysseus will say later at the court of King Alcinous. Unvisited, that is, until he, Odysseus, clinging to the keel of his shattered vessel on the tenth night after his shipwreck, was washed up on Ogygia.

Meanwhile the tales travelling over seas, lands and cities had given a genealogical account of her divine descent. The being who looked like a woman and who, as the story went, took in the stranded mariner and lovingly tended him, was now *the daughter of Atlas, Calypso ... the seductive nymph with lovely braids* (O, F 7, 283). Her relationship to the circle of the gods was later reflected in a portrait on an Etruscan relief stela of the mid-fifth century BC, now in the Museo Civico Archeaologico Bologna, showing her as a winged being. This, incidentally, is the only work of antiquity apart from a Lucanian water pitcher of about 385 BC to depict Calypso and Odysseus together. Her beauty deserved more artistic homage; it is all the more regrettable that a famous picture by Nicias of Athens, dating from the second half of the fourth century BC and showing a radiant portrait of the nymph (Pliny saw it) has now vanished without trace.

And she promised more than good food and drink and the pleasures of love. Her tempting offer *to make me immortal, ageless, all my days* (O, F 7, 296) was meant to induce Odysseus to stay on the lonely island. He spent seven years on Ogygia, and not, as on Circe's island, of his own free will. The offer of eternal youth did not seduce him. He wanted to go home to Ithaca and Penelope. So he sat on the beach and on rocks day after day,

> Wrenching his heart with sobs and groans and anguish,
> gazing out over the barren sea through blinding tears.
>
> (O, F 5, 174).

Only one picture from antiquity – and its provenance is dubious – shows Odysseus in this situation. It is on the cheek guard of a bronze helmet of the first half of the 4th century BC, now in the Berlin Antiquities Collection. It depicts Odysseus in the typical pose of a desperate man deep in thought, railing against the gods, leaning on his left arm, his head laid on his right hand as he goes over the questions in his mind again and again – why? When? A very fine later depiction is reproduced as the frontispiece of the famous edition of the *Odyssey* translated into German by Rudolf Alexander Schröder, published by Harry Graf Kessler at the Cranach Press in Weimar: Odysseus, sitting bowed over on a rock surrounded by water, props his head on his hands in grief.

If we take Panarea to be Calypso's island, no more suitable place can be imagined for Odysseus staring into the distance, bedewing the clothes given him by the nymph with tears, than the beaches of Cala del Moro, Cala Junco, and Capo Milazzese in between them. And there could be no finer moment to transfer these Homeric lines into ideas of visual beauty in a beautiful landscape setting than in twilight, at a time of year when you can sit alone on the fantastic natural terrace of the headland here, legs outstretched on the large threshold stone of a Bronze Age house, giving yourself up to the tender duet of the rushing wind and the gently lapping waves, watching the close of day in quiet enchantment, until the most magical and strangest moment of all comes, when the basalt rocks around the bay are merely black, bizarre contours seen against the fading light of the evening sky, and the sea has turned to flickering light.

LEAVING OGYGIA. At last the time came. After the gods had consulted together twice, and Odysseus had spent seven years on Ogygia, Calypso had to set her human lover free. In spite of the promise of immortality and eternal youth and the nymph's unstinting devotion, Odysseus could not return her love to the same extent. Now she, who had wanted to keep the man washed up by chance on her lonely island there for ever, was transformed into an unselfish adviser.

After they had made love for the last time in the cave, day dawned. With swift, sober determination, Calypso began obeying the orders of the father of the gods: she must help Odysseus to go home, and sent him off to build himself a raft. She gave him tools, showed him the trees on her island that he was to fell, and provided cloth for the sail. On the fourth day the work was finished, on the fifth day divine Calypso let Odysseus go, not without first preparing a bath for him, laying fragrant garments ready, and supplying him with water, wine and food.

Last of all, she gave him clear astronomical directions for his voyage: he was to make sure that he kept the constellation of the Great Bear on his left. That meant that Odysseus had to steer a course from west to east if he was to reach the land of the Phaeacians from Ogygia. So did he go from the Liparian Islands to the Calabrian mainland, which the Wolfs assume to be Phaeacia? Uvo Hölscher would not have said so in such detail. In his book, however, in a chapter entitled 'Geography of the Wanderings', he concedes that the fairy-tale myth contains some geographical features, and the voyage of Odysseus from Ogygia to the land of the Phaeacians is evidence of one of them. 'It would be absurd,' he writes, 'to assume that Homer's audience was not expected to form any idea of the geographical circumstances implied by the story. It cannot be pure coincidence that the final return to Ithaca from Phaeacia is a journey from the west, described in realistic nautical detail (...) The voyage into uncharted waters had to take Odysseus west, since he could not return home from any other point of the compass. It was a false defence of the poetic element to situate the adventures of Odysseus in the Nowhere of fairy tale: the audience of the epic saw them linked to their own experience by clear navigational directions.'[81]

The realistic description of the building of the raft, which has to be based on real-life observation; the following passage in the text describing Calypso's practical provision of skins full of water and wine for the departing Odysseus – the waterskin is larger than the wineskin for obvious reasons – as well as a basket of food; finally, the nymph's explicit direction to steer strictly by the stars: these passages, and many more, allow us to assume all the time that we are not concerned simply with stories of voyages and adventures from the unreal world of fairy tale, but with what, although it may also be a literary fiction, is one with its feet on the ground. The account drew on sources of real experience or credible report, and the state of contemporary knowledge at the time.

The moon is bright enough to read by on the terrace of our hotel; the reed awning that keeps the sun off in summer has been taken down. We have a clear view of the stars, including those that showed Odysseus the way to go as he journeyed east.

And now the master mariner steered his craft,
sleep never closing his eyes, forever scanning
the stars, the Pleiades and the Ploughman late to set

and the Great Bear that mankind also calls the wagon:
she wheels on her axis always fixed, watching the Hunter,
and she alone is denied a plunge in the Ocean's baths.
Hers were the stars the lustrous goddess told him
to keep hard to port as he cut across the sea.

(O, F 5, 297).

However, the light of the moon and stars alone will not enable me
to read Uvo Hölscher's useful commentary on the geography of the
hero's wanderings in the *Odyssey*. The print is rather small, the light
of the heavenly bodies not sufficiently bright, and so a flashlight is
called into service to help.

By night, we see the constellations seen by Odysseus, with the
Pleiades pursued by Orion the mighty hunter, the ploughman
Boötes, the Great Bear. By day we enjoy a Homeric idyll in the
flourishing gardens of the east coast of Panarea, with their wealth
of flowers, bushes and trees, of angels' trumpets or brugmansia, wild
roses, oleander, with hibiscus, bougainvillea, grape vines, lemon and
olive trees, palms, larches, cypresses, while smoke rises here and there
from burning fires of leaves and wood.

A great fire
blazed on the hearth and the smell of cedar
cleanly split and sweetwood burning bright
wafted a cloud of fragrance down the island.

(O, F 5, 65).

We leave Ogygia with the memory of an impressive female form,
youthful, with beautiful braids of hair, terrible in her loving ardour,
her voice full of melodious magic, but when necessary very practical
and nobly ready to help after making her painful renunciation. A
goddess of love in every way.

On Foot Through the
Land of the Phaeacians

Land of the Phaeacians – *the Calabrian isthmus and east coast*

THE GREAT BEAR TO PORT. At first all went well. Calypso *summoned a wind to bear him onward, fair and warm* (O, F 5, 294). Since Odysseus had observed the nymph's instructions to leave the Great Bear on his left hand all the time, that is to say to port, the wind finally brought him to the coast of the land of the Phaeacians:

> And seventeen days he sailed, making headway well;
> on the eighteenth, shadowy mountains slowly loomed...
> the Phaeacians' island reaching toward him now,
> over the misty breakers, rising like a shield.
>
> (O, F 5, 305).

How glad at heart he was! At last there was nothing in his way, no difficulties, no disasters, no deadly danger. But he had rejoiced too soon, failing to remember the grudge that angry Poseidon bore him. The god now ruthlessly pursued him with the powers at his command: storms, dark clouds, the fury of the sea. A great wave sent the raft spinning round, destroyed the mast and sail, and threw Odysseus into the rough water. However, he managed to haul himself back on board his craft. Superhuman powers were battling for his destruction or survival: Poseidon battering him with terrible waves, the sea-nymph Leucothea who gave him her veil to save him, and the goddess Athene who commanded the winds to die down. By this time the raft is in pieces and the tree-trunks it was made of are scattered. Odysseus makes a brief attempt to save himself by riding one of them *like a plunging racehorse* (O, F 5, 408). Tearing off his clothes, he ties Leucothea's veil around him – the only depiction of the incident so far known is on the Etruscan relief stela in Bologna mentioned above – and plunges into the waves. He drifts for two days and two nights in the water, finally sights land, feels hope revive, but it is disappointed again when he sees rugged rocks nearby. A wave throws him up on the reef, he clings fast, the next wave sends him back once more, with scraps of skin torn from his body. Coming up above the surface, he looks this way and that, swims around, and finally sees something that means safety: a sheltered beach and the mouth of a river.

In Homer this is a dramatic scene: the vengeful god threatens a man with torment and destruction, yet divine help brings safety. There are descriptions of terrible storms that send the sea towering up, with waves like mountains of water destroying any craft beneath them, and the human protagonist appears to be helpless, abandoned by the gods. *Wretched man, what becomes of me now, at last?* (O, F 5, 329) exclaims Odysseus. His desperate cry expresses the despair that overcomes him. But Athene stands by her protégé after all, for otherwise the promise given by Zeus to let the patient sufferer go home at last could not be fulfilled. However, he has to swim and fight the water for two days and nights to *reach the land of the Phaeacians.*

Incidentally, even the lay reader of the *Odyssey* will notice the close duplication of themes. The erotic Circe episode is soon followed by the first shipwreck, then comes the also erotic Calypso episode and the second shipwreck. What does this mean? Scholars will explain that Homer was the first to introduce the tale of Calypso into the epic, and the duplication of the shipwreck is his work too.[82] In the old seamen's yarns and tales of adventure that surround the character of Odysseus there is only one shipwreck, and Odysseus saves himself from it unaided, landing directly on the coast of the Phaeacians. One shipwreck would surely have been quite enough to convince us of Odysseus's capacity for withstanding the hardships he endures, so why a second one to increase the patient hero's suffering to an almost inhuman degree? Hölscher sees the Homeric *Odyssey* as a story of home-coming, suggesting that as such it required a long absence on the hero's part, and then a plausible explanation was needed for that long absence. The story of his seven years with the beautiful nymph suited the purpose.

THE DIRECT ROUTE. The journey from Calypso's island of Ogygia to the land of the Phaeacians is described in Books 5, 7 and 23 of the *Odyssey*. But how does the passage from line 275 onwards of Book 19 fit into the episode? It comes in the first conversation between Penelope and Odysseus after his return to Ithaca, while he is still pretending to be a stranger and telling his famous lying tale. It may all be lies, but it is not far from the facts, as the narrator of the epic comments: *Falsehoods all, but he gave his falsehoods all the ring of truth* (O, F 19, 234). For instance, the account of the sinking of the ship in a storm off the island of Thrinacia is true. But in this very brief account of events, the story of the Calypso episode between the shipwreck off the island of Helios and his coming safe ashore on the Phaeacian beach remains untold – a lie in itself? Or did Odysseus perhaps deliberately fail to mention his seven-year liaison with the nymph, into which he had to some extent been forced, out of thoughtfulness for the constant Penelope?

In fact classical scholars have a different explanation: the sequence of adventures as we know it with Odysseus' seven years on Ogygia, and the version without the Calypso story, belong to two literary layers dating from different periods, and both have their own 'truth'. In the pre-Homeric tales of the wanderings of Odysseus, there was no Calypso episode; he came ashore on the land of the Phaeacians directly after the shipwreck. It was Homer, scholars say, who added the figure of Calypso: 'Calypso is not a character of legend but a poetic invention.'[83] This means that there are two versions of the way in which Odysseus reached the land of the Phaeacians after escaping Scylla and Charybdis: in the older story by the direct route; in the *Odyssey* as we know it with a landing on Ogygia and seven years spent there before he reached Phaeacia. In other words, we are in the fortunate position of being able to follow Odysseus' journey from Charybdis to the land of the Phaeacians by two different routes.

The direct route, coming from Charybdis, follows a coastline where there were *no coves, no harbours that would hold a ship, nothing but headlands jutting out* (O, R 5, 405) all the way to the flat beach with the river mouth in the land of the Phaeacians. He comes safely to shore

(...) abreast of a river's mouth,
running calmly, the perfect spot, he thought ...
free of rocks, with a windbreak from the gales.

(O, F 5, 486).

Even today the passage from the Strait of Messina through the Gulf of Gióia, past looming Capo Vaticano to the Gulf of Sant' Eufemia, is a voyage in no way inferior to a journey overland. It takes only a few hours to cover the fifty sea miles. Homer leaves aside the question of how long Odysseus would have needed, drifting and swimming, to reach Scheria. In the first account of his journey from the time of the shipwreck off Thrinacia to his arrival in Phaeacia, as given by Odysseus to Penelope in seven lines of direct description, there are no details of the duration of his desperate journey, struggling through the waves perched on a beam from the raft.

Whether a ship takes the northern course from the Strait of Messina along the coast and through the Gulf of Gióia, or goes eastward past the Liparian Islands, it will steer towards a landmark of majestic beauty visible on a clear day even from Sicily: Capo Vaticano, the Taurianum Promontorium of the Romans, its rugged rocks familiar to all seafarers sailing along the west coast of Calabria. Further along the rocky coast, ships pass Tropea, an enchanting little town on a plateau above precipitous cliffs, and Pizzo, built into the slope around the central Piazza della Repubblica.

North of Pizzo the mountains fall back, and the land levels out into a plain with the mouth of the Fiume Lamato in the Golfo di Sant' Eufemia. The long, flat shoreline forms a crescent shape here before the Apennines approach the sea again to the north. Was it here, at the mouth of the Lamato, that Homer brought his hero safe ashore after days of struggle at sea, pursued by the vengeful Poseidon?

A COUNTRY LIKE A SHIELD. Whether he came direct from the whirlpool of Charybdis, or took the longer way from Calypso's island, Odysseus was finally rescued by a gentle wave and washed up on the Phaeacian shore, totally exhausted:

> Out of danger he swam on, scanning the land, trying to find
> a seabeach shelving against the waves, a sheltered cove,
> and stroking hard he came abreast of a river's mouth,
> running calmly, the perfect spot, he thought ...
> free of rocks, with a windbreak from the gales.
>
> (O, F 5, 486).

Again, the question arises: was it on the Gulf of Sant' Eufemia? The ong, level bay with its soft sand would provide good conditions for an exhausted shipwrecked mariner to be gently washed ashore. We can imagine Odysseus being carried into the mouth of the Lamato by one last wave, and lying unconscious on the slope of the shore for a little while until he came back to his senses, when he immediately recovered his usual presence of mind, powers of pragmatic reasoning, and determination. He quickly decided to go a little further into the forest, where he finally found shelter under the inextricably tangled branches of a cultivated and a wild olive.

But wait – had Odysseus landed on the west coast of Calabria? Was that the 'island of the Phaeacians' from which he would finally set out on the voyage home to Ithaca? That is what the Wolfs think. Their thesis, in short, runs: leaving the Sirens behind, Odysseus and his companions passed through the strait between Scylla and Charybdis going south. After the shipwreck and the loss of his entire crew, Odysseus saved himself on a few beams that were still afloat, and was driven back to Charybdis. The crucial question is: what happened next? According to the Wolfs, after Odysseus had jumped down from the fig tree standing above Charybdis and landed on the beams as they resurfaced from the whirlpool, he went on into the Tyrrhenian Sea and finally reached the west coast of Calabria in the region of the mouth of the Fiume Amato, whether as in the older version direct or, as in the Homeric version, by way of Ogygia (the Liparian Islands). His way back to Ithaca could then be only overland to the eastern coast, from where his home island was within easy reach by ship. The country and city of the Phaeacians must therefore be somewhere between the west and east coasts of Calabria. This thesis is based on the fact that, in the *Odyssey*, there is no evidence that Odysseus passed through the strait a third time, now going south again, which would be necessary if he were to go straight home across the Ionian Sea. All attempts so far 'to point to a geographically feasible route for the *Odyssey* have failed on this point (...). The contradiction seemed insoluble in the light of the rest of the voyage. It has therefore been found necessary either to alter the geography at this juncture or to depart a long way from the Homeric text.'[84]

At this point between the Golfo di Sant' Eufemia and the Golfo di Squillace, Calabria is compressed on the eastern side into a wasp-waisted isthmus. If we follow the map from here north and south a little way in both directions past the 'waist', the shape of the isthmus has some similarity with the dipylon shield of Homeric times. The

Wolfs link this similarity to the passage in Book 5 of the *Odyssey* where Odysseus, after seventeen days of voyaging, sights *the shadowy mountains of the Phaeacians' country*, which *looked like a shield laid on the misty sea* (O, R 5, 280). They saw the suggestion of a shield shape in this topographical passage as an argument supporting their theory that Calabria was the land of the Phaeacians, and it was from here that Odysseus returned home to Ithaca. One may object that such pictorial impression can be gained only from an aerial view, which of course was impossible in Homer's time. On the other hand, there is a point about the shield comparison noted by Uvo Hölscher, who does not usually indulge in conjecture over locations for the wandering of Odysseus. In the landscape descriptions of the *Odyssey* he sees 'the evolution of fairy-tale and wonderful elements into realism. (...) By comparison with the *Iliad*, the perception of landscape is perceptibly sharper, and can extend to a distant view. To Odysseus on his raft the land of the Phaeacians in the distance appears "like a shield laid on the misty sea". This sounds like a personal experience of an optical impression.' [85]

But whose experience? The poet Homer's? The experience of other informants? Perhaps, then, the line may depict either some one's own observation, or impressions conveyed through stories and other narratives, of the striking landscape with curved indentations both on the side facing Greece – where there was already a 8th-century settlement at the village of Skylletion – and on the side facing the Tyrrhenian Sea?

Another question arises. Was the land of the Phaeacians an island as is generally postulated? The traditional opinion that Scheria was an island is opposed by the Wolfs, citing a mistake in one of the German translations (by Johann Heinrich Voss), which in fact the translator himself corrected in the third edition of his version of the *Odyssey*, but he could not dispel the general idea of an island. 'The crucial point is that not only does the Greek text never call the land of the Phaeacians an island, it does call it "Scheria" (...) meaning literally continent or mainland.' [86]

NAUSICAA. So if Calabria is the land of the Phaeacians, if Homer brings Odysseus ashore to its west, on the coast of the Tyrrhenian Sea, and then, with Phaeacian help, sends him home to Ithaca from the east, he has to cross the Calabrian peninsula.

'North of Pizzo the land levels out into a plain (...). The Mafioso building industry has been established in this flat, monotonous region for decades, trying, with considerable assistance from the European Union, to waste as much concrete and asphalt as possible in building huge road junctions that will not be needed in a hundred years' time, and bridges leading nowhere.'[87]

No doubt the destruction inflicted on the peninsula between the Gulf of Sant' Eufemia and the Gulf of Squillace (which is also the valley between the north and south part of the Appenino Calabro, with two rivers passing through it), as the quickest traffic link between the west and east of Calabria, is to be deplored. But we can still form an idea of the charm and beauty of the pre-industrial Calabrian landscape if we leave the fast highway near the Ponte Calderaio, instead striking out into the fields and small woods through which the old country road leads along the Fiume Lamato.

Are we following in the footsteps of Odysseus? If we assume that the Phaeacian episode is set in the Calabrian landscape, then it is along the Lamato that we shall find places able to provide pictorial illustration of the poetic scenery of Phaeacia.

The landscape in the valley of the Lamato, also known as the Fiume Amato, is one of bucolic charm when you look across the fields: you see flocks of sheep here and there, a few farmhouses, groups of trees, small plots of arable land, and looking on past thickets of reeds the hills and mountains of the wooded Sila range in the north. A sturdy stone bridge arches over the narrow river that winds its way past a little wood, through wild plants, undergrowth and rushes. A solitary large, rounded, light grey rock stands on a broad strip of the bank, a surprising sight in the Amato valley, where rocks are few and far between. Was it a washing stone on the bank of the river, a stone on which clothes could be beaten, kneaded and brushed in the clear water coming down from the granite mountains of the Sila? The Wolfs were told by two men from the nearby hill town of Tiriolo that up to the time when modern water mains were built, this place was a popular traditional spot for washing clothes. Did the tradition go right back to Homer's time? Could this even be the place where Nausicaa and her maids washed clothes?

Early in the morning Nausicaa, daughter of King Alcinous of Phaeacia, and her maids had left the city with her maids on a mule-drawn cart laden with clothes for washing. Her mother Queen Arete had given them plenty of food and a goatskin container of wine to take too, since the washing pools were some way from the town. The goddess Athene, taking the shape of a friend of Nausicaa, had advised her to ask her father to let her take a wagon, *the tall one with the good smooth wheels.*

> Once they reached the banks of the river flowing strong
> where the pools would never fail, with plenty of water
> cool and clear, bubbling up and rushing through
> to scour the darkest stains – they loosed the mules,
> out from under the wagon yoke, and chased them down
> the river's rippling banks to graze on luscious clover.
> Down from the cradle they lifted clothes by the armload,
> plunged them into the dark pools and stamped them down
> in the hollows, one girl racing the next to finish first.
>
> (O, F 6, 95).

We can certainly imagine this cheerful scene enacted here: the young women washing clothes by the Lamato, which is narrow at this point but tumbles fast along its stony bed, laying the washing out to dry, eating their well-earned picnic, and then preparing to take a bath and rub themselves afterwards with the oil that Nausicaa's mother had given them in a golden flask.

In the little wood nearby, Odysseus was sleeping the deep sleep of exhaustion. Nausicaa and her maids were already preparing to go home, the mules were harnessed to the cart, the beautiful clothes neatly folded, when Athene put it into the mind of the king's daughter to throw a last ball at one of the maids. Perhaps Nausicaa's thoughts were already on the return journey, but anyway she missed her aim and the ball fell into the swirling water. What did the girls playing their game do? They screamed aloud, says the *Odyssey*. It was probably more of a happy, crowing cry, but anyway it woke Odysseus who now emerged from the bushes, concealing his manhood with a leafy branch.

We are now sitting on the wall of the bridge, imagining the scene played out below us. A party of cheerful, pretty young women playing ball, the uncouth, naked, salt-encrusted man with his tousled hair coming out of the woods, sending the maids scattering in panic while Nausicaa – *a head taller than any of them* (O, R 6, 107); the nobility and height of her figure could not be more succinctly expressed – stays where she is, composed and fearless. After all, she has the support of Athene. And now conversation begins between Odysseus, Nausicaa and the maids. Its tone is delightfully human and respectful as the characters come together, showing a level of good manners that in itself, even if only this passage were preserved as evidence, shows a high stage of cultural development in the people of the time. Yet we should not forget how Odysseus and his comrades behaved in Ismarus, or the merciless and indeed barbaric way he deals with the faithless maids on his return to Ithaca. When we remember those dark depths of his character, we cannot help shuddering.

This scene, notable for its dialogue, was difficult to transfer to the language of the visual arts. There are few pictorial depictions of Odysseus in the land of the Phaeacians. One fine example is on the Attic red-figure amphora of about 440 BC by the so-called Nausicaa painter, now in Munich. The figures surround the body of the amphora, bright orange on a black ground. On the front there is a group of four: Odysseus, Athene, Nausicaa and one of her maids. The depiction of the human characters is full of variety in suggesting their state of mind and emotions, from the divine and imperious statuesque attitude of the goddess who, unseen, is directing the course of events, to Nausicaa, about to turn away at the sight of the wild man, but still poised to resume her conversation with Odysseus. He is leaning over as he steps out of the bushes, aware of his nakedness, his attitude following the line of the amphora up to its neck. The maid is running away in alarm. On the back of the amphora, three girls are busy with the washing, and sure enough, the picture shows a washing stone very much like the big rock on the Amato.

TIRIOLO AND SKYLLETION. Finally Nausicaa asked Odysseus to accompany them to her father's palace, and first to pay his respects to her mother, so that all would go as it should. *When she had finished, Nausicaa used her shiny whip on the mules, and they soon left the flowing river behind them, their legs weaving a pattern as they trotted steamily along* (O, R 7, 316), cart and mules keeping up a good pace to reach the king's city of Tiriolo before darkness fell.

For it is to Tiriolo that we are now bound; up there, at a height of 690 metres, is the place where the Wolfs assume that the city of the Phaeacians lay. Since antiquity it has promised a spectacular and enticing sight: the isthmus here is so narrow that almost at a glance, or at least with only a slight movement of the head, you have two views of the Mediterranean, the Ionian Sea to the east, the Tyrrhenian Sea to the west. This climactic view is matched by panoramic opulence if the weather is kind. A helpful hint from Armin Wolf, who has a holiday home in the nearby mountain village of Squillace and knows the area well, makes us stop at a sharp left-hand bend in the road a few metres above the village of Marcellinara. Here, for the first time, is the visitor's chance of seeing two seas at once. But today the sky is covered by grey cloud, the low-lying land near the coast and the surface of the water seem to merge almost indissolubly with each other and the sky in the diffuse light. We go on to the mountain town of Tiriolo. Our second chance to see 'the view' could be here in the little piazza, where in principle it is safe for ever, since the place is a protected monument and cannot be built over. But a hideous white monument to Odysseus obscures the view. We swiftly turn our backs on it and climb through the steep, narrow Old Town to the castle ruins of Sant' Angelo. From here the eye can wander unimpeded over the undulating hills all around. The roofs of Tiriolo add contrast to the picture, buttercups in the meadow near the Castello are like fresh splashes of paint in the wan light. But still the two seas can hardly be distinguished from the sky; there is no brightness, no clarity, in a word, no sun. However, a little window of sky above the Golfo Sant' Eufemia does seem to be opening to it; there is a patch of blue looking through the grey curtain. So we go towards the sun, and perhaps we may come back in its company this evening.

Sure enough, not half an hour later we are sitting on the deserted beach of Falerna Marina looking up at the last clouds, our backs against an upturned boat, a prosciutto sandwich in one hand, a glass of red wine in the other. Now to climb to Monte Tiriolo, 150 metres above Tiriolo itself, the place from which you have the finest double view of the Tyrrhenian and Ionian Seas: eastward over green valleys and mountain ridges, on one of which the capital of the Calabrian region, Cantanzaro, lies; then down to the Golfo di Squillace, which forms the horizon with the sky, now tinged with delicate shades of pale grey and blue – sfumato! To the west the eye is caught first by the hill where the fortress stands, with the houses of the Old Town above it, then your glance moves to a landscape which, back-lit at the moment, has lost all its sharp edges and sinks to the silvery gleam of the Golfo di Sant' Eufemia. On the horizon is the pyramid shape of Stromboli.

The Wolfs think that the city of the Phaeacians could have been

n Tiriolo or a little lower down. The place where Odysseus spent the
night and where the girls came to wash clothes would then be close
to the spot where the country road crosses the Amato. The journey
of Nausicaa and her maids to the washing pools, and then the return
from the Amato to the city on foot or in a cart, might be estimated as
taking three to four hours. Tiriolo and its surroundings are regarded
as very fertile, a region where the west wind almost always blows –
both of which are also features of the land of the Phaeacians. Here is
the city of Alcinous as described by Nausicaa:

> But once we reach our city, ringed by walls
> and strong high towers too, with a fine harbour either side ...
> and the causeway in is narrow; along the road the rolling ships
> are all hauled up, with a slipway cleared for every vessel.
> There's our assembly, round Poseidon's royal precinct,
> built of quarried slabs planted deep in the earth.
>
> (O, F 6, 288).

Tiriolo, beside a place where the waters divide, is a mountain town; it
commands the Calabrian peninsula and thus the way from sea to sea.
Two seas, and with them the possibility of two bays offering harbour
at the western and eastern river mouths; that is how the Wolfs try to
resolve the difficulty of adjusting the quite detailed description of
the city of the Phaeacians as a seaport to the fact that Tiriolo is in the
mountains. The city is enclosed on two sides by its harbour, to which
a narrow access leads, probably not far from the market place with
the temple of Poseidon – here it does become difficult to reconcile
the contradictions, faced with the facts of the Calabrian landscape
at this point. The Wolfs wonder if it is possible to understand the
passage about the harbour on both sides of the city as being a harbour
beside one of the seas, and another harbour on the side of the other.
'The way between them, however, would have to be short enough for
both harbours to be visible from the city (...). And there is indeed a
town with such a view: Tiriolo.'[88]

Even if we put this construction on the passage, there are still a
good many questions. Why did Odysseus fail to notice any bay or
harbour when he came to land at the mouth of the river? Hoe can
the clear description of a narrow causeway (between the two sides of
the harbour) be reconciled with the topographical circumstances of
the mouth of the Lamato and the mouth of the Fiume Corace in the

Ionian Sea? And does not the text suggest that we should imagine a walled city by the sea, with a double harbour, reached by a narrow access – the space could have been narrow because ships were moored on both sides of it – and a fine temple standing in the market place? Then again, how could Odysseus reach Ithaca from the Tyrrhenian Sea without going through the Strait of Messina again in a southerly direction? On foot across the Calabrian peninsula?

In spite of many doubts, then – after all, we cannot follow Homer's trail and the wanderings of Odysseus without any questions and doubts at all – we come to the third part of the way leading from the city of the Phaeacians to *the good ship and the sea shore* (O R 13, 65), in other words from Tirioli to the Golfo di Squillace and the mouth of the Corace, which has its source in the Sila mountains flows into the Ionian Sea, and was navigable in antiquity. Perhaps the ship that was to carry Odysseus to Ithaca was initially anchored not in the harbour by the sea but further up, halfway towards the city. The Wolfs point to the subtle difference in the fact that when Alcinous himself stowed the bronze vessels taken to the ship by the Phaeacians so that they would not hamper the oarsmen, there is no mention of the sea but only of the ship, while later Odysseus and his companions *had come down to the ship and the sea* (O, R 13, 70). From this they conclude that the city of the Phaeacians was not directly beside the sea, but a little way inland and higher up, and that perhaps ships could approach the city upstream by a river.

In antiquity the Corace was presumably navigable in its lower reaches, south of Catanzaro, where you can accompany the river to its mouth along a quiet country road through a pretty valley that makes you forget the dismal expanses of concrete, at least briefly. Emerging from the green hinterland, the river cuts its way past the sand of its banks, leaving the land and the mountain range from which it springs with a graceful curve to the right. To the north, the almost entirely flat coast runs in what is nearly a straight line to the Marina Capo Rizzuto, with its four capes, close to the old Greek city of Crotone; to the south the strip of land along the shore soon ends in the foothills of the mountainous Le Serre region, overgrown with evergreens, and part of the Apennines.

Here, where there is nothing to be seen now at the mouth of the Fiume Corace but a few anglers and fishing boats, and the uniform grey of the scene is enlivened only by two long lines of fishing nets the colour of oxblood stretched out on the road leading to the river

– here we may perhaps think of the place where Homer describes the swift ship of the Phaeacians putting out to sea to take Odysseus, well provided with guest-gifts, food and drink, home to his own land of Ithaca (*Odyssey* 13, 70 in the original Greek).

Skylletion, founded by Achaeans in the 8th century BC, lay only a little way south of the mouth of the Corace. Its importance was in its special geographical position as a settlement by the sea and close to a navigable river, at the eastern end of a trade route in the narrowest part of a region settled by the Greeks along both coasts from the middle of the 8th century onwards. Was that the information that reached Homer's ears, and perhaps inspired him to identify this place with the spot where Odysseus, homeward bound, left the land of the Phaeacians? And was that, in the heightened interaction of myth, the source of the legend of the founding of Skylletion, the only city in greater Greece to claim Odysseus as its founder? At least, a delightful story has come down to us in a commentary on the *Aeneid* by the Latin grammarian Servius, according to which Odysseus built a city here from the wreckage of his ship (*de navium fragmentis*) and called it Navifragum Scyllaceum. And the famous Roman statesman and scholar Aurelius Cassiodorus, who held high office under the emperor Theodoric the Great, born in AD 490, communicating the spirit of antiquity to the early Middle Ages, reports: 'Scyllaceum is the first of the cities of the Bruttii people of which it is said that Odysseus, the destroyer of Troy, founded it.' So the Phaeacian memorial erected by the Gulf of Squillace in 1974 allows no doubt of the mythological reality of the place, and links it to the historical reality of Cassiodorus: QUESTO/IL NAVIFRAGUM SCILADEUM/DI ULISSE. QUI/NE L'AMPIO GOLFO/LA TERRA DEI FEACI/ LA GRECA SKILLECION/IL VIVARIUM DI/MAGNO AURELIO CASSIDORO. The monastery of Vivarium, founded by Cassiodorus a little further south close to the present seaside resort of Copanello, had a great library and was a centre of scholarship.

Not two kilometres south of the Corace, in a beautiful grove of olive trees up to three hundred years old, lies the Parco Archeologico di Scolacium. Passing the mighty apses and walls of the ruined Norman or pre-Norman church of Rocalletta, which was built with bricks from ancient Scolacium, its red, brown and ochre mingling with the olive green and silver of the surrounding trees in a visually pleasing manner, the road leads into the Roman city. All that is left of its Greek predecessor is the *Fama* – and perhaps some remains still unexcavated; we detectives would like to think they might go back to ancient times close to the Homeric period. Here we are happy to agree with the Wolf brothers when they suggest to archaeologists that they 'excavate the places in the Calabrian isthmus, at Tirioli and Skylletion, to which Homer erected a poetic monument in the *Odyssey* as the city and harbour of the Phaeacians.'[89]

For the time being we must content ourselves with the remains from the Roman period, and again there is a theatre – the only Roman theatre yet excavated in Calabria – which has a view from the upper tiers over the Parco Archeologico, the gently hilly coastal land, and the sea, giving an idea of the beauty, charm, and pleasant residential areas of the ancient coastal cities of Magna Graecia. This is the place to wish the Phaeacian ship carrying the sleeping Odysseus a good voyage and a happy return, and beg Zeus to calm his angry and vengeful brother Poseidon. And if we want to keep the retreating ship in view a little longer – for it will soon be gone beyond the horizon, it is a Phaeacian ship and could not be overtaken even by *a wheeling falcon, the fastest creature that flies* (O, R 13, 87) – then we should follow it from the nearby mountain village of Squillace, continuing the ancient name of Skylletion or Scolacium, 350 metres above the coast. There you look down on the little town lying below, over the roofs of the houses and church, strongly tinged in many shades of earthy brick colours. And over the hilly land, with its light green pastures and dark groups of trees, the view is down to the sea, now blurred in shades of blue and green.

Viewing conditions today are not ideal for us to watch the Phaeacian ship leave. But our thoughts go with it: safe voyage, good luck, until we meet again on Ithaca.

Home Again ... Home?

Ithaki – *Ithaca*

ITHACA. Faster than the falcon, that swiftest of birds, the Phaeacian ship carried Odysseus home to his own island as he slept the deep sleep of exhaustion, and soon, *still fast asleep* (O, R 13, 119), he was laid on the beach with the rich gifts he had been given. Then the ship turned back, and had almost reached her own harbour when Poseidon appeared, to take vengeance on the kind and humanitarian Phaeacians who had brought Odysseus home so swiftly. He struck the ship *and with one blow from the flat of his hand turned her into stone and rooted her to the sea-bottom* (O, R 13, 162). At this good King Alcinous ordered his people never again to take home any travellers who happened to come to their city.

But what about Odysseus?

> That very moment
> great Odysseus woke from sleep on native ground at last –
> he'd been away for years – but failed to know the land.
>
> (O, F 13, 213).

Where and in what region was the 'native ground' to which it was his dearest wish to return from his adventures both dangerous and amorous? That will to return, ultimately overcoming all difficulties, was what had motivated the hero and kept him alive. It is not at all outlandish to suppose that Homer knew about the island home of Odysseus from seeing it himself, or from a wealth of information deriving from the extensive knowledge of traders and seafarers.

So what island can be regarded as the one that Homer called Ithaca? It has always been unquestioningly taken for granted that it was one of the Ionian islands off the west coast of Greece. Wilhelm

Dörpfeld, the great archaeologist and excavator, favoured the attractive area around Nidri on the east coast of the island of Lefkada, with its fine natural bay and a few smaller islands nearby. Other classicists have named Corfu (Cercyra) and the small island of Atokos between modern Ithaca and the mainland. There has also been strong support for Cephalonia, the large neighbouring island to the west of Ithaca. John V. Luce, however, sees little reason to doubt that it is the present island of Ithaca, traditionally identified with the home of Odysseus anyway. In his book *Homer's Landscapes* he has put forward many arguments, and says that: 'The evidence assembled in this study should at least make it hard to deny that Homer's picture of Ithaca is well grounded in reality and that it relates to the island that still bears the ancient and celebrated name.'[90] Trusting in him., we will take him as our guide for the final stage of the Homeric journey. He will have the company of another very interesting supporter of Ithaca: Prince Herrmann Ludwig Heinrich von Pückler-Muskau. In his travel book *Südöstlicher Bilderatlas* [South-Eastern Pictorial Atlas] published in 1841, he too devotes a delightful chapter to the island of Ithaca, clearly expressing his conviction that he has been able to trace the course taken by Odysseus on the island as set out by Homer: 'In my viewing of the various remarkable features of the island, I believed I could do not better than to follow Ulysses himself, with Homer's poem in my hand. Some even claim that Ithaca was Homer's birthplace, and he must at least have known it very well, as his description of the localities most remarkably reveals.'[91]

It is true that there are also several quite weighty arguments against this assumption. We do not even need to visit Ithaca to notice the discrepancy, in relation to the neighbouring islands, between its real position and that of the place described by Odysseus himself in Book 9 of the *Odyssey*:

> My island
> lies low and away, the farthest out to sea,
> rearing into the western dusk
> while the others face the east and breaking day.

(O, F 9, 27).

The map shows that not Ithaca but Cephalonia to the west of it matches this account better. On the other hand, the details show so many similarities between real topographical features and those cited

in the *Odyssey* that John V. Luce (see the Notes) was firmly convinced of Ithaca's claim. 'I conclude that the topographical setting for the events of the last twelve books of the *Odyssey* is in full and accurate correspondence with the terrain of the island still known as Itháki.'
[92]

> And then, that hour the star rose up,
> the clearest, brightest star, that always heralds
> the newborn light of day, the deep-sea-going ship
> made landfall on the island ... Ithaca, at last.
> There on the coast a haven lies, named for Phorcys,
> the old god of the deep, with two jutting headlands,
> sheared off at the seaward side but shelving toward the bay,
> that break the great waves whipped by the gales outside (...).
> Here at this bay the Phaeacian crew put in –
> they'd known it long before – driving the ship so hard
> she ran up on the beach for a good half her length,
> such way the oarsmen's brawny arms had made.
>
> (O, F 13, 109 f., 127 f.).

There is a wide choice of bays. An enchanting landscape of Mediterranean fjords lies at your feet if you stand on the south-east slope of Neriton, the highest mountain on Ithaca, as it falls steeply to the Gulf of Molo. The funnel-shaped gulf narrows from the open sea in the east to the bay of Aetos on the wasp-waist of the island, which is only 600 metres wide, and is bordered to the west by the Ithaca Channel (Stenos Ithaki), the narrow waterway between Ithaca and the neighbouring island of Cephalonia. The meandering coastlines with their many bays, and the perspective limitations of the contours of the mountains on both islands, which look like little inland lakes but really represent the sea washing the islands, create a wonderful play of water and land, rich in variety of form.

THE BAY OF PHORCYS. In spite of the many bays, however, the choice narrows down to two. Vathy Bay thrusts far into the south-east part of Ithaca, and is shaped approximately like a leaf with its stem. At its end lies the town of the same name, nesting between mountains rising to a moderate height with fertile land beyond them. 'Bright and clear, the gulf or harbour of Phorcys lies here in the shelter of the mountain. Its deep waters duplicate the mountain itself and the coastline in a picturesque reflection. The eastern end of this lake-like bay surrounds Vathy in an idyllically beautiful position. The lines of the *Odyssey*, Book 5, 96–104, describe the place to us clearly,' [93] says the Estonian traveller Otto Magnus von Stackelberg, who visited Ithaca in January 1813, assuming that it was the island of Odysseus.

The long bay, surrounded by mountains that shelter it from the wind, connects with the Gulf of Molo only by a narrow passage, and is thus protected from the rough waters of a stormy sea. It is one of the best natural harbours in Greece and offers safe anchorage. One wonders if Homer had it before his mind's eye when he describes Phorcys Bay, saying that *large ships[can] ride inside without tying up, once they are within mooring distance of the shore* (O, R 13, 100). Or was it the smaller Dexia Bay, next to it and directly to the east?

The ferry from Patras to Ithaca does not make for Vathy as its main destination, but puts in at Pisaetos Bay on the west coast of the island – directly below the conical mountain peak of Aetos, which since the English traveller William Gell published his *The Geography and Antiquities of Ithaca*[94] in 1807 has been described on several occasions as the probable site where the palace of Odysseus stood.

Crossing a col, you reach the other side of Aetos Bay. Then the road bends sharply around a rocky promontory covered in bushes – and you are looking at pretty little Dexia Bay, surrounded by green hills. Two rocky headlands face one another at the entrance to the bay, which has a slightly curving flat, sandy beach with a grove of olive trees. Steep hills rise beyond the bay. Where the olive groves merge with the *macchia* a pale patch marks the entrance to the cave of Marmarospilia, which can now only be guessed at.

This, then, must be the place, in the opinion of John V. Luce anyway and, as he writes, of many scholars who expressed the same opinion before him: the Bay of Phorcys. Wonderful water, bright and clear, pale green near the flat shore, invites you to bathe at the place where we can imagine the exhausted, sleeping Odysseus being gently laid down by the Phaeacians.

> There on the coast a haven lies, named for Phorcys,
> the old god of the deep – with two jutting headlands,
> sheared off at the seaward side but shelving toward the bay,
> that break the great waves whipped by the gales outside

so within the harbour ships can ride unmoored
whenever they come in mooring range of shore.
At the harbour's head a branching olive stands
with a welcome cave nearby it, dank with sea-mist,
sacred to nymphs of the springs we call the Naiads.

(O, F 13, 109).

If Homer really did envisage Dexia Bay as the Bay of Phorcys, he
was doing an honour to this modest indentation in the coastline of
the island, which like an amoeba assumes many forms. Phorcys, after
all, is one of the 'old men of the sea' – the others named by Homer are
Proteus and Nereus – and thus a member of the very ancient mythological nobility, one of the pre-Olympian deities. In the sacred books
of Orpheus, Phorcys was a son of Oceanus and Tethys, and therefore
went back to the beginning of time, for according to Homer Oceanus
(I, R 14, 246) is the *forefather of all.* With Oceanus we are 'at the
beginning of all things', the words with which Karl Kerenyi begins the
first volume of his history of gods and men. In his *Theogony,* Hesiod
has Gaia and Pontus as the parents of Phorcys, and calls him strong
and virile.[95] If by virile we understand the ability to father many children, and in Phorcys' case children who themselves achieved fame
(most of them in a gruesome manner) then the Old Man of the Sea
deserves this epithet. He was the father of the dreadful Scylla, yet
had paternal feelings of affection for her; when she was killed by
Heracles for stealing his cattle, Phorcys burned her body, boiled it
up, and remade her from the resulting brew. Whether she reappeared
more beautiful than before or even more terrible we do not know.
He, the most ancient of the Old Men of the Sea, was also the father
of ancient daughters, the white-haired yet fair-cheeked Graiai and
the black-skinned, snake-haired Erinyes. He also fathered the sisters
of the Erinyes, the Gorgons, and the snake goddess Echnida, mother
of the most terrible dogs in Greek mythology, Cerberus and Orthus,
who with his mother brought into being such impressive creatures as
the Sphinx and the Nemean lion. If we mention that other daughters
of Phorcys were the Sirens and the Hesperides, only the last-named
can be considered figures not imbued with ideas of terror, horror and
destruction. They were linked to the star of Aphrodite, the evening
star, and had beautiful names inspiring confidence: Hespera, the
Evening One; Aigle, the One of Light; Erytheia, the Red One;
Arethusa, the goddess of springs; as well as Chrysothemis, golden

order; Hygeia, health; and others. One is tempted to imagine this ancient, pre-Olympian, undomesticated family of deities, the Old Man of the Sea with his many daughters and grandchildren, bathing in the open air at Dexia Bay during a family party.

THE CAVE OF THE NYMPHS. Homer situated the sacred Cave of the Nymphs near the olive tree, and therefore also close to the Bay of Phorcys. If Dexia Bay is regarded as the Bay of Phorcys, then the Cave of the Nymphs, described as 'a welcome cave nearby' (O, F 13, 116) should be found not far away. However, 'nearby' is a phrase allowing is some latitude in assessing the distance. For an early Greek, whose natural frame of reference could be very different from ours today, did 'nearby' mean just round the corner, as it does to us, or could the distance be rather longer by our own standards, perhaps going some way up a mountain? To a Greek of the time, that would still not be very far off.

There was a cave very close to the bay when William Gell visited Ithaca in 1801 and 1806, publishing his account of his experiences and his observations in 1807. He, even more markedly than his travelling companion Edward Dodwell, was able to reconcile Homer's topography quite easily with the Ithaca of his own time,[96] and to see the reality of the *Odyssey* reflected in the remains of buildings and archaeological finds. His book soon became a standard work used as a guide by travellers to sites on Ithaca connected with Odysseus.[97]

Several classical scholars joined the ever-growing stream of visitors at this time. The German scholars among them in particular, after seeing conditions on the island, expressed fundamental doubts of the historicity of Homer's Ithaca, and more especially of Gell's identifications. His claim to have found the palace of Odysseus on Aetos was vehemently rejected. The classical scholar and teacher Rudolf Hercher of Berlin was biting in his criticism of Gell ('As a consequence of his antiquarian hallucinations, he detected the poet's hand even in the smallest details')[98] and did not spare the travellers who had followed him either. Only the classicist Rudolf Menge of Halle, after a visit lasting four months to the Homeric sites in 1890, particularly Ithaca and Troy, put an end to 'German scepticism', as the English geologist David Thomas Ansted has called it, by observing, 'And so we do not doubt that the poet of the *Odyssey* saw Ithaca with his own eyes, just as we do.'[99]

Prince von Pückler-Muskau, as mentioned above, visited Ithaca in 1836 and shared this opinion, and so did Heinrich Schliemann, who came here in 1868 and 1878. But they could not agree on the precise identification of sites in the *Odyssey* as stated by Gell after only brief visits to the island. The Prince expressed his scepticism in his typical light style, with ironic amusement: 'Gell, in short order, gave us the entire plan of the city and the palace so precisely that you can see for yourself the place from which Ulysses shot at the suitors – however, to my shame I must confess that except for the great terrace and the two cisterns I could not make out a single one of the many lines tracing the buildings offered with such certainty in his plan. Perhaps my imaginative powers were too much affected by the enormous heat and exhausted by the great effort of the climb, so that I even allowed myself the heretical notion that Ulysses could not possibly have lived anywhere so uncomfortable.'[100] As for Schliemann, he called the 'Reproduction of the "citadel of Odysseus"' in Gell's book on Ithaca 'a work of pure fantasy'.[101] John V. Luce too is unimpressed by the identification of this site. However, Aetos is still a worthwhile destination for a strenuous walk, and the hiker's efforts will culminate in the sight of what is presumably a Mycenean fortification wall, and be rewarded by a wonderful view. The city of Odysseus, however, must be sought elsewhere.

And what about the Cave of the Nymphs? Gell was quick to locate that too, identifying it with a cave not far from the shores of Dexia Bay. Later travellers could not check his findings for themselves because the cave had been partially destroyed when a road was built, and as the German archaeologist Carl Haller von Hallerstein said in 1814 'resembles nothing so much as a stone-quarry',[102] so he himself withheld his verdict on its Homeric identity. It was for Pückler-Muskau to raise doubts: 'Gell instantly declared it to be the cave of the Naiads, and although Homer's description was in no way analogous, he arranged items to suit his hypothesis to the best advantage, as classical scholars are only too apt to do.'[103]

But then where *was* the cave with the springs of the nymphs? Pückler-Muskau continues: 'Even at the time, all this contradicted Gell's theory, but since then a very remarkable cave has been found a few hundred paces further up the mountain, where olive trees still grow today, corresponding in every particular to Homer's account and, I may add, doing so in the most poetic manner.'[104]

He meant the limestone cave of Marmarospilia, as it is known today. If we allow the premises set out above, then this cave in the north-east slopes of Mount Merovigli, above Dexia Bay, also fulfil the criterion of being 'nearby'. I say 'also' because its other feature already make it a prime candidate for identification as the Cave of th Nymphs in the *Odyssey*. Luce goes so far as to say that Homer's detaile description 'puts its identification beyond reasonable doubt'.[105]

Today you can reach the cave comfortably along a little roa making its way through gardens, orchards and olive groves. A ma in Vathy, asked the way, warns us that at present it is closed for road works. There are no roadworks and the cave is not closed. We ar glad – but also at first sorry to see the poor condition of the area i front of the cave, surrounded by an ugly wire fence. A notice pro claims that this is EPILAIO NYMPHON (and CAVE OF TH NYMPHS is added in scrawled handwriting in English). It is har to believe this in view of the overflowing dustbins, a crooked set c struts with no sun awning, and a rusty green gatehouse. The heav iron door at the entrance to the cave is open, so we can see the narro wedge-shaped entrance to the Cave of the Nymphs familiar fro illustrations in books. Once I step in, I would like to abandon myse to the sense of awe I had expected to feel as soon as I entered th Naiads' sanctum, but first, by the faint light of a pocket torch, I hav to take care not to stumble over broken wooden stakes and brick wrapped in ragged lengths of plastic. It does not look as if any wor is going on at present. The eyes gradually become accustomed to th darkness, and I can see the place and its shape better. On the le the floor of the cave goes some five metres down over slippery step separated only by a structure of lathes with a rope to hold on to fro the main cave, which is almost circular, dropping to a considerabl depth on the other side. Where there is a barrier to climbing an further down, I see a stalactite wall projecting in a slight curve wit a ridged, almost pleated surface, a stone chiton in grey, black an pale pink. Or is there some similarity to a loom? Is it one of the *long stone looms [...] where the nymphs weave out their webs from clouds sea-blue wool* (O, F 13, 120)? Up in the height of the domelike vaul there is a small opening which lets in a little faint sunlight to fa on the floor of the cave some twelve metres below. Several adjoinin spaces on different levels, opening off the main hall, give the Naiad an underground palace of many rooms adorned with stalactites an stalagmites, although the light is so faint that I can admire its beaut only in the places closest to me.

Back in the light of day the junk and garbage are forgotten, like the ugly fence, the unimaginative bank of earth outside the entrance to the cave, the rotting gatehouse. Before you, if you look over the fence, lies Homeric country. Seen in a sober light, the slopes of Mount Merovigli, planted with olives and cypresses, fall away to Dexia Bay and the Gulf of Molo, while the mountains opposite rise to their highest peak, Mount Neriton. However, a poet may have seen the same view over 2700 years ago, and have been enchanted by the sight of the land and the sea. Perhaps, like visitors much later, he had just looked at the glittering palace of the cave by the light of a torch, had seen the stalactites and stalagmites and was reminded by them of looms, pitchers and urns, had seen the light coming in through the roof, heard a constant dripping, and the buzzing of bees near the entrance where they built their combs. And then, we may suppose, he took all these impressions away rooted in his mind, to be transformed one day, like the stalagmites formed by water dripping on the limestone of the cave, into material for the beautiful tale of the landing of Odysseus in his homeland of Ithaca. It is told with both dramatic effect and humorous enjoyment of the hero's tall tales, and has an aura of kindly divine clairvoyance.

The cave of Marmarospilia could indeed have been the one that Homer made into the Cave of the Nymphs, turning its rock formations and stalagmites and stalactites into stone bowls and jars and looms:

> There are mixing-bowls inside and double-handed jars,
> crafted of stone, and bees store up their honey in the hollows.
> There are long stone looms as well, where the nymphs weave out
> their webs from clouds of sea-blue wool – a marvellous sight –
> and a wellspring flows for ever.
>
> (O, F 13, 118).

The cave has two openings, one through which human beings may enter and one in the vault above. Birds could get in but for the prosaic wire netting now closing off the aperture in the rock. Of these openings, we are told, there is:

> One facing the North Wind, a pathway down for mortals,
> the other, facing the South, belongs to the gods,
> no man may go that way ...

it is the path for all the deathless powers.

(O, F 13, 123).

Facing north and south, the northern entrance is for men, the southern entrance for the gods. Well, there is no doubt that I am a man and
I am standing in the evening sunlight outside the cave. My shadow
falls almost directly on its entrance, which should really mean that
it faces west and the entrance for birds is more to the east. Pückler-
Muskau and after him Luce disagree, and think the entrances lie, as
Homer wrote, to north and south. All the same, I am standing outside
the cave in the evening sunlight, and the sun is spreading golden light
over the western slopes of Mount Meravigli, casting my shadow on
the narrow entrance for humans. But let us not quarrel over a little
matter of 90°. Let us agree that Homer is right.

COMING HOME. As he was promised, the traveller is home at last.
Odysseus, laid on the sand asleep, wakes – and does not recognize
his native land. Pallas Athene has shrouded everything in mist. He
think he is in yet another foreign country and has been betrayed by
the Phaeacians after they promised to take him to Ithaca. And so
his homecoming begins with a heart-rending moment, described
by Schiller in his distich 'Odysseus'[106] with what Johann Gottfried
Herder admired as great simplicity:

> Odysseus sails many waters in search of home,
> Past the barking of Scylla, the dangers of Charybdis,
> Through the terrors of the hostile sea, through the terrors of the land,
> His wanderings take him even to Hades' realm.
> Fate brings him at last, sleeping, to the coast of Ithaca,
> Where he wakes, and laments, not knowing his native land.

Now Athene appears in the guise of a handsome young shepherd,
and in answer to his question describes the general features of the
land that he has failed to recognize, ending with its name, Ithaca.
His joy is great. But Odysseus would not be the man so well known
to both gods and men if he were to tell the boy the whole truth, and
reveal his identity. He tells a story that is a tissue of lies, much to the
amusement of Athene, who now appears in the new form of a beautiful and accomplished woman and compliments him on his cunning,

subterfuge, and inventive mind. But the man who has been through so many trials, who has been so often disappointed and betrayed, and has equally often betrayed and disappointed others, still fears that he has not really reached *my bright Ithaca* (O, R 13, 325) and that Athene is mocking him. Pleading with her, he begs: *Tell me, am I really back in my own beloved land?* (O, R 13, 328) And for the second time she describes Ithaca, but now in detail, naming the features that appear before the eyes of Odysseus once she has made the mist disperse. At last he sees the place that has been his destination in his wanderings for ten long years, his eyes rest on the familiar landscape, and he is overjoyed. He kisses the fruitful earth and prays to the nymphs. Athene urges him to conceal the Phaeacians' precious gifts in a safer place, hidden in the Cave of the Nymphs, and Odysseus *set about bringing in all his belongings, the gold, the indestructible bronze and the fine fabrics* (O, R 13, 366). Then the goddess seals the entrance with a stone. Now they sit down by the trunk of the sacred olive tree and plan the ruin of the over-confident suitors.

Book 13 is framed by dramatic events – the turning to stone of the Phaeacian ship as it sets out for home, and the coming massacre of the suitors – but serves as the prelude to the part of the action set on Ithaca. There is something playful about it in the hero's swings of mood between deep despair and great rejoicing, in Athene's double change of shape, the lying tale that Odysseus tells her, and the goddess's amused respect for the intellectual gifts of a man with a nature so close to her own.

There are three passages in Book 13 where Homer has woven descriptions of Ithaca into the course of the action. In the first, the narrator of the epic provides the listener or reader with information about the specific features of the Ithacan coastline where the Phaeacian ship is about to land. The scene, already confined to a small part of the island, is focused on a particular place there, the Cave of the Nymphs, describing it in such precise detail that we, coming long after Odysseus, feel we can recognize the cave of Marmarospilia as the cavern described by Homer. The detailed attention paid to it prepares for the moment when at last Odysseus believes that he is truly back in his own homeland, and the grateful hero is moved to offer pious prayers to the immortal daughters of Zeus, the Naiads, and promise gifts if, with divine assistance, he lives to see his son grow up. (There is no mention here of his faithful wife, eating her heart out as she waits for his return.)

The two following descriptions are given by Athene, first in the shape of a handsome boy, then as a beautiful and stately woman. The idea of the second is to give a kind of survey of Ithaca to the questioner, Odysseus. In Athene's opinion, she says, he is *either a simpleton or [has] travelled very far from home*, since he does not know on what island, with a name *far from inglorious*, he has landed. The goddess mentions several general features in outline, using the rhetorical trick of making light of the merits of Ithaca at first, but then painting the picture of a land blessed by fertility. Odysseus is delighted to hear of his homeland. But this is not enough; it is all too vague and described in terms too general for him.. He must see his land, the details that he still remembers, and that finally show him beyond all doubt how – in spite of his constant persecution by the apparently almighty Poseidon – he has come home at last. Athene opens his eyes, disperses the mist, *and the countryside stood plain to view* (O, R 13, 352).

At last he has reached the place he remembers. This is a moving moment, for the hero himself and for listeners and readers. But Odysseus soon turns to business again; his emotion does not last long. Advised by the goddess herself, his guardian spirit, he makes his plan to kill the suitors.

Initially, if we study Odysseus' return to Ithaca, his total failure to realize where he is at first because of the mist conjured up by Pallas Athene, the necessity for the goddess's two descriptions of the island to remove all doubt from the hero's mind, it may all seem to slow down the course of the action and the narrative flow – but we can also see all this as a leisurely prelude, striking the keynote of what is to come, the reunion and recognition of husband and wife, Odysseus and Penelope.

It makes no difference to the visitor today, seeking the trail of Odysseus on Ithaca, whether Homer is making Athene show the hero his native land from the shores of the Bay of Phorcys or from the Cave of the Nymphs. Here is the view from the entrance to the cave of Marmarospilia, as described by bright-eyed Athene:

> But come, let me show you Ithaca's setting.
> I'll convince you. This haven – look around –
> it's named for Phorcys, the old god of the deep,
> and here at the harbour's head the branching olive stands
> with the welcome cave nearby it, dank with sea-mist,
> sacred to nymphs of the springs we call the Naiads.

> Here, under its arching vault, time and again,
> you'd offer the nymphs a generous sacrifice
> to bring success! And the slopes above you, look,
> Mount Neriton decked in forests!
>
> (O, F 13, 391).

Olive groves cover the steep hills that fall to Dexia Bay, with its two headlands overlooking the Gulf of Molo.

> There on the coast a haven lies, named for Phorcys,
> the old god of the deep – with two jutting headlands,
> sheared off at the seaward side but shelving toward the bay.
>
> (O, F 13, 109).

And opposite rise the dark flanks of the highest mountain in Ithaca, turned away from the sun, its peak surrounded by white cloudbanks, Neriton, *decked in forests*. This mountain was mentioned earlier, in Book 9. When Odysseus, at the court of Alcinous, finally came to tell the tale of his wanderings since leaving Troy, he introduced himself briefly and without false modesty, going straight on to mention his origin and the topographical features of his home:

> Sunny Ithaca is my home. Atop her stands our seamark,
> Mount Neriton's leafy ridges shimmering in the wind.
> Around her a ring of islands circle side by side.
> Dulichion, Same, wooded Zacynthus too.
>
> (O, F 9, 23)

Mount Neriton is older now than in Homer's time, and its peak has become bald, but it still bears the same name.

And on the horizon beyond Cape St Ilias, where the mountains around Neriton fall to the east, we see the neighbouring island of Lefkada outlined to the north. Its 'White Rocks' are the place where the poet Sappho, in despair over her unrequited love for the beautiful youth Phaon, is said to have thrown herself into the sea. But that is another story.

THE RAVEN'S CRAG AND THE SPRING OF ARETHUSA. After Athene and Odysseus have decided that the insolent suitors must die, she transforms him into an ugly old beggar wrapped in rags to keep him from being recognized too soon. Then the goddess tells him to go to the swineherd Eumaeus:

> But you, you make your way to the swineherd first,
> in charge of your pigs, and true to you as always,
> loyal friend to your son, to Penelope, so self-possessed.
> You'll find him posted beside his swine, grubbing round
> by Raven's Rock and the spring called Arethusa.
>
> (O, F 13, 461).

Where the old names have survived for thousands of years, it is not surprising to find that others too are still extant today: *Kórakos pétri*, the raven's rock or crag, and *Krini Arethoúsi*, the Spring of Arethusa. A huge cliff and a spring bearing these names lie in the south-east of the island. The way there could still be the same that Homer himself may once have known, the path he made his hero take from the 'harbour' to the farm of Eumaeus, or in terms of modern topography from Dexia Bay to the Marathia plateau. It is a strenuous walk of at least four hours. That would have been no great problem for a man like Odysseus, used to great rigours and extreme physical stress, particularly if we imagine his physical condition as portrayed by Kirk Douglas to film-goers in *Ulisse*, for instance in the scene of the killing of the suitors. So there is no mention of the time and effort it took him to reach his destination, or of the natural beauties surrounding him on the way. He had more important matters on his mind. Many hours and days of constant and concentrated effort still lay ahead, all with a single aim. We are therefore given only a laconic account of the way he reached the swineherd's house:

> So up from the haven now Odysseus climbed a rugged path
> through timber along high ground – Athena had shown the way –
> to reach the swineherd's place, that fine loyal man
> who of all the household hands Odysseus ever had
> cared the most for his master's worldly goods.
>
> (O, F 14, 1).

If you go from Dexia Bay to the Marathia plateau, the way leads past the Cave of the Nymphs. Not far above it you come upon a *monopati*, one of the many narrow footpaths criss-crossing Ithaca. There is an abundance of Mediterranean flora here: vine-covered slopes as far as the eye can see; fig, olive and laurel trees; cypresses and shrubs that release refreshing scents to be carried on the strong wind. The chirping of grasshoppers and the bleating of lambs provide acoustic accompaniment to the Arcadian scenery. The path winds uphill and then runs along the side of Mount Merovigli, often only half a metre wide, bordered by sage, furze and laurel bushes. You come to an old threshing-floor where a gnarled, windblown laurel tree grows. The view below is down to Vathy Bay, which from this perspective looks like a lake. Beyond it rise the Poros hills, and then more sea and more islands; Atokos is clearly visible, Kalamos and the contours of the mainland are blurred. And as you go on you always see the landscape from a new angle, for instance looking from the ruins of Paläochora, the old capital of Ithaca, at other islands and inlets, or from the village of Perachoro – by now the path is passing through fertile farmland – where there is a view of the east coast of Ithaca with its many curves and bends, and the west coast of the mainland with the islands that lie off it. Land and sea seem to be playing a pleasant game with their inexhaustible variety.

Finally the 'path of Odysseus' joins the new road to the Marathia plateau. First, however, a *monopati* branches off it, passing through fragrant, bright green *macchia* and leading along the eastern side of Mount Merovigli and down to the Spring of Arethusa. Fine silver threads of cobweb with spiders hanging from them cross the path again and again. Often all you can see of the webs is the spiders' little black bodies, apparently hovering above the sea or against the sky. You feel you do not want to destroy these elaborate works of art, you dive under the threads or try to go around them. A sudden delicate touch on your face, no more than a breath, the faintest resistance, a slight sound as something gives way, and you know, regretfully, that the wonderful metre-long cobweb rope has broken, the tightrope dancer has fallen and must begin its work again. The deep inky blue of the depths and the emerald green of the water closer to shore play around each other, giving the sea a magical dual colour. The white sails of the boats lying at anchor in the quiet bays put the finishing touch to the peace that presides over the landscape.

A last bend, and then you are presented with two major attractions for any visitor who comes to Ithaca on the Homeric trail: the Raven's Crag dropping vertically from the Marathia plateau, and the nearby Spring of Arethusa, emerging from the rock. Here we are, *by Raven's*

Rock and at the spring called Arethusa (O, F 13, 465), as Athene briefly describes them to Odysseus in her account of the whereabouts of Eumaeus. Over the last few metres outside the entrance of the cave where the spring rises, the path is once again spanned by long, glittering threads that, when you come close to them, seem to pass above the bushes on the steep slopes and the walls of Raven's Crag – light grey with flecks of rust-colour – and are lost like filigree lines of vapour in the infinite sky.

It takes the eyes a little while to adjust to the dark depths of the cave where the spring rises. Then you can see the water that you have already heard, dripping musically from the walls into the spring hidden in the rock as it draws its waters up from underground. You see and hear the rhythm of the falling drops like a measure of passing time. The flow of time itself is made up of drops falling every four seconds, a musical sound echoing all the way to eternity. The water glints briefly as each drop falls, and then a dark ring of ripples spreads, ebbing away against the rock walls.

There is a small stone bench where a visitor can rest, leaning against the rock in the shadow of trees. A good opportunity to let your thoughts wander, imagine herdsmen driving their animals to this spring, the only one for far around: their goats, sheep – or pigs. A book published in 1821, *Views Dedicated to T. Maitland*, by the Englishman Joseph Cartwright,[107] contains a colour print showing such a scene: herdsmen with their animals, in the clothing of their time, which seems more different from today's garments than from those of the herdsmen's ancestors in the Homeric period of the Odyssey. In this picture, which as a whole is very close to the present features of the landscape, we see a stream falling from the Raven's Crag and pouring through a ravine, passing close to the spring. Once the spring had a basin here, filled with water by the wintry stream from above and the spring from the side. However, earth tremors have destroyed the walled receptacle, and now only the spring can be seen in June. You would have to come back at another time of year to enjoy the blessing of water flowing from the Marathia plateau to little Ligia Bay with its white sands.

Like Eumaeus, perhaps, who had his farm close to the edge of Raven's Crag, and drove his pigs here to drink from the basin of the spring? It would certainly have been a steep climb down and up again. But the life-preserving water was here and nowhere else. Eumaeus, says Athene, will be found:

... posted beside his swine, grubbing round
By Raven's Rock and the spring called Arethusa,
Rooting for feed that makes pigs sleek and fat,
The nuts they love, the dark pools they drink.

(O, F 13, 464)

The dark pools they drink, or in another (English) translation *drinking water from deep pools* (O, R 13, 410) – the epithets allow us to conclude that the water the pigs drank was not glittering in bright daylight, but was flowing somewhere hidden in dense bushes – or in a rocky cavern, and thus in shade: *dark pools, deep pools.*

THE FARM OF THE SWINEHERD EUMAEUS. Did Telemachus too quench his thirst here when he returned from his travels in search of his father, after visiting the court of Menelaus in Sparta, moored his ship down in Ligia Bay, and made haste up to the faithful swineherd's farm? But more of that later. Perhaps following the trail that Homer intended for him, I strike out into the *macchia*, I climb, stumble, and scramble uphill, find a narrow path crossing a south-facing slope, and come upon a steep area of scree leading to a cave. The sweat is dripping off me faster than the Spring of Arethusa flows. A little way outside the cave, I sit down on the ground, which is padded only slightly with dried herbs, all around me there are thistles a metre tall, presenting their silvery barbed spears and beautiful bright purple flower-heads to flocks of yellow butterflies. They make no sound as they fly, land, and suck pollen from the flowers. Briefly, the noise of a plane intrudes into the vast noonday silence, quickly turning to a hollow droning sound and swiftly ebbing away again, like an acoustic comet tail following the plane as it flies past. Then the envelope of silence closes in once more, except for the broad, warm buzzing note of a swarm of wasps in a little tree near me. I am in luck. It is even better when I see a notice claiming that this is the cavern of Eumaeus.

It lies in a rock looking south, with a low stone wall in front of it. Animal droppings lie on the ground. These features show that it is sheltered from the north winds.

First over his broad shoulders he slung a whetted sword,
wrapped himself in a cloak stitched tight to block the wind,

and adding a cape, the pelt of a shaggy well-fed goat,
he took a good sharp lance to fight off men and dogs.
Then out he went to sleep where his white-tusked boars
had settled down for the night ... just under
a jutting crag that broke the North Wind's blast.

(O, F 14, 597).

Odysseus had lain down to sleep near the fireplace in the swineherd's house. The faithful Eumaeus, meanwhile, who did not like to sleep apart from his boars, went out to spend the night with them. In this 'Cavern of Eumaeus', perhaps?

Or perhaps, as Luce thinks, under an overhanging ledge at the foot of Raven's Crag? There is one weighty argument against that: the Raven's Crag curves from north to north-east in a rather concave shape, and is thus exposed to the north and north-east winds. The boars and their swineherd would have been better off in the cave called after Eumaeus, with the solid shelter of rock to the north, even if it was a little way below the foot of the rock wall. It would have been rather difficult for a man, if not for boars, to climb up and down the very steep, stony path.

So I reach the Marathia plateau, rather out of breath, and almost at once I am in the garden of a small farm. Or is it a garden? A plot of land with rocks scattered around, partly shaded by mighty olive trees, surrounded by a dry stone wall reinforced with thorny bushes here and there. And is it a farm? Surrounded by heaps of stones, rubble, and rubbish stands a small, single-storey, poorly whitewashed house, built of the stones naturally found here – this is the dilapidated property of a late counterpart of the swineherd Eumaeus. It is obvious that farming is not very profitable here.

You used the available stones to build a house and a garden wall, adding thorny bushes to ward off unwanted visitors – we can be sure that such was always the essential material for a house and home, as the description of Eumaeus' farm makes clear:

The swineherd made those walls with his own hands
to enclose the pigs of his master gone for years.
Alone, apart from his queen or old Laertes,
he'd built them up out of quarried blocks of stone
and coped them well with a fence of wild pear.

(O, F 14, 9).

Homer obviously visualized a considerably better place as the model for his farm. Herdsmen lived in modest circumstances themselves, but on the whole Homer gives us the impression of a well-managed farm with an impressive number of animals: 600 pigs and piglets, not counting the boars.

The present farm lies almost directly by the Raven's Crag on the Marathia plateau. The situation of the farm of Eumaeus is described as having *a long view*. And indeed there is a wide view from here, bounded only by the horizon. At its most distant, a straight line divides the rather darker sea from the sky or, if you go only a little way south up the slightly rising land, among tall flowering thistles and stately mullein, under ancient olive trees with mighty trunks on which many centuries have left their mark, the contours of mountains hint at the surrounding islands and the mainland.

Another factor in favour of the theory that Homer envisaged the Marathia plateau by the Raven's Crag as the model for the farm can be gleaned from a remark by Odysseus to Eumaeus:

> But if your master doesn't return, as I predict,
> set your men on me – fling me off some rocky crag
> so the next beggar here may just think twice
> before he peddles lies.

(O, F 14, 450).

Earlier, while telling a tissue of lies about his personal story – for his incognito must still be preserved – he has assured the doubtful swineherd for the second time that his king will soon return. If he is wrong, he says, let them throw him off the crags. If we take all the descriptions and comments in Book 13, and in the books in which Eumaeus features (Books 14–7), together with the topography of the swineherd's farm and its immediate surroundings, we can hardly agree with Luce that Homer has 'precisely and comprehensively (...) envisaged the whole location.'[108] It is easy to suppose that there was already a farm or a shepherd's hut here in ancient times because of the nearby spring of water, such a rarity in the south of Ithaca. The first travellers on Homer's trail in the early 19th century, W. Gell and E. Dodwell, who deliberately looked at the Raven's Crag and the Spring of Arethusa in the light of their reading of the *Odyssey*, found what they wanted so much to find: a herdsman's hut on the Marathia plateau. After them, these sites repeatedly became the destination of enthusiastic classicists.

The swineherd occupies a special place among the characters in the *Odyssey*. So does the description of the place where he and his farm hands live. The books containing Eumaeus represent a breathing space, a moment of rest amidst the upheavals at the Ithacan court, left without its king, where the riotous suitors are planning to murder his son Telemachus – while we have also heard the dramatic tale of the wanderings of Odysseus on the one hand, and on the other his humiliation when he comes to his own palace as a beggar. Then there is the suspense factor of Penelope's constantly postponed decision, and finally the terrible punishment of the suitors and the faithless maids.

Even apart from the swineherd's repeatedly expressed deep grief for the fate of his lost master, and his bitter complaints of the useless, dissipated young aristocrats, Eumaeus conveys a touching sense of humanity: he offers hospitality to a stranger with unpretentious goodwill; his violent outburst of tears expresses his joy at the surprising return from Sparta of Telemachus, whom he had thought dead; he has a sense of justice, ensuring that the hands too get their full share of everything; and all these qualities are based on an unquestioning devotion to the gods, which Eumaeus takes for granted, for he trusts the gods who *honour justice, honour the decent acts of men* (O, F 14, 197). The swineherd, without being idealized, is a genuinely good man.

Realistic and particularly attractive scenes are conjured up by the dialogues between Eumaeus and Odysseus in the guise of a beggar, as well as the passages of narrative in between. Uvo Hölscher, in the chapter about the background to the epic in his book, discusses the question of the landscape, the social and historical atmosphere of the *Odyssey* – here comparing it to the *Iliad* – and pays special attention to the descriptions of Ithaca, especially those relating to the swineherd and life on his property. "The scenes on the pig farm are described with unusual pleasure. They seem to stand on their own, to relish their account of the simple, natural life.' [109] Several times Hölscher mentions the sympathy, which the reader too cannot help noticing, that Homer feels for this character: 'But the liking of the poet for his figure and for the way he lives is striking. Eumaeus is the one character whom he distinguishes by the poetic means of apostrophizing him by name: 'To him you answered, swineherd Eumaeus.' [110] As a rule the conversational exchanges are in the third person, on the pattern of *And the great Odysseus, long in exile, answered/And the good swineherd answered, foreman of men.*

There could be no better place to read the touching books in which Eumaeus appears than in the shade of one of these mighty olive trees. Leaning against a great trunk, I sit looking at the high Marathia plateau. It seems to extend into the sea and the mountains of Cephalonia. To the south-east stretch the contours of the island of Oxia, one of the little islands to the west of the Acheloos delta with its many lagoons, in Homer *Oxeiai*, the cleft place. Telemachus passes it on his way home from Sparta. These are the Odyssean views, close to the Raven's Crag and far from the sea and islands, with which Homer enriched his Ithacan geography.

Into the Pan-like silence of early afternoon breaks the loud, rising cry of a cockerel, destroying the fine tissue of silence for a brief moment. After this onslaught, the silvery sound of bells worn by a slowly approaching flock of sheep, carried on the wind, is like angelic music.

In Search of a Father

Ithaca, Pylos, Sparta – *Ithaca, Pylos/Epano Engliano, Sparta*

Telemachus has returned to Ithaca, and first of all he seeks out Eumaeus. He can have no idea that the purpose of his journey, to discover something of his father's fate, is to be realized here at the loyal swineherd's farm in a manner surpassing his hopes – he will actually see that father again in person.

He had left Ithaca a week before on a journey undertaken at the urging of Athene. In the opening scene of the entire *Odyssey*, describing the assembly of the gods, she had already planned a double strategy (Book 1, 84f): she sent Hermes to visit Calypso on Ogygia and tell her that she must set Odysseus free, and she herself went to Ithaca to prepare Telemachus for his role as assistant to Odysseus in his father's final act of revenge, the killing of the suitors.[111] From now on Homer develops two parallel strands of plot, with father and son as the protagonists of their respective stories, keeping strictly to the time scheme of a week. While Odysseus, after leaving Ogygia, spends two days at sea, three days with the Phaeacians, and then after reaching Ithaca two days with Eumaeus, his son Telemachus travels from Ithaca by way of Pylos and Pheae to Sparta and back again. On the morning of the eighth day, they meet at the swineherd's farm.

In Books 1 and 2 of the *Odyssey* – they, with other passages in the first four books and part of Book 15, make up what is called the *Telemachy*, in which the leading character is Telemachus, the son of Odysseus and Penelope – we hear of the difficult situation at the court of Ithaca while its king is gone: a pack of spendthrift suitors have come to woo Penelope and are urging her to make a decision, while Telemachus is about to come of age, and the unhappy queen has almost entirely lost hope that her husband Odysseus will ever return. It is an account of a crisis coming to a head, and it provides the dramatic tension of the background in the final part of the story of the return of Odysseus, beginning from the time when he leaves Calypso's island. The *Telemachy* may be regarded as the poet's own invention, the expression and evidence of his poetic imagination with the aim of developing 'an art of perspective'.[112]

As part of Athene's plan, Telemachus is to visit his father's old comrades in the Trojan War, Nestor in Pylos and Menelaus in Sparta, and ask them about the fate of Odysseus. And so he does. The goddess, taking the shape of Mentes, Odysseus's oldest friend, and swiftly flying to Ithaca, tells him what to do: if Telemachus hears from Nestor and Menelaus that Odysseus is still alive and will come home, he is to put up with the suitors for another year; if he is told that his father has died, then now that he has reached manhood himself he should give his mother another husband. He determines to do so, calls an assembly and tells the suitors of his decision.

Now taking the form of another old friend of Odysseus, Mentor, Athene helps him with his preparations for the journey, and so does the faithful Eurycleia, formerly nurse to both Odysseus and Telemachus. However, Telemachus tells his mother Penelope nothing, so that she will not *mar her lovely face with tears* (O, F 2, 416). Perhaps that is not the only reason, and it is also one of several ways in which he makes it clear that he is now an adult. 'The *Telemachy* is an example of those folktales in which adolescent sons, placed in an epic situation, become men.'[113] That evening the time comes. Athene and Telemachus have taken their places on deck at the stern of the ship, the oarsmen are on their benches, the mast is raised, the sail hoisted, the goddess brings them a favouring wind – the ship putting out to sea, we may assume at sunset, must have been a fine sight as the wind *sent it singing over the wine-dark sea* (O, R 2, 421).

Athene's clear topographical directions are very useful to anyone on the trail of the *Odyssey*. We do not always have an easy time with the tale of the hero's wanderings, but the voyages of Telemachus are comparatively simple to trace. Is that perhaps because the *Telemachy* may be regarded as a genuine invention on the part of the poet? The events that occur in it have a more realistic touch than the wanderings of Odysseus in which the poet reworked ancient Mediterranean legends and traditional tales. Situations are described that could well have been those of Greek princely courts of the Mycenaean and the poet's own period. And similarly, such a voyage may relate to facts as known to Homer.

When Telemachus sets out on his journey of inquiry, the story told in Books 3, 4 and 5, we may imagine him setting out from the harbour of the capital of Ithaca. If the most likely site for the capital itself was near the present village of Stavros in the north of the island, the harbour may be identified with nearby Polis Bay. While the setting sun tinged the waves purple, *wine-dark*, the ship put out to sea. Her destination was Pylos, the city of Nestor, reached by sailing in an almost straight course south-east, first passing through the channel between Ithaca and Cephalonia (then called Same), then along the east coast of Cephalonia and Zakynthos, and over the open sea to Pylos. The night fell fast, the mountains of Samos were already dark, the peak of Mount Neriton glowed in the last gold and purple of the sunset light. Soon there would be only the dark of the night.

> And the ship went plunging all night long and through the dawn.
> As the sun sprang up, leaving the brilliant waters in its wake,
> climbing the bronze sky to shower light on immortal gods
> and mortal men across the ploughlands ripe with grain –
> the ship pulled into Pylos, Niles' storied citadel.
>
> (O, F 2, 477 and 3, 1).

Neleus was the founder of Pylos, king of a domain on the west coast of the Peloponnese that was extended considerably by his son Nestor. In its Mycenaean heyday, it probably reached from the river Alpheus, flowing past Olympus, to the Gulf of Messenia.

PYLOS. Three places in the western Peloponnese bore this name in antiquity.[114] Was it Pylos in Elis? The position of that Pylos, quite far inland and east of the Pinios reservoir, at the centre of the old region of Elis, would seem to suggest that it was not. The Pylos mentioned by Strabo, on the Gulf of Kiparissia in nearby Tripylia to the south, was the favourite option for a long time. This identification gained archaeological support when Dörpfeld found two Mycenaean tholos tombs (burial chambers roofed by a dome or vault) and the remains of a palace at the place known as Marmara, near the fishing village of Kakovatos, and identified it as Nestor's Pylos. That would match the account of a voyage from Ithaca by night, lasting some twelve hours, to a Pylos located here, given a distance of about 130 kilometres and assuming a sailing speed of ten kilometres an hour.

At present this archaeological site is in a pitiful condition. Although it is on a hillside only a few hundred metres from the main road to Patras, it seems to have been forgotten. If it were not for a dilapidated, closed gate, with a fence half broken down, obviously by people climbing over it from time to time, with a notice beside it saying 'Archaiologos choros/Archaeological site', no one would think that this was a place where Mycenaean remains had been found, let alone one with a claim to share some of the glory of the *Odyssey*. At first all you see is apparently impenetrable bushes on the edge of a meadow gone wildly to seed, with an approximately round area enclosed by rock walls behind it. The rock is still clad by masonry only in two small places, almost covered by undergrowth. There is no sign of a dome; the place is open to the sky. Not a very royal tholos. The hilly landscape rises to the east, undulating and green, first with olive trees, then other bushes and trees, and climbing to the Minthi mountains soon leaves the sea for the fertile plain typical of wide expanses of the west coast of the Peloponnese. The features of the landscape and topography of this place could well make it seem a candidate for a Mycenaean centre, but the particularly scanty archaeological finds raise considerable doubts.

Authors of classical antiquity up to Pausanias unanimously located Nestor's city much further south in Messenia, on the rocky peninsula of Coryphasion north of the Bay of Navarino. The place occupied by a Venetian citadel – now known as Paleokastro – was called Coryphasion by the Spartans and Pylos by the Athenians, and there was a small Mycenaean city there, a place dating from Neolithic times and inhabited, with some interruptions, up to the Middle Ages. It has a commanding situation with much to offer the eye. But is it enough, without important archaeological finds, to give us a satisfactory idea of the *royal palace* (O, R 3, 388) of the wise and mighty ruler Nestor, praised by all?

Discussion of the site of the Homeric Pylos received a considerable boost from excavations in 1939, and then again after the interruption of the Second World War from 1952 onwards. They were carried out by a team from the University of Cincinnati under Carl W. Blegen, and uncovered a large Mycenaean palace in the hilly landscape above the Bay of Navarino, near Ano Engliano. As no even faintly comparable ruins have been found in a suitable situation anywhere else, historians and archaeologists overwhelmingly agree that in the excavations of Ano Engliano they are looking at the site of Nestor's palace, although they bear in mind Blegen's scepticism about the historical reality of the famous mythical king: if there ever was a Nestor, said Blegen, then he lived here in the palace of Engliano, which was in its prime in the 13th century.[115]

A Mycenaean palace which must have been magnificent in the past, on the site of a landmark that, taken with a grain of salt, can be seen to suit the nautical information in the *Odyssey* reasonably well if not in every particular – this is the place that, we may argue, was perhaps the first destination of Telemachus in his journey to find his father and himself. For whatever the name of the king who lived in this palace – and maybe it really was Nestor – the archaeological finds leave us in no doubt that this place was an archaic power centre at the time of the Trojan War, with influence reaching far beyond its boundaries. Bearing in mind all the information that we can say, with a fair degree of certainty, was available to the poet about Ithaca, not so very far away, we may assume that Homer knew of the ruins of Nestor's palace. Presumably they were still impressive in his time, a testimony to the glorious Mycenaean past.

So let us imagine Telemachus standing expectantly in the bows of his ship, keeping a lookout for Nestor's radiant palace in the light of the rising sun. His gaze wanders over the hilly landscape that rises *across the ploughlands ripe with grain* beyond the coastline. There would have been two bays available as harbours, the large Bay of Navarino, a huge natural harbour, and the small Voidokilia Bay north of the foothills of Coryphasion. Access to the latter is so narrow that it does not appear on the official map of the Peloponnese, where the bay looks like a small lake. But to say so deprives it of a considerable part of its breathtaking beauty, for its link to the open sea, narrow as it is, is an essential ingredient in the wonderful landscape here seen as a whole.

A beautiful path leads down to it. On the sandy landing stage between the northern Bay of Navarino and the Divari lagoon, you approach the Coryphasion promontory. On the left, the flat curve of the shore swings in a wide curve towards the little town of Pylos in the south – founded in 1820 and given the name of the Homeric Pylos – a natural harbour safe from the violence of the open sea behind the island of Sphakteria, which acts as a barrier. At the foot of Coryphasion the path runs over what little soil is left between the steep rise of the promontory and the shallow waters of the lagoon, with mountain flora on one side and maritime flora on the other, until Voidokilia Bay shows us that it is close: white sandy underfoot in a dune landscape, where sea plants and mountain plants happily co-exist. From a small height, you see the bay like an enchanting eye in clear, cool shades of blue, changing from the indigo of the deep sea to the light blue of the water near the shore, where the presence of sand turns it paler. It all instantly suggests more poetic associations than might be suggested by its name of 'ox eye', Voidokilia.

The entrance to a cave is visible from some distance, half-way up Coryphasion, crowned here to the north by the Frankish castle of Paliokastro. You trudge uphill through the deep sand of a dune, make your way over a small slope criss-crossed by little ledges and covered by violet-hued flowers, climb a very steep, stony path through *macchia*, and then you are facing the large, almost triangular mouth of the cave.

The cave itself is a tall place reminiscent of Gothic architecture, almost like a church, or it would be if it did not turn a corner, leaving the back of it in the dark. Caves are the oldest of human dwellings: Neolithic remains from the 6th century BC have been found here, as they have on the Coryphasion plateau and other heights nearby. These remains are further from Nestor's time than we are from his. Since early peoples were reminded of animals and animal skins by the shape of the stalactites in caves, they may have turned the inorganic into the organic and allowed Nestor's flocks and herds, in a mythical transformation, to find shelter and safety here, giving the cave the king's name. But it was not only his cattle, goats and sheep who were at home there. A divine thief had once hidden the profits of his crime in these stables, part of the herd of fine cattle stolen by Hermes from his half-brother Apollo on the lush meadows of Mount Olympus. He left the rest of the stolen cattle in a cave by the river Alpheus.

Hermes was something of an infant prodigy. As soon as his mother the nymph Maia had given birth to him in the deep darkness of a cave in the Arcadian mountain of Kyllene – like so many others, he was fathered by Zeus – he invented the lyre, fashioning it from a tortoise shell, and he did not stop at that. He was the first to kindle fire, the first to make an animal sacrifice. The art of prediction from casting the dice, astronomy, the musical scale, the cultivation of olives, and much else, some of it more like conjuring tricks and magical practices – they were all invented by the clever brain of the god Hermes. However, his cunning and astuteness also brought him into conflict with the law. What would his career be like if he could commit robbery and cattle-rustling on his first evening alive? Those were his crimes, but they were glossed over by his divine relations; it was all in the family. Apollo, enchanted by the child's singing and playing, was ready to let him have his beloved cows in return for the wonderful lyre, and the deal was done. They shook hands on the bargain, and Apollo went happily away from Nestor's Cave with his instrument, on his way down to the Alpheus to play to the cattle still there, and console them for the claustrophobic time they had spent in captivity with the musical notes that had enchanted him so much himself. So the baby Hermes was already the owner of a fine herd of cattle. If you are on a high induced by the effort of the climb to the cave and your pleasure in the delightful place, you can easily think you see the skins of two of the animals that he killed hanging among the stalactites.

From the entrance of the cave, the eye wanders over a varied landscape that we can imagine as the heart of Nestor's kingdom. The little island of Proti is the last bulwark of land in the boundless expanses of the Ionian Sea, barely separated from Pelops' huge island, on which the peaks of the low mountain ranges of Egaelo and Likodimo mark the horizon beyond the plains and hills of the land in between, and you can just make out the palace precinct of Epano Engliano in the muted blue of the distance. The waters disclose a panorama full of variety to delight the eye. To the west the sea lies along the coastline in broad, blue abundance. But not far from Nestor's Cave it is broken; the Coryphasion promontory running out into the sea and a headland opposite – where there is a Mycenaean grave said to be that of Nestor's son Thrasymedes – form a gateway beyond which, like a sealed-off bubble or a charming pendant to the great sea, you see the perfect curve of Voidokilia Bay: the shimmering iris of an eye surrounded by its white, a regular, gently rising sandy strip. The bay is separated from the water nearest to it only by a narrow strip of shore and dune, and then comes the shallow lagoon shining in matt tones of lead and ochre, and in its own turn sharing the long projection of the sandy Gialova plain with the neighbouring Bay of Navarino, where the sea glows in its familiar colours.

The fine sand of the flat shore of Voidokilia Bay, protected by the rocky ledge thrusting into the sea, is an invitation to any seafarer to land and enjoy a picnic on the beach. And of course it would be exactly the place for a banquet in honour of a god whose element is the sea.

The ship pulled into Pylos, Neleus' storied citadel,
where the people lined the beaches,
sacrificing sleek black bulls to Poseidon.

(O, F 3, 4).

What luck for Telemachus! Nestor himself, the man he had come to visit, and his sons and friends were preparing a sacrificial feast to Poseidon, not inland in the palace, but sensibly enough on the sea shore. Encouraged by Athene in the shape of Mentor, Telemachus overcame his bashfulness. Together they approached the men of Pylos sitting to eat, were welcomed kindly and invited to join the meal.

Nestor's son Pisistratus, first to reach them,
Grasped their hands and sat them soon at the feast
On fleecy throws spread out along the sandbanks.

(O, F 3, 39).

After Athene and Telemachus had also poured a libation to Poseidon, they all shared the meal. Nestor followed the civil custom of showing hospitality to strangers before asking them their names, their origin, and why they have come. Telemachus, his confidence bolstered by the support of Athene, gave a clear and heartfelt account of his story, and a confidential conversation developed between him and the king, skilfully arranged by the poet as a dramatic dialogue in which encouraging remarks by Nestor, who considers the return of Odysseus perfectly possible, are countered by Telemachus' all but hopeless belief that his father will never come home – *long ago the undying gods have sealed his death, his black doom* (O, F 3, 274). This scene is beautifully represented in the one known pictorial version of it, on a red-figure Apulian mixing-bowl from the Collection of Antiquities of the Berlin State Museums, dating from around 370 BC: white-haired Nestor, bent with age and emphasizing his words with two outstretched fingers of his right hand, which rests on a gnarled staff, turns to the youthful figure of Telemachus, who wears the garments of a travelling warrior – he is upright, but has removed his helmet and bends his head slightly as a gesture of respect – while behind the king a maidservant stands in a relaxed, almost casual attitude, her left hand lying lightly on her hip, her right hand holding a gift for the guest.

The defeatism of Telemachus was an essential element in his development, with Athene's guidance, into a mature man who would abandon the timidity and fears of an adolescent and actively take the initiative. His real aim should be to remove the suitors – as with his father's help he eventually does. As an example to spur him on, Nestor tells him of the revenge of Orestes on the treacherous murderer of his father Agamemnon. Evening has come on as the old king tells his tales of Menelaus and Agamemnon on their return from Troy, and their very different fates, recommending Telemachus to visit Menelaus in Sparta and ask if he has any news of his father Odysseus. At this point Athene rather surprisingly departs in the shape of an eagle. Telemachus is given an invitation to spend the night in the palace, and so the company sets off for it.

Voidokilia Bay would have been an extremely suitable place for the morning sacrificial banquet *along the sandbanks*, and the meeting between Telemachus and Nestor. However, one would be more inclined to situate the kingdom's harbour and wharves in the spacious moorings of the Bay of Navarino, protected by the island of Sphakteria, which forms a natural mole almost five kilometres long. Nestor's kingdom is ranked directly after Agamemnon's in the *Odyssey* in terms of importance and influence. Agamemnon's kingdom sent a contingent of a hundred ships to Troy, only ten more than Nestor's. Such a large fleet could have been accommodated only in the Bay of Navarino, the sole natural harbour along the entire west coast of the Peloponnese.

O Imathóeis Pylos, sandy Pylos – the epithet used by Homer, which later became a standard description through constant use – suggests the geomorphological character of Nestor's country. Pausanias thought it referred to the poor soil of the province of Pylia, which was sandy and thus unsuitable 'to provide enough pasture for cattle. Homer himself testifies to it, always calling Nestor the king of sandy Pylos when he mentions him.'[116] But the visual evidence does not agree with him. The entire land near the coast, first a flat plain and then gently hilly, is fertile; only the shores themselves were and still are sandy.

The ploughlands ripe with grain (O, F 3, 3), *the fruitful earth* (Rieu translating the same passage) – it would only be doing justice to the landscape rising from the plain with its lagoons by the sea to the palace of Ano Engliano to emphasize that feature of it in Homer's description. Olive groves covering the hills and valleys, terraced fields here and there, small groups of cypresses are all obvious evidence of his image of the fertile soil giving nourishment and thus life. Not a place of extremes but a pleasant landscape that, with its agricultural and maritime resources, has always offered good ground for those who knew how to exploit it. With the addition of a sense of security, no threat from enemies at home or abroad, a palace culture similar to that of earlier Cretan models could have developed without the necessity for massive defensive walls, in contrast to the Mycenaean centres of power in the north-east of the Peloponnese, which increasingly had to defend themselves against Greek tribes coming up from the south, and were probably also exposed to political tensions at home.

The colourful reconstructions of Nestor's palace by Piet de Jong, a member of the excavation team led by C.W. Blegen and based on comparison with the more abundant fragments of painting and architecture found in such centres as Mycene and Tiryns, give us an attractive and delightful idea of the architectural beauty and enchanting decoration of its halls and courtyards. The floor and ceiling of the spacious throne room are shown covered with vivid linear patterns, while figurative frescos adorn the walls: a girl playing the lyre, a flying dove, as well as lions, griffins and stags in a discreetly sketched forest landscape. Opposite the great central hearth stands the royal throne, probably made of wood and richly decorated with ivory, lapis lazuli and other precious substances, with a basin nearby, intended for libations that could be poured by the occupant of the throne.

One they were back in the palace, Nestor did indeed pour a libation to Athene. Then the company went to bed. While the old king withdrew to the interior of his palace, Telemachus and Nestor's son Peisistratus, who was about the same age as the guest, slept in the hall.

The reality of the palace ruins today is of course considerably less spectacular than de Jong's reconstructions. However, the location of the complex is impressive, standing in its landscape setting on a plateau 170 m long and 90 m wide. The plateau was inhabited in the Middle Helladic period, between 2000 and 1600 BC. Instead of the natural landscape a domesticated and cultivated one will have developed as the result of human ingenuity, and standing outside what was once the palace entrance we may assume that it has not altered much today. Agricultural land with many olive trees falls gently to the sea and the Bay of Navarino, with the island of Sphakteria protecting it, while to the north and east the Egaleo and Likodimo mountains are the outstanding features of the landscape.

It is easy to find a rock at the palace entrance where one could sit early in the morning – for rosy-fingered Dawn has just woken – waiting for the king when he

> (...) climbed from bed,
> went out and took his seat on the polished stones,
> a bench glistening white, rubbed with glossy oil,
> placed for the king before his looming doors.
>
> (O, F 3, 452).

He has gathered his six sons around him to sacrifice to Athene. Telemachus has taken his place too, and his companions are also to be present. Someone is swiftly sent *to brave Telemachus' ship* (O, F 3, 482) to summon them. Once Nestor's wife Eurydice and all their daughters and daughters-in-law have come to attend, a heifer is sacrificed. Now it is time for the banquet, and Odysseus' son prepares for it with a pleasant bath:

> During the ritual lovely Polycaste, youngest daughter
> of Nestor, Neleus' son, had bathed Telemachus.
>
> (O, F 3, 521).

Then she anoints him with oil and wraps him in a magnificent tunic and cloak. The archaeological remains suggest some unusually attractive items to help us to imagine the scene: close to the queen's chambers there was a wonderfully well preserved terracotta bathtub, imitating the shape of the human body with a slightly concave curve in the central area. A spiral pattern on the upper rim may symbolize the stimulating effect of water on the circulation, as well as the way in which it was applied – gently poured from shallow bowls (nine have been found) by maids, and in this particular case by the king's own daughter, over the body of the man in the bath, both cleansing and relaxing him.

After the banquet that followed the sacrifice, Nestor gives orders for a team to be harnessed to a chariot in haste so that Telemachus can drive to Sparta, accompanied by Peisistratus. Following the sacrifice and the banquet, it will now have been around midday, and they could not have reached Sparta before nightfall, but must stop in

Pherai, also a part of Menelaus' domain, on the Gulf of Messenia on the site of modern Kalamata, about 60 km from Ano Engliano.

It is a pleasant journey, beginning with a drive through the hills with their extensive olive plantations. In the nearby village of Chora the museum, its displays consisting almost exclusively of Mycenaean finds, gives us an idea of the palace culture of Ano Engliano in its prime. In the higher regions of the mountainous country linking Egalea in the north and Likodimo in the south any green plants are *macchia*, with now and then a small area of woodland or vines. There is not much traffic on the small byroads, so little, in fact, that snakes seem to feel safe. If a car does come along, they ignore reality, allow themselves too much time to get out of the way, and next moment the car has hit them. Several dead snakes, not as elegant as they were in life, bear witness to their carelessness.

In the little village of Daras – here the olive has taken over as the dominant feature of the landscape again – you cross a plateau with a wide view of the wall of the Taygetos mountain range, obstructing the entire eastern horizon. The Pamisos valley, one of the best fruit-growing regions of the Peloponnese, flourishes in its shelter. Another hilly stretch, and then we reach the plain, with the Pamisas river that brings water even in summer, and is bordered by dense thickets of reeds. Now the provincial capital of Kalamata is in sight.

It is known as 'the white city by the sea', and the term seems particularly apposite when you see it from the south, coming from the Mani peninsula that impressively dominates the landscape. On many days you can see a shimmering white bank of cumulus cloud lying over the long, flat shore of the gulf and then, as the patches of white grow fewer, merging into the gardens and fields around. Behind them, the lizard-shaped contours of the mountain ranges seem to meet as they converge from left and right. The perspective appears to leave only a wedge of land free, the Pamisos plain going north. Happily Kalamata, which suffered from a severe earthquake in 1986, has begun to prosper again after several years of stagnation.

Even before that natural catastrophe, however, it was a town without many major sights, certainly not from the period of antiquity. We may look at the literature instead, and here there is a truly outstanding source: Homer. Let us assume that the city of Pherae, mentioned in both the *Iliad* and the *Odyssey*, is the same place as the later town of Pharai on the Gulf of Messenia and Kalamata – which also gives its name to the Kalamatiano, a dance already known in

Homeric times, and described by Durrell as the most attractive and earthily seductive of all Greek dances. The heart of the town is the rock on the north-east periphery of the urban area, on which stands the *castro*, built in 1208 on the site of the acropolis of Homeric Pherai by Geoffrey de Villehardouin I, the Frankish knight who was co-founder of *la France d'outremer*, France overseas in Greece. From here there is an unimpeded view on all sides, over Kalamata and down to the Gulf of Messenia, which lies as if embraced in the strong arms of the western and central foothills of the Peloponnese, defended by high mountains. Beyond the heights to the west lies the palace of Nestor, beyond the peaks on the other side the sites associated with Menelaus and Helen. To the north are the stately foothills of the Taygetos mountains, and opposite them, separated by the Pamisos plain, the Ithomi mountains. Behind them, in a broad and fertile valley, lay Messene, the ancient capital of Messenia, a city that over the centuries tried to defend itself, often in vain, from the threat from Sparta.

Pherae is mentioned in the *Iliad* as one of the seven cities that Agamemnon offered to Achilles, with many other gifts, hoping to soothe his wrath and induce him to take part in the fighting again. In vain, as we know; before Achilles returned to the fray his friend Patroclus must die. The town is mentioned again in the *Odyssey* as the place where Telemachus spent the night on his way to Sparta:

> The sun sank and the roads of the world grew dark
> As they reached Phera, pulling up to Diocles' halls,
> The son or Ortilochus, son of the Alpheus River.
> He gave them a royal welcome; there they spent the night.

> (O, F 3, 546).

As chance would have it – or was it a dispensation of providence, even a good omen? – Telemachus' father Odysseus had stayed with Ortilochus the father of Diocles when he was young and went on an expedition, on behalf of his own father Laertes and other Ithacan elders, to bring back cattle stolen by raiders from Messenia. And now came Telemachus, although only to stay one night in order to set off for Sparta early next morning. Presumably the place then, as now, lay directly under the crags.

Homer described the drive from Pherai to Sparta very briefly. But we are given clear information about its timing: Telemachus set off in the morning and arrived in the evening, so it was a day's journey, which seems a realistic estimate if we regard Homeric geography as compatible with the conditions. A bare 60 kilometres divide Kalamata from Sparta, although the way is almost exclusively uphill along a road winding through the Taygetos mountains. However, the mountain range was not an insuperable obstacle even in antiquity, as the three Messenian Wars and the centuries of occupation of Messenia by the Lacedaemonians show us, since they entailed the movement of large bodies of men between the valley of the Eurotas and Sparta on one hand and the Pamisos valley on the other. Peisistratus spurred on the team to make haste, so that he and Telemachus could reach their destination by evening.

Passing the spur of rock where the castle stands, the main road from Kalamata to Sparta climbs briefly into hilly terrain, and soon leads down again, with many bends in the road, to the deep valley carved out by the river Nethonas. The hillsides are densely covered with bushes, and the rock itself, grey and rust-coloured, lies bare only where the slope is very steep. The valley floor is full of the green leaves of May, which almost hide the river and let only the sound of its rushing come through until summer, when that sound too dies away. Only when the road has climbed up from the valley again is there space for a few villages, lying among olive groves on terraces reclaimed from the *macchia*. Magnificent chestnut trees show that there is enough humidity in the air for good growing conditions. And the coniferous trees seem to be saying: these mountains are high enough; we would feel fine here but for harmful environmental influences, bark beetles that make our lives difficult, and foresters who don't get up here very often. But the trees have sufficient vitality to flower and lure bees, with the result that along the road you can buy 'Meli Taygetou. Apo Elati-Anthi', Taygetos spruce honey. However, the great huntress Artemis would not have much chance of hunting stags, chamois and wild boar with her seven swift hounds in the forests of today, which are not so dense as in her own times.

From the height of the pass the road passes through an Alpine landscape, dramatic in places. Nature has used her imagination in shaping the eastern side of the mountain range. The waters of a river, grinding, scraping, eroding – although now in May they are running dry again – have carved a deep groove through the rocks. They tower above us small human beings as we drive towards the Spartan plain, trusting in the skills of the road-builders. But other dangers too can threaten here, as witness the monument to a fire chief who, we are told, died here in July 2000 fighting the fires in the Taygetos which raged, devastating the area, for three months on end. It is not yet the season for forest fires. And there, where a deep abyss opens up – it was used by the Lacedaemonians as a place of execution; and victims were thrown from the rocks above – the wild landscape opens out, the hills are lower and olive trees grow on them again as they curve down into the fruitful Eurotas valley between the Taygetos and Parnonas mountains. Sparta lies at its centre.

Ancient Sparta, one of the leading powers in Greece for many centuries and noted for its militarism, did not make a great show of its fame as the first Greek military state by erecting impressive public buildings. When we consider the pompous and ostentatious bad taste often shown by the architecture of dictatorships and tyrannies in promoting their own view of themselves, which tends to oscillates between megalomania and an inferiority complex, that might be seen as a point in favour of the state, saying something positive about the Spartan spirit. The Spartan warrior caste clearly thought it unnecessary to erect magnificent and artistically outstanding buildings of the kind put up everywhere else in ancient Greece, to the greater glory of the city states, more particularly by Sparta's great rival Athens. Very little architectural evidence is left to remind us of the great days of Sparta, and if we had only the remains of its buildings to judge by we could still agree with the historian Thucydides in saying that, at the time of the Peloponnesian Wars, Sparta could be thought rather unimportant, since it had no temples or fine buildings but was made up of village communities in the old Greek way.[117]

The young Philhellenic King Otto of Greece, of the Bavarian royal house of Wittelsbach, hoped to reclaim it from the insignificance it has suffered later, right up to the liberation of Greece, by founding a new kingdom in opposition to Athens, which had acted as the flourishing capital of Greece since 1834. Now, thought Otto, they would be on terms of friendly rivalry in the new Greece. But nothing came of the plan. Today Athens is a metropolis, a city where millions live, a Moloch, a cultural magnet – and Sparta is a little country town able to boast of only a moderate number of antiquities. There is some evidence of Bavarian neo-classical architectural ambition, but the place still has no railway connections, although recently there have been signs of improvement in that respect.

However, Telemachus was not going to visit such a figure as the legendary founder of the state, the lawgiver Lycurgus, or the kings who, as descendants of the Doric conquerors, followed him. Odysseus' son was on his way to see Menelaus, a pre-Doric Achaean from the heyday of Mycenaean culture. So we are not looking at the Sparta of today, a community first created by the amalgamation of four villages around 950 BC, but the hill of Aghia Kiriaki five kilometres further south, near the village of Amikles, which took its name from the older Amyklai, famous in antiquity, where the shrine of Apollo Hyacinthus stood.

The hill in the plantations west of the Eurotas has fertile land at its feet. There is a little church at the top of it, surrounded by coniferous trees and a few tall cypresses, telling the country round about: here is the place where you must imagine the palace of Menelaus, great and gleaming, made even more radiant by the presence of the famous Helen and her beauty, her charm, her kindness, her sensitivity. (Unfortunately, however, it cannot be concealed that from a sober historical viewpoint the realm of Menelaus, located by Homer in Laconia with its palace in Sparta, is pure poetic fiction. The facts about it given in Homer 'contain not a trace of historical truth.'[118] The information is unwelcome because it destroys our illusions. Yet surely it is enough that Homer thought of the lovely valley of the Eurotas, with the mountain ranges around it, as the scene for the magnificent court of the Achaean hero Menelaus. That poetic truth is sufficient.)

Amyklai lay in an area where a complex network of Mycenaean settlements formed after 1500 BC. It was the pre-Doric Greek centre in Laconia, and an independent dynasty was based there until the 9th century BC. After that it was incorporated into the league of villages forming the post-Mycenaean 'new foundation' of Sparta – whether after conquest by the Spartan king Teleklos, as Pausanias says, or as the result of a peaceful take-over is a moot point.[119] In the famous ship catalogue of the *Iliad*, enumerating the Achaean forces drawn up outside Troy, the contingent commanded by Menelaus contains the ships of Amyklai as well as others. At a time when the place had long been part of a village community, then, the poet allows it to feature as genuinely Achaean in the fiction of his epic.

Can we imagine a woman of Helen's gifts and charisma in the disciplined male society of historical Sparta? No adultery to cause world-shaking incidents, no important Achaean prince like Menelaus, captivated by his wonderful wife, magnanimous enough not just to overlook her failings but to raise her again to the place of an honoured princess at a great court. (Although not much is left of

Menelaus' nobility in Wolfgang Hildesheimer's radio play *Das Opfer Helena* [Helen the Victim], which presents the beautiful and clever woman as the victim of the bellicose lords Paris and Menelaus; in Hildesheimer's play Menelaus unscrupulously forces her to beguile Paris and let herself be abducted to give the Achaeans a reason to wage war, and Paris abducts her with the similar intention of giving the Achaeans such a reason, for the Trojans too want war.)

Homer gives Helen the last word in the touching scenes in Menelaus' palace, even bestowing the gift of prediction on her, and she tells Telemachus that his avenging father will be back. Was it perhaps the family relationship with Zeus, her father, who will have known all about the fate of Odysseus, that gave her prophetic power?

On the southern side of the hill lie huge quarried stone blocks, some still piled up, some scattered. What is now a comfortable place to sit in the shade of the cypress trees, with a fine view of the plain of the Eurotas and the Taygetos mountains, was once part of the temple of Apollo Hyacinthus, a singular building designed like a throne and adorned with gold and ivory. The huge statue of the god, approximately 14 metres tall, stood in the middle of it. Behind the double name lies a myth about a vegetation deity, his downfall, and the rise of a new and younger god. Hyacinthus is the pre-Greek name of the older divinity, and there was a shrine to him here in the Mycenaean period; Apollo is the younger, Olympian god, whose worship was merged with that of Hyacinthus after the Doric invasion. The myth makes this connection into a friendship between the two, one that must end tragically because, in the natural course of succeeding generations, the older must give way to the younger. In a discus-throwing combat with Apollo, Hyacinthus was killed when the discus struck him, but despite this accident the god was still worshipped. In high summer, the time of drought and the death of vegetation, the three-day Hyakinthi were celebrated under the aegis of Apollo, beginning with funeral rites for the death of nature, then striking a cheerful note in anticipation of its revival.

It is surely legitimate to imagine the palace of Menelaus here on the hill, or close to it where old Amyklai formerly stood, surrounded by the fertility guaranteed by the river Eurotas as it flows between two mighty mountain chains. The king's mythological genealogy is fascinating too, and the succession of ancient names linking people, mountains and rivers has captivated us from very ancient times to the present day.

Lelex, the first legendary king of the Lelegians who lived in Laconia, had a strong son who drained the low-lying swamps of the land that was to become Sparta, letting the water run away to the sea, an agricultural measure of prime importance. It is appropriate that the river bringing fertility to the valley was given his name: Eurotas. His successor was Lacedaemon (as the region governed by the Spartan state was later called), a son of Zeus and the nymph Taygete, who had her home by the rivers of the great mountain range called after her, the Taygetos (one of the highest in Greece, rising to 2404 metres). A great-grandson of Lacedaemon was Tyndareus, who with his wife Leda officially had four children, famed beyond all measure: Helen (with such qualities we may assume that Zeus himself and not Tyndareus was her father), later to be the wife of Menelaus; Clytemnestra, the wife of Agamemnon; and the Dioscuri Castor and Pollux (their nickname of Dioscuri, sons of the god, gives the game away: again Zeus had a hand – or something else – in it; think of Leda and the swan). Menelaus succeeded Tyndareus. He could look back, then, on a very impressive family tree, and he himself was described as *warlike Menelaus* (I, R 3, 21), *master of the battle-cry* (I, R 3, 96).

> The sun sank and the roads of the world grew dark (...)
> At last they gained the ravines of Lacedaemon ringed by hills
> and drove up to the halls of Menelaus in his glory.
> They found the king inside his palace, celebrating
> with throngs of kinsmen a double wedding-feast
> for his son and lovely daughter.
>
> (O, F 3, 546; 4, 1).

In the evening Telemachus and Peisistratus reached Sparta. They found a great feast in progress, in celebration of the double wedding of the king's two children, and they were welcomed and invited to eat before Menelaus asked who they were. The size and magnificence of the palace impressed them:

> They marvelled up and down the house of the warlord dear to Zeus –
> a radiance strong as the moon or rising sun came flooding
> through the high-roofed halls of illustrious Menelaus.
>
> (O, F 4, 51).

Nestor himself, when recommending Telemachus to travel on to Menelaus, had spoken of his home in *lovely Lacedaemon* (O, F 3, 367). Was there once a palace in Amyklai as magnificent, large, and elaborately designed as the palace in Pylos, before the iconoclasm of Sparta and Nature combined put an end to it? Judging by the description of the imposing building, the luxury inside it, the civilized manners and aristocratic culture of the court of Menelaus as a whole, it was in no way inferior to Nestor's court. A bath, for instance, was taken in Homeric Sparta in as much comfort as in Pylos – in tubs for which the terracotta cladding of the one found in Pylos might have been the model. *Into the burnished baths they climbed and bathed* (O, F 4, 56). The long conversations held with Telemachus by Menelaus and Helen, interspersed with various stories of incidents at Troy and during Menelaus' long voyage home, circle around the fate of Odysseus, and Menelaus encourages his friend's son to hope. Telemachus politely but firmly turns down his host's fervent and pressing invitation for him to spend another eleven or twelve days in the palace. Very confident now – his initiation into adult life is well advanced – he even refuses the fine gift generously intended for him by Menelaus, *three stallions and a chariot burning bright* (O, F 4, 683), on the sensible grounds that there is:

> No running-room for mares in Ithaca (...) no meadows,
> goat, not stallion land, yet it means the world to me.
> None of the rugged islands slanting down to sea
> is good for pasture or good for bridle paths.
> But Ithaca, best of islands, crowns them all!
>
> (O, F 4, 681).

Menelaus accepts Telemachus' rejection of the gift without demur; he takes his hand and tells him, in friendly tones:

> Good blood runs in you, dear boy, your words are proof.
> Certainly I'll exchange the gifts. The power's mine.
> Of all the treasures lying heaped in my palace
> you shall have the finest, most esteemed. Why,
> I'll give you a mixing-bowl, forged to perfection –
> it's solid silver finished off with a lip of gold.
> Hephaistus made it himself.
>
> (O, F 4, 686).

This description reminds us of the two famous and splendid golden cups now in the National Museum in Athens, found in a tholos tomb at Vafio, two kilometres south of the hill of Aghia Kiriaki. The way leads through an area full of memories of characters in the *Iliad*. Votive offerings of the 6th and 5th centuries BC dug up locally include figures that could be interpreted as depicting Agamemnon and Clytemnestra, others as the heroine Alexandra, equated in Laconia with King Priam's daughter Cassandra.

The tholos tomb, which is shaped like a huge pan, lies in a hilltop site surrounded by carefully tended olive trees, at the foot of deep, slanting excavation ramps. Its diameter is 10 metres, and the path leading to it, the dromos, measures 25 metres. It is true that only the foundation walls of the dome of the beehive are preserved, to a height of about a metre. But if we think of the so-called tomb of Agamemnon at Mycene, we can easily imagine a royal tomb here too – and ascribe it, following local tradition, to the royal hero Menelaus. Certainly the two cups of around 1500 BC are royal. Fortunately, in spite of the tomb robberies of antiquity, they were still here to be found during the systematically conducted excavations of 1888. The outsides of the cups are elaborately covered with depictions of bulls in a meadow landscape. Today we can still get an idea of the splendour of these animals in their natural surroundings by visiting a good Spanish cattle-breeding farm or going to a bullfight in one of the major arenas. Such a work, one feels, can have been created only by the skilled smith of the gods, Hephaistus himself.

The company in the palace has gone to rest. Peisistratus enjoys quiet slumbers, but Telemachus lies awake; he cannot get the still unknown fate of his father out of his mind. As he broods, Athene visits him by night, telling him to go home to Ithaca quickly; above all, he must avert the imminent threat of his mother's remarriage. She also tells him about the murderous intentions of the suitors, and the measures that he can take to escape their plot. Here she proves a very co-operative colleague to us in our attempt to trace the journeys of father and son – in this case the latter – by mentioning a number of localities which have the same names as real places, or at least can be seen as such. More of that to come.

Telemachus wants to set out at once. He wakes Peisistratus, who thinks, however, that *we cannot drive a team in the dead of night* (O, F 15, 55). It would be better, he says, to wait for morning. In the incident of the waking of Peisistratus Homer shows what a close observer he is with a wonderful little detail:

> Telemachus woke Nestor's son from his sweet sleep;
> he dug a heel in his ribs and roused him briskly:
> 'Up, Peisistratus.'
>
> (O, F 15, 50).

He dug a heel in his ribs – exactly what we might do to rouse a fellow traveller staying in simple accommodation on a journey, sleeping in a tent or on mattresses – hey, wake up!

Menelaus and Helen continue to show touching concern for Telemachus next day. The king even offers to take him on a tour of the rest of Greece. On the other hand, he knows very well that a traveller must not be held up, particularly one on such an urgent mission. Telemachus says goodbye, taking with him as gifts the wonderful mixing-bowl made by Hephaistus and the finest of the robes from Helen's chest of clothes, which she gives him as a gift for his future bride. They feed him well again for the strenuous journey back over the mountains, and he is finally encouraged by the queen's prophecy of a happy ending to the story. This time Telemachus is driving the chariot. He and Peisistratus will be on the road until evening again in order to reach Pherai, the castle of the noble Diocles.

We know the way they took now and need not accompany them; instead, before we rejoin the travellers in Pherai/Kalamata, we can visit another place linked to the noble king and queen of Sparta. From Vafio there are delightful pathways through luxuriant groves of oranges and olives and across the meadows down to the Eurotas. The thickets of reeds, poplars, and in general lush, almost tropical growth on the banks owe their magnificence to its waters. The waters of the river are shallow now, in early summer, and we can cross it over a ford. Directly accompanied by the Eurotas, we go a few kilometres upstream to a road on the right leading to the hill of Aghios Ilias, which rises steeply from the plain, and the Menelaion. It is a beautiful road, bordered by olive trees on terraces skilfully reclaimed from the hillsides. The gradient becomes steeper, but it is well worth climbing up to the plateau on top of the hill. For now that we have a clearer view we can see important elements in the landscape: the course of the river makes its way, curving gracefully, through the green of the vegetation, which is relieved by sandbanks; its stream alternately flows on and stands still; this is the softer aspect of Sparta, and arriving on the crest of the hill we also have a view of the mountain chains all the way to the eastern horizon. For all its variety, the continuo to this great orchestration of the landscape is ever-present: it is the view of the Taygetos mountains.

And its peaks also form the background to the little stony range that rises on the plateau, consisting of a solid platform of mighty stone slabs serving as the base for a little temple of which only the rudiments are preserved. This place was known in antiquity as Therapne, 'the place worthy of veneration'. Pausanias' statements have been clearly confirmed by dedicatory inscriptions found here: on the hill lay the Heroon, a place of worship dedicated to Menelaus and Helen, and also, with some masculine bias, known as the Menelaion. Originally intended for the worship of a vegetation goddess in Mycenean times, then abandoned in the so-called Dark Ages and brought back into use as a place of worship in the late 8th century, the place acquired more architectural importance when, in AD 500, building began on several terraces, the remains of which can be seen today. The votive offerings found in large quantities near the Menelaion – above all lead figures of warriors only a few centimetres tall, but with plumes on their helmets, shields and spears, as well as elegantly dressed women with strikingly small waists – suggest that the Spartans went on pilgrimage to this place to worship the royal couple, the men to assure themselves of the courage and dignity of Menelaus in future battles, the women to pray to Helen for at least a little of her beauty and charm for themselves and their children. Not that the woman depicted on the famous funeral stela of the early 6th century BC in the Museum of Sparta, said to show Helen, suggests much of these qualities, but that is only because the visual arts of the time had not scaled the heights of the literature of the same period. If we take this picture as a portrait of the royal couple, the obvious equality of the partnership is impressive: husband and wife stand face to face, each with an arm about the other's shoulders.

The Mycenaean past of the narrow mountain range, between the valley of the Eurotas in the west and a rivulet in the east, has come to light in several places, only a few hundred metres from the Menelaion, in Helladic settlements which go back to the 15th century BC and are among the most important in Greece. The most carefully excavated remains are the walls, steps and paths of two lordly Mycenaean dwellings built between 50 to 100 years apart, on top of each other in some places, and although obviously fixed with much modern mortar they stand on a plateau falling moderately to the east before you reach the Menelaion. It takes more imagination here than in Mycene or Tiryns to visualize the walls complete and the buildings decorated in colour. Their dominating situation, however, is abundantly clear.

Traditionally the Menelaion, as well as the tholos tomb of Vafio, is one of the sites considered to be the place where Menelaus was buried, but here with Helen beside him. It must have been a worthy resting-place for the couple, high above the fertile valley of the Eurotas, which lies like a river oasis between the hills culminating in the heights of Mount Parnon, and the severe, powerful Taygetos range.

Just as the sun is setting, Telemachus and Peisistratus reach shelter in Pherai. The rest of the journey to Pylos also follows the course of the outward journey; they set off early in the morning from Pherai, whipping the horses on to make haste, with the result that they are *approaching Pylos soon, the craggy citadel* (O, F 15, 215). Telemachus goes on past the palace and straight to his ship, which lies at anchor in the bay, fearing, as Peisisratus confirms, that Nestor will not want him to leave without observing the ancient rules of hospitality by entertaining him further. So he puts out to sea that same day, taking with him a man from a far country, a stranger called Theoclymenus, who has killed a man – the incident is not explained in detail – and has sought refuge in Argos. Before night falls, Telemachus has gone a good part of the way home:

> Now bright-eyed Athene sent them a stiff following wind
> blustering out of a clear sky, gusting on so the ship
> might run its course through the salt sea at top speed –
> and past the Springs she raced, and the Chalcis' rushing stream
> as the sun sank and the roads of the world grew dark and
> on she pressed for Pheai, driven on by a wind from Zeus
> and flew past lovely Elis, where Epeans rule in power,
> and then Telemachus veered for the Jagged Islands,
> wondering all the way –
> would he sweep clear of death or be cut down?
>
> (O, F 15, 325).

This passage is a gift to those of us who do not regard Homeric geography as purely imaginary. Hölscher too speaks of 'experiences of reality (...)in the *Telemachy* that clarify the *Odyssey* ...'[121] Landmarks are named, offering realistic identifications. Luce comments as follows: 'Krounoi and Chalkis, as Strabo informs us, were the names of small streams. They cannot now be identified with certainty, but they serve as an indication of the coast of Messenia north of Pylos. Pheai was a place of some importance (...). It is plausibly taken to be the Bronze Age predecessor of the Classical town of that name which stood on a bold promontory near the modern town of Katakolo. (...) The ship then followed the coast of Elis as far as the promontory of Chelonatas. Then, instead of turning in towards the Gulf of Corinth, Telemachus struck north to the "sharp islands".' [122]

Sandy Pylos – almost the entire west coast of the Peloponnese would fit that description if we take it as referring to the sandy shores. It is far removed from the general infertility of sandy soil. From Pylos a belt of fields, orchards and gardens, a strip of land that is sometimes quite narrow but well worth cultivating, runs north along the coast, clearly growing wider after Pyrgos and extending inland, then narrowing again outside Patra because of the mountainous hinterland. So you pass through a flat, fertile coastal strip from the Bay of Navarino towards Kyparissia, and in winter several rivers bring water down from the Egalea and Kyparissia mountains, although they dry up in summer. Among them may be the rivers called Krounoi and Chalkis. A ship setting out from its moorings in the Bay of Navarino and bound for Ithaca would not follow the long line of the Gulf of Kyparissia, tracing a concave curve to the east, but would take the more direct route and hold course to the north-west. At its end, however, the coastline of the bay turns capriciously south, in other words, a narrow promontory thrusts out southward, and when such a cape has a lighthouse on it sailors are glad of its help. Katakolo is the name of the harbour settlement lying here in the shelter of the promontory. It is not ancient, not even old in Greek terms, founded only in 1857, and these days it is often intermittently busy when the huge cruise ships anchored in Katakolo Bay let their passengers go on land to visit the sanctuary of Olympia, taking them back on board a few hours later. Then the long street full of souvenir shops does good business, and later, perforce, falls idle again. The Frankish castle of Pontiko Kastro stands on a wooded height on the isthmus of the promontory, apparently the only building that has a past history.

Where is Pheai? In a hotel in one of the little bays the man at the reception desk answers my question in two syllables, accompanying his laconic information by pointing his forefinger at the sea: *Kato*.

Down there, under water. Swallowed up by an earthquake in the 6th century BC, it was probably the Bronze Age predecessor of the town to which Homer referred as Pheias in the *Iliad* and *Odyssey*. It comes into Book 7 of the *Iliad*, and the nearby river Iordanos is also mentioned. It still bears that name today, and you cross it after driving a few kilometres from Pyrgos towards Patra. The brief mention in the *Odyssey*, where we are told of the ship, *on she pressed for Pheai*, was presumably based on familiar seafaring knowledge of the striking landmark that is the headland on the cape of Pheai, a literally outstanding aid to sailors to help them find their way. It is much the same today. There is a lighthouse at the southernmost point of Cape Pheai, and it is not just ending its days here as a romantic relic of the seafaring world of the past, but is manned by computer staff working to aid shipping, people who have little in common with the usual idea of lighthouse keepers.

The journey goes on through Porthmos Zakinthou, the broad passage between the island of Zacynthus – which in Homer's time bore the same name as it does in ours – and the westernmost part of the Peloponnese, which also still has its old name. Elis (today Ilis) is low-lying hilly country near the sea, made fertile by the rivers Alpheus and Pinios with their tributaries. Was it this quality of flourishing fertility that earned it the Homeric epithet which in Greek literally means 'divine', for the blessing of the gods obviously lay on it? On their left, then, lay the coasts of Zacynthus, on their right they *flew past divine Elis*, past the Chlemutsi headland, in whose shelter the strategically important settlement of Cyllene has stood from time immemorial; it was an important port for transhipment to the Greater Greek regions, an anchorage for the Spartan fleet in the Peloponnesian War, the place where the Frankish Villehardouins settled ... and today, going by the name of Kyllini, is a small port much visited by tourists because of the nearby long, sandy beaches. Once you have passed the headland you reach the Gulf of Patra, and now a ship could steer straight for Ithaca, perhaps for Vathy Bay, today the site of the largest town on the island, or into Polis Bay near the village of Stavros, where the model for Odysseus' palace may once have stood.

What will Telemachus decide to do as he approaches his own island? What plan will he make for his return from Pylos to Ithaca, remembering Athene's warning?

And another thing. Take it to heart, I tell you.
Picked men of the suitors lie in ambush, grim-set
in the straits between Ithaca and rocky Same,
poised to kill you before you can reach home (...)
Just give the channel islands a wide berth,
push on in your trim ship, sail night and day.

(O, F 15, 31).

Telemachus takes that second warning to heart. But he still has to heed the more important one, not to go straight to the harbour in Polis Bay, through the straits between Ithaca and Samos – or in present terms the Ithaca Channel, between Ithaca and Cephalonia. Luce is convinced that the suitors were lying in wait where the straits run between Polis Bay and the northern tip of Cephalonia, planning to capture Telemachus if he ran into his home harbour by the route that might have been expected.. Athene advises Telemachus to *give the channel islands a wide berth*. So he must not on any account come through the Ithaca Channel. She alludes to the dangers threatening him, the island of Samos or Cephalonia, and the west coast of Ithaca itself. If, taking her advice, he avoided this area but still wanted to come in to Ithaca, he would have to approach his island from the east, past the islands described variously by translators as *jagged,* (Fagles), *pointed* (Rieu), and *sharp* in Luce's own version. Considering the prime importance of avoiding the western route, it would seem geographically obvious to accept the series of small islands lying off the mainland as those meant by Homer, for instance Vronomas, Makri and Oxia. The matter of the real significance of the epithet rendered so differently in translation must remain an open question. Anyone approaching Ithaca from the east or south-east will see the first landmark, Cape Jannis with its lighthouse, as clearly as Homer could have done, following Athene's clear and succinct advice to Telemachus.

At your first landfall, Ithaca's outer banks,
speed ship and shipmates round to the city side.
But you – you make your way to the swineherd first.

(O, F 15, 42).

There is no way to anchor at the inhospitable rock of Cape St John, but only a little further on the stony rocks of the east coast withdraw from the sea for a short distance, giving way to a secluded bay with white sand, a very suitable place to land for anyone who wants to climb to the Marathia plateau. This place is Ligia Bay at the far end of the bed of the stream coming down from the Raven's Crag.

Telemachus has sailed through the night and reached Ithaca. The men on the ship eat one more meal together. Then the crew and Theoclymenus row on with the ship to 'the town', while Telemachus sets off at once and walks in haste to the swineherd's farm. The story is now making for one of its high points, the meeting between father and son. The two carefully managed twin streams, the tales of Odysseus and Telemachus, will soon merge into a torrent swelling as it reaches the murderous cleansing of the final tableau, and the quiet drama of the scenes in which husband and wife recognize one another and are reunited. And here again there will be two strands to the plot: the one that has followed the hero's wanderings all this time, and the other which has told of the sufferings of his wife, left at home.

When Telemachus arrives at Eumaeus' farm, he and the swineherd greet each other warmly, and then the 'beggar' is introduced by the swineherd as a stranger from Crete. They discuss the delicate situation at the palace. Telemachus tells the swineherd to go quickly to the town and Penelope, to let her know that her son is safely home. That evening Eumaeus returns. Meanwhile, there has been plenty of time for Odysseus to reveal himself to his son, and they embrace in tears. Once their emotions have died down, Odysseus in his usual rational manner quickly comes to the point, which is the detailed plan for the terrible punishment of the suitors. Early next morning Telemachus sets off, *striking out for the city* (O, F 17, 6).

Where was *the city*, how far away was it? In Book 17 there is a remark by Odysseus, spoken in his role as a stranger, which Telemachus and Eumaeus are not, referring directly to the distance between it and the farm. *And town, you say, is a long hard way from here.* (O, F 17, 25). That would seem to mean that the town was in the north, a long way off, if Homer had imagined the swineherd's farm in the south of Ithaca. So what would be the best place if we are to reconcile Homeric geography with the real facts?

The German scholar Carl Haller von Hallerstein, who went to Greece in 1814 on a mission from the Crown Prince of Bavaria, later King Ludwig, to acquire antiquities, and who visited the island of Ithaca, had already suggested that the region around the village of Staurus – today Stavros – was also the most densely populated part of the island in antiquity. However, he still backed Gell's opinion that the capital had been on Aetos. Wilhelm Dörpfeld, who began his excavations on Ithaca in the year 1900, was investigating 'first and foremost the surroundings of the village of Stauros in the northern part of the island, because only this place, in our view, can be considered as the location of the palace of Odysseus (…) The plateau above Stauros was the site of the most intensive investigation. As the property of the Pilikas family, it is now known as Pilikata.' [123] In fact he discovered no Mycenaean or prehistoric pottery, but he said he thought that such material might be found some day, and his assumption proved correct, as systematic excavation campaigns carried out by the British School of Athens in the 1930s showed. They made it possible to establish that there had been a centre of settlement of the late Bronze Age in the vicinity of Stavros. 'These results confirmed that Ithaca formed part of the Mycenaean world and for the first time proved a firm factual basis for the Homeric tradition,' says Luce.[124] He expresses his conviction that the city and palace of Odysseus lay near Stavros, in the middle of flourishing agricultural land, and near three navigable bays, one of which still bears the name Polis – city.

So now that we know the way to go, let us set off from south to north through Ithaca by the routes that Homer could have given his characters to use. Eumaeus walked to the city and back in a day. Considering the lie of the land, that would have been about 40 kilometres, 'a long but far from impossible walk for a hardy Greek herdsman,' writes Luce.[125] However, there is a passage in Book 17, 599 ff., that makes such a calculation rather tricky. The conscientious Eumaeus, who has accompanied Odysseus to the city, wants to go back to his pigs the same day. Telemachus recommends him to wait until he has had his supper. German translators differ on this point, Weiher has Telemachus recommending Eumaeus to, *Eat your evening meal first and then go.* Schadewalt gives the swineherd a little more latitude, with Telemachus recommending him to go when he has had something to eat. But in all these cases, even if 'something to eat' was a snack at about five o'clock in the afternoon, he would not have been home until far into the night. However, maybe the moon was shining, and maybe Eumaeus really had it in him to be an Olympic walker. Be that as it may, he is back punctually next day at the palace with three fine pigs.

Telemachus sets off early in the morning, when it is still cool. The stranger says he will follow later, with Eumaeus, *once I'm warm from*

the fire and the sun's good and strong (O, F 17, 22). At first the way
they take could have been the reverse of the route taken by Odysseus
on his way to Eumaeus' farm, this time from the farm to the Bay of
Phorcys, then from the Marathia plateau to Dexia Bay. In line with
the natural conditions, you still skirt the shore around Aetos Bay,
except that now you drive along a paved road.

It is eleven in the morning. The sea to the east lies before us like
a beautifully painted water-colour. A fine mist hovers over the water
from which the Atakos, Kalamos, and Kastos islands and the mighty
Boumistos massif on the Acarnanian mountains of the mainland
coast rise, covered with a thin veil of haze. We are ahead of the two
travellers of antiquity, who will not reach this spot until early in the
afternoon. Then the mist will have dispersed and the contours of the
mountains will be more clearly outlined. As we go along the road the
time of day and climatic conditions change – *you'll find it colder with
nightfall coming on* (O, F 17, 207), Eumaeus warns Odysseus – and
impressions vary – *the road is treacherous, full of slips and slides* (O,
F 17, 212) and also *rugged*. Homer describes the two men's walk as
one through space and time – a new *Iliad* in that 'the time of day in
the *Odyssey* (…) is perceived as a sensuous medium.' [126] Finally they
cross the Aetos isthmus and are now on the other, western side of the
island. It will take them some hours yet to reach the city.

Travelling by car today, we have long ago left the wasp-waisted
Ithacan isthmus behind and are resting at the village of St John under
the ancient olive tree known locally as 'Laertes' olive'. Four gigantic
trunks grow from a single root, with branches as thick as columns.
The tree is so huge that its age of 2000 years, as claimed by the local
authorities, does not seem entirely improbable. Laertes' olive? Is
this where we should imagine the estate of Odysseus' father? To the
scholar and philhellene Friedrich Thiersch of Munich, when he stayed
here in 1832, one clue in favour seemed to be the local name of 'St
John's in the gardens' given to the area. However, the appearance of
the country around St John (Aghios Ioannis) is against it. The terrain
falls away to the sea with rocky ground below, leaving enough space
for a garden attached to a house, but not for extensive orchards of
fruit trees, fields and large gardens. For that is the impression we get
of the estate run by Laertes as the scene is evoked in Book 24, when
Odysseus, his task completed, goes to his father with Telemachus and
two herdsmen to reveal himself at last to Laertes. If we believe the
Homeric text, the estate must have been near 'the city', for

Odysseus and his men had stridden down from town
and quickly reached Laertes' large, well-tended farm.

(O, F 24, 226).

We shall see.

Having passed Polis Bay, we reach the village of Stavros, the largest in northern Ithaca. We know where we are here; Odysseus himself is present, obviously fit and well, with a vigorous expression, beard and hair well groomed under the *pilos*, the felt cap worn to line the helmet that is typical of him. A chiton is thrown over his powerful chest. He looks as if he had just risen from the bath, refreshed after the massacre in the throne-room, lovingly anointed with oil by the maid Eurynome and clad in a fine cloak and tunic. But Eurynome alone did not succeed in restoring the hero to himself. Athene put her hand with its masterly touch to the work:

And Athene crowned the man with beauty, head to foot,
made him taller to all eyes, his build more massive,
yes, and down from his brow the great goddess
ran his curls like thick hyacinth clusters
full of bloom.

(O, F 23, 174).

This is how his bust, the work of a nephew of Schliemann's Greek wife, stands before us in the village square of Stavros. The tall plinth is inscribed with the words 'Offering to Odysseus'. This is not an expression of the sculptor's feelings, but a quotation from a much older time, the 1st or 2nd century BC, found as a votive inscription on the fragment of a terracotta mask with remains of a female bust, now the crown of the Ithacan collections in the Stavros museum. It was discovered – and this is the exciting part, both for local patriots and for the follower of the Homeric trail of Odysseus – in a cave on the north shores of Polis Bay: a memento of the veneration of Odysseus from the Hellenistic period, found on 'his' island, in a cave temple on the harbour of 'his' city.

Stavros lies on a col between the mountains Anogi, which also still bears its Homeric name of Neriton, and Exobi. Around the village the land spreads over hills and falls to three bays. It is well farmed, and is the most fertile part of the island. A hill called Pilikata in the north of Stavros has on it, besides a number of properties with attractive gardens, the little museum containing some very important finds – important both for the prehistoric and Mycenaean past, and for the question of Homer's historicity. First and foremost, these are the 'Odysseus shard' with the votive inscription, and some bronze tripods of the 8th to 9th centuries BC from the cave known as the Louizos Cave on Polis Bay, as well as earthenware vessels and animal figures going back to the early Helladic period of 3000 BC onwards, coming from several excavation sites near Stavros.

We are able to repay the museum attendant a little for her kindness and readiness to give information by letting her take a good look at our copy of the German version of *Celebrating Homer's Landscapes* by John V. Luce, which she saw once in the original English some years ago. It contains many photographs and an attractive jacket of good quality showing the main town of Vathy with its surroundings of mountains and water, but of course it is not a bibliophile's treasure. However, the lady seems to venerate it as if it were.

Polis Bay, lying below Stavros to the south-west, fits perfectly into the impressive series of beautiful bays on the island. The terrain, covered with fields, olive groves and *macchia*, rises like an amphitheatre to the outskirts of the village on the yoke between the mountains. A few fishing boats lie in harbour, there are some sailing boats further out, a little restaurant with a handful of guests – it is a peaceful place. It may have been more bustling in antiquity.

The Louizos Cave is inaccessible. Several earthquakes have blocked it with rock-falls, and it is under constant assault by seawater. In 1930 onwards it was systematically explored by W.A. Heurtley and Sylvia Benton with their team from the British School of Athens.[127] As well as finds from the pre-Mycenaean and Mycenaean periods in the deepest stratum of the excavations, exciting evidence was found of its settlement from the Bronze Age to the 1st century AD, when the cave was a place for the worship of the nymphs and also, at least in the Hellenistic period, of a cult of Odysseus. Besides the shard with the votive inscription, Miss Benton found fragments of twelve bronze tripods intended as votive offerings to the cave shrine, finds that are also of special importance for Homeric research. The British archaeologist Lady Waterhouse thought it perfectly possible that some at least of the tripods were votive offerings given in honour of Odysseus by victors in local games.[128] The Israeli archaeologist Irad Malkin even proposed the theory – as you can read on a notice near the cave – that it had in fact been a site of the veneration of Odysseus since the 9th century BC, not just by the local population but by Greeks in general. He therefore ranks the Louizos Cave one of the most important archaeological sites in Greece, probably a place of pan-Hellenic worship long before Olympia and Delphi.

Was Homer one of its early visitors, visiting the place perhaps not just to offer pious prayers, but also to collect material for his epic? Luce points out the possibility of a fascinating connection between the find of (in all) thirteen tripods, and certain scenes at the court of Alcinous in Books 8 and 13. One passage mentions twelve princes and the king of Phaeacia, Alcinous himself, who give the stranger gifts. When he leaves, Odysseus, whose identity is now known, receives a further present: *come*, says Alcinous, *each of us add a sumptuous tripod, add a cauldron* (O, F 14, 13). Is it just coincidence that Homer mentions gifts of thirteen tripods, among other items, from the friendly Phaeacians, and exactly thirteen bronze tripods were found in a cave on Ithaca now identified as a site of the veneration of Odysseus?

Luce ventures the interesting hypothesis that Homer was playing a kind of practical joke. Staying on Ithaca, thinks Luce, he had seen the sacred cave with its thirteen tripods, and heard of the cult of Odysseus – and gave the votive offerings a place in the *Odyssey* as part of the generous gifts of the good spirits who brought the hero home to his island at last after so many trials.

The hill of Pilikata is a magical place. As you go up the road to the village square, it broadens, and at the top there is a view of an extraordinary panorama: if you turn once on your own axis, the same landscape passes before your eyes in three variations, V-shaped configurations of steep, green mountain slopes embracing triangular areas of sea down below, from which, depending on their distance, island mountains rise in different shades of blue, while in the foreground the *campagna* makes its own lush contribution with a vineyard on one side, an olive grove on the other, and on the third a colourful mixture of rose hedges, oleander bushes and cypresses. The three glimpses of the sea are at Polis Bay in the south-west, Phrikes Bay in the north-east, and Aphales Bay to the north, with the islands of Cephalonia, Atokos and Lefkada in the backgrounds.

A magical picture, in which the enchantment of the imagination, together with fantasy, can flourish on a factual background. Most of the scholars who see modern Ithaca as the Homeric homeland of Odysseus agree that on Pilikata Hill we are probably on the site of a palace complex going back to Mycenaean times. It is tempting to assume this was the palace of Homer's Odysseus, since we can call for support both on archaeological facts and the many parallels between the text of the *Odyssey* and the features of the landscape – for instance, Phrikes Bay, visible from Pilikata.

Coming from Olympus, Athene seeks out Telemachus in the palace and appears to him in the shape of the trader Mentes. Asked who he is and where he comes from, the visitor replies:

> My ship is not berthed near the city, but over there by the open
> country, in Reithron Cove, under the woods of Neion.
>
> (O, R 1, 186).

Luce interprets this as meaning that the mountain of Neion was Exogi, and the bay of Reithron was Phrikes Bay, into which the largest stream in Ithaca, the Phrikes, flows. As 'Reithron' means river or torrential stream, this name could also be taken as indicating the 'city of the stream', and identified with the little modern harbour of Phrikes. In summer the bed of the stream is dry, and its course, which has been channelled to run through the village, is thickly covered with the foliage of eucalyptus trees standing as tall as a man on the neatly walled banks. When the stream flows again in winter it will wash the leaves into the sea.

Odysseus and Eumaeus have now reached their journey's end. After their long walk, their dry throats and tired limbs need refreshment, and they see it on the outskirts of the city ahead: a *solidly built, clear-flowing fountain*, surrounded by poplars, the site of an altar to the nymphs. There are no traces of a well running from a spring in Stavros. But there is a stream, the Pilikata stream, that runs from the village down the slope to Polis Bay in the wet season. Close to the bed of this stream, at a place called Asprosykia, Mycenaean shards have been found. A basin of water fed by the Pilikata stream would thus fit well into the picture of a small capital city on the col of the range between the mountains.

However, the travellers cannot stop to enjoy the fresh, clear waters, perhaps because they have no chance to drink them. For just as they reach the spring Odysseus, in his guise as a beggar, is coarsely insulted and kicked by the goatherd Melanthius. Odysseus has to steel himself to put up with the insults in silence at first, since his immediate instinct, to kill the man on the spot, could have wrecked the plan for killing the suitors. So they follow Melanthius as he hurries ahead. Then, after twenty years, Odysseus stands before his palace again. He is allowed to marvel at the building, but not give away the emotion he feels. That must be done more discreetly, in the form of the one small gesture that Homer does allow him:

> And the master seized his servant's hand, exclaiming,
> 'Friend, what a noble house! Odysseus' house, it must be!'
>
> (O, F 17, 290).

We do not see the walls, the gate or the columns of the magnificent palace. But we have the text. With that, we can sit down on Pilikata Hill in the roofless ruins of a chapel, on the wall of a vineyard, or under the branches of an olive tree and give free rein to the imagination, like the poet who was so taken by this place – and presumably it had a *polis* on it in ancient times – that he made it the central setting of his epic – a work that is 'more like a historical novel than an epic poem' (Luce)[129] – as many scholars agree.

On this level, the presentation of poetic form is overlaid and permeated by a whole variety of figures and images: the good and friendly swineherd, the shameless and bad goatherd; the sturdy beggar; the faithful and the amorously faithless maids; the dog, weak with old age but with his memory strong; the pack of suitors and their frustrated attempt to bend the bow of Odysseus; his own golden shot through the twelve axes; the fast and furious killing of the suitors; the cruel punishment of the faithless maids and the goatherd Melanthius; the drama of the reunion between Odysseus and Penelope, who is torn between hope and fear. And if you do not mind weighing down your hand baggage on a journey in search of Odysseus with a magnificent illustrated book, *Odysseus. Mythos und Erinnerung* [Odysseus. Myth and Memory], then the magic peculiar to many of these scenes can be heightened as you study the pictures: for instance the touching scene in which the old dog Argos recognizes his master, sniffing him and wagging his tail, while Odysseus puts out his hand to pat the dog (shown on a Roman sarcophagus of around AD 130 in the Museo di San Martino, Naples); the dramatic scene when Eurycleia recognizes Odysseus by a scar as she washes his feet, and is prevented from announcing the glad news – which at this point can be conveyed only in the text – by Odysseus himself, taking her by the throat, because he does not want disclosure yet (shown on a Thessalian votive relief of the 4th century BC in the National Museum of Athens). The book contains various depictions of Penelope in what became established from the 5th century BC onwards as her typical pose: a woman deep in thought and sunk in melancholy, her legs crossed, her attitude one of concentration (for instance on the beautiful red-figure drinking cup by the 'Penelope painter' of Chiusi in 440 BC). Finally, there is the massacre of the suitors, particularly impressively shown on the Campanian bell-shaped crater of the 'Ixion painter' of the end of the 4th century BC, with its ochre figures against a dark brown background, now in the Louvre; despite the many figures it is a well-ordered composition in an area that is only vaguely indicated, with the attackers Eumaeus, Odysseus and Telemachus approaching from the side. Telemachus, like the suitors, is shown in his youthful and athletic nakedness, beardless and with a shock of russet hair, while the two older men wear chitons and cloaks and have their heads covered. Eumaeus is wielding his gnarled herdsman's staff with deadly effect, while Odysseus appears as an archer in the thick of the fray. The tables that the suitors, taken by surprise, hold before them, as recommended by Eurymachus – *Swords out! Tables lifted, block his arrows winging death!* (O, F 22, 77) – do not shield them from the avenging fury of the three. Later, after a last wild hacking and stabbing between the friends and followers of the dead men, and Odysseus with his small group, the story comes to a kind of happy ending, ushered in by Athene's call for peace:

> Hold back, you men of Ithaca, hold back from brutal war!
> Break off – shed no more blood – make peace at once! (...)
> Royal son of Laertes, Odysseus, master of exploits,
> hold back now! Call a halt to the great leveller, War –
> don't court the rage of Zeus who rules the world!

(O, F 24, 584).

and by the laconic decree by the father of the gods that precedes it:

> Let us purge their memories of the bloody slaughter
> of their brothers and their sons. Let them be friends,
> devoted as in the old days. Let peace and wealth
> come cresting through the land.

(O, F 24, 535).

An extraordinary resolution! As a criminal gang, the suitors are punished with death in accordance with the decision taken by the council of the gods. But so that the society to which they belonged will not collapse, and peace can return, total amnesia is ordained for the dead men's followers, extinguishing their terrible memories and making them capable of peace through oblivion.

Last of all, Odysseus reveals himself to his father Laertes, who is bowed with grief at the supposed loss of his son, and has allowed his outer appearance to reflect his sad state of mind. But his farm and his land are in good order. His farm workers care for them, but Laertes himself still lends a hand. There is mention of *the well-worked plot*, the *great orchard* full of fruit trees. Odysseus, still incognito, praises his father:

> You want no skill, old man, in tending a garden,
> all's well kept here; not one thing in the plot,
> no plant, no fig, no pear, no olive, no vine,
> not a vegetable, lacks your tender, loving care.

(O, F 24, 271).

There are two indications of how far the estate of Laertes is from the palace (O, 24, 204; 24, 357). If we imagine ourselves on Pilikata Hill, we can assume that the *well-worked plot* with its gardens, orchards and fields is in the fruit-growing region of Ithaca, the gentle landscape near Stavros, marked out by the three mountains of Neritos, Exogi and Marmakas as if by three mighty watch towers, and linked to the sea by three bays. A few villages and country villas lie in the beautiful orchards and olive groves that cover the hill, their silvery foliage shining cheerfully. Only a few cypress trees are dark, grave notes.

'This region is marked off from the rest of the island by its agriculture,' wrote Haller von Hallerstein to Crown Prince Ludwig, describing the country around Stavros. 'Here we find the country houses of Ithacans and Cephalonians in pretty places, among plantations of trees and vineyards, with many cypresses. I believe it may well have looked the same in antiquity.'[130] There are indeed fruit trees and vines here, and Odysseus praised them as well tended on his visit to the estate of Laertes. After he has revealed his identity, he proves it by telling his father, who still doubts him, all the kinds of fruit trees that Laertes gave him as a boy

Trailing you through the orchard, picking our way,
among those trees, and you named them one by one.
You gave me thirteen pear, ten apple trees
and forty figs – and promised to give me, look,
fifty vine rows, bearing hard on each other's heels,
clusters of grapes year-round at every grade of ripeness,
mellowed as Zeus's seasons weight them down.

(O, F 24, 375).

The scene of the reunion between Odysseus and Laertes is visually illustrated in only one work, as a fragment of a Roman sarcophagus of about AD 50. It is marvellous, then that this one find is extremely beautiful in its language of gesture and expressive power. As we look, we witness an entirely spontaneous moment that needs no words. Father and son hold one another in a close embrace.

And so the *Odyssey* ends, even in its memories of happy childhood days, in the almost idyllic atmosphere of fairy tale. The hero has returned to his wife and son, peace is ensured by divine decree, his rule is restored and its continuity shown in the patriarchal triad of heroes represented by Laertes – who in fact engaged in the last battle wielding his spear – Odysseus and Telemachus. Now there was nothing in the way of a pleasant old age for Odysseus until gentle death took him – as Tiresias had prophesied. First, however, he must set off once more on a difficult and dangerous journey to be reconciled for ever with Poseidon. He tells his wife Penelope this during their recognition scene – that intense, oppressive, captivating episode – but at first only in outline; she wants to be told more now, and in detail. Odysseus complies with her wish, and tells the circumstances of this last trial, after which, however, the course of their lives will be peaceful:

And at the last my own death will steal upon me ...
a gentle, painless death, far from the sea it comes
to take me down, borne down with the years in ripe old age
with all my people here in blessed peace around me.
All this, the prophet said, will come to pass.
'And so,' Penelope said in her great wisdom,
'if the gods will really grant a happier old age,
there's hope that we'll escape our trials at last.'

(O, F 23, 321).

A happy ending, then, for a family, a small nation, after all the trials, suffering and cruelties that have been inflicted and suffered? That was what Homer obviously wanted. It was probably expected by his aristocratic audience, with whose ideals he identified, and by the schools that would soon come into being in which his epics were regarded from the first as handbooks for Greeks. If the *Odyssey* was also intended to show how the human spirit can finally overcome all obstacles, how the will to live, together with practical intelligence and ingenuity, make up the new Greek ideal of a human being who has left behind the stage of magic and enchantment with his faith in the Olympian gods as they appear in the Homeric epics,[131] then the story, presented as credible, of the figure in whom all those qualities were united would probably provide such a satisfyingly well-rounded conclusion.

Homer lets the curtain fall.

'But the legend did not fall silent, it worked on in a kind of Flying Dutchman theme about Odysseus, a late, wild, unknown Odysseus.'[132] Up to our own day, post-Homeric mythmakers, poets and writers have been unable to accept the happy ending. The character of Odysseus, we may suppose, has too much human depth for other times to be satisfied with that domesticated finale. The period of what was announced in the *Odyssey*, if only as a prophecy, as his happy retirement is described by authors from Sophocles to the Byzantine scholars of the 12th century as a difficult phase of his life, with the violent, tragic death of Odysseus destroying the family unit: Odysseus banished by the law for ten years to Thesprotia in Epirus in Greece, where he marries the queen of the country and has a son, while Telemachus is sent into exile to Cephalonia because an oracle has foretold that Odysseus' own son will kill him. The banishment is in vain; back in Ithaca Odysseus is killed, because he went unrecognized, by his son by Circe, Telegonus, who has come in search of his father. Meanwhile Penelope is ruling the island as regent for a son, not yet of age, called Polyporthis. However, her regency is not entirely up to the Homeric standard. Some authors even claimed she had slept in turn with all the suitors, which is surely just gossip and slander.

Dante's *Divine Comedy* holds out the prospect of the hero's life taking a different turn from that in the *Odyssey*, long before the end of the adventurous Homeric journey. This is an entirely new dynamic, or perhaps the old dynamic driving him on and refusing to let him grow old, a pensioner king sitting by the hearth, accepting the human fate of decline and a gentle death. Dante's Odysseus remains in the turmoil of impatience, a longing to explore the world, to cross generally accepted frontiers. And for the seafaring man *par excellence* that can mean only to put out to sea again, with a small but loyal crew, to travel far into foreign lands. He cannot be kept from it by either 'love for his son, nor pity for his old father, nor the dutiful love he owes Penelope.' [133] Consequently, the life of this driven man, like that of another driven man who perished later in the sea of erotic storms, ends in the element destined to be his fateful stage: the ocean. There is a storm, the ship founders, 'until the sea closed over us', as the soul of Odysseus, wrapped in flames in the Inferno section, replies to Virgil when he is asked about the circumstances of his death.

Ernst Bloch has devoted a chapter to this Dantean variant on the life of Odysseus, which diverges from the canonical version, calling him one of the leading figures among those who cross borders, and headed it: 'Odysseus did not die in Ithaca but travelled to the uninhabited world.' Certainly it is more than right that a hungry man would wish to be fed, a freezing man would long for the fire on the hearth, and a traveller for his wife and child. But all the same ...

'But when the name of a father who has been all around the world is Odysseus, the return is not so straightforward (...). The wanderer did not just suffer trials, he was also a traveller who saw the cities and lands of many men, and Calypso and Nausicaa as well. Superficial interpretations have seen a moral in the story to the effect that an ingenious husband and father will always, in every danger, strive to return to his own (...). The return is certainly an important factor, but all the greater are its dangers and drawbacks, just as those of repose are.' [134]

This was probably how Greek and Roman mythmakers understood the subject. So did Dante later. With him, Odysseus is the victim of his own hubris and dies, but for Bloch he is also 'the first titanic figure, descended from knights and not from patient men.' [135] To name only a few more names, this is also how Alfred Lord Tennyson sees him, in the heroic emotion of his dramatic monologue *Ulysses*: 'Vile it were/For some three suns to store and hoard myself,/ And this grey spirit, yearning in desire/To follow knowledge like a sinking star,/Beyond the utmost bound of human thought.' [136] So does Inge Merkel, who gives a final slant to the theme of curiosity and longing: 'This strange homesickness, in his limbs and stirring his cool blood, had nothing to do with cheerful seafaring. Nothing to do with a desire for knowledge, or curiosity to see marvels never seen before that the sea and the islands had withheld from him. He was curious about death.'[137]

Since Homer's own time, many others have gone on weaving the immeasurable fabric that embraces what is great, what is all too human, what is shameful, in fact all that makes up mankind. It offers much. Just how the towering mythological figure of Odysseus stimulates us to continue his story depends on our personal qualities, values and circumstances; do we put the *Odyssey* aside when we have finished reading it, happy with the prophesied end, or do we regard it as an open book into which, bringing our imagination to bear on the tale of Odysseus, we project our own desire for a free and unconfined life? Odysseus as a kind of Flying Dutchman, a sailor opposing storms for all eternity, might be one sequel; a Wandering Jew of the sea, bearing the stigma of having left the aura of the magic to enter the circle of light of the Olympian gods, who were then liquidated by the philosophers – although they survived in art – making way for Western rationalism and scepticism. Where the heavens disappear the world cries out to be discovered and conquered in thoughts, words and deeds. Curiosity, activity, a hunger for experience, a longing for knowledge, ambition, the striving for fame and power, desire, an aim, an action, fulfilment (although brief), emptiness, new desire, new activity, and again and again journey on the sea of restlessness, the ocean of events.

Could there be any help for this Odysseus, any way to bring relief to the Odysseus in ourselves? Perhaps it could be the calm cheerfulness of the older Montaigne, whose philosophy takes leave of the will to plan and conduct our lives actively, aware now of the arbitrary nature of human fate? Or by dipping into the jade jar of Lao Tze's wisdom, with a few drops of wu-wei mixed into the foaming brew of the Western urge to keep offering the ego a new playground for its wishes and desires – to mute so much activity at least, if not to end it entirely?

But must he turn his back on travelling? Be content with the journeys in his head? Should we emulate Lao Tze? 'Not going out of the door, yet to know the world/not to look out of the window, yet to see the way of heaven:/If we go far out/we know little.'[138] Or the Roman stoics, who advised against travelling since it only disturbed your leisure and was evidence of an unsteady mind? But in this attitude – and its heroic ethic of death – Montaigne was unable to follow the stoics in his later years, although otherwise he was on a very familiar footing with them. He was too fond of the joys of life, its surprises, its imponderability, and emphasizes the variety and constant change of the outer world as a mirror of its inner abundance,[139] to wish to deprive his flexible mind of travel as the source of rich experiences and observations of contemporary life. He was not concerned with reaching his destination but with travelling, with movement, in which he liked to recognize intensified paradigms of man's personal journey through life. 'I travel for the sake of travel.'

Does the way, then, lead back to Odysseus, to the Odysseus of the *Second Odyssey*,[140] the title of a poem by Constantine Cavafy? Probably not, for as even the epigraphs of that poem – 'Dante, *Inferno*, Canto XXVI' and 'Tennyson, *Ulysses*' – suggest, we shall meet an Odysseus here who does not envisage a royal retirement, one who will set off from his home without any firm intention of coming back again. Disillusion is evident in the first verse:

> A second great Odyssey,
> Perhaps even longer than the first. But sad to say
> Without Homer, without hexameters.

Then we learn of the comfortable and pleasant conditions on Ithaca, of the love and liking of his family, friends and people, of the peace of his home, all of which 'pierce the seafarer's heart like rays of joy.' But one line further on: 'And like rays they are extinguished.' The urge to go to sea and the longing for travel are felt once more and cannot be suppressed. The love of his family, friends and people, the peace of his home 'oppressed him. And he went away,' sailing westward to the Pillars of Hercules and who knows where?

> And his heart, lusting for adventure,
> Rejoiced, cold as it was and empty of love.

This time Penelope, Telemachus and the people of Ithaca cannot expect him to return. They must give up the idea of Odysseus as husband, father and king.

But as for us, to whatever end the *Second Odyssey* comes, let us not fail to be touched by the magic wand of the first, the Homeric *Odyssey* complete with hexameters.

Notes

As there is not a single extant document about the life of Homer, nothing certain can be said about the poet's place and date of birth, his career and how long he lived. Briefly, what we surmise can be summed up thus: Homer was born around 770 BC in Ionia in Asia Minor; the *Iliad* is thought to have been created around 730 and the *Odyssey* around 710. Whether the *Odyssey* can in fact be considered Homer's work is a matter of controversy to the present day. According to Latacz,[141] expert opinion is now much more inclined than it once was to give him credit for authorship of the second work as well as the first. It therefore seemed to me permissible, for the sake of simplicity, to refer to the poet of both the *Iliad* and the *Odyssey* as 'Homer'.

After completing this work I came upon the book *Odysseus Unbound*, by Robert Bittlestone (Cambridge 2005), in which not Ithaca but the peninsula of Paliki on the neighbouring island of Cephalonia is described as the home of Odysseus. After I had been to Cephalonia and studied Haliki closely, I wrote a literary account of my visit in reaction to Bittlestone's exciting ideas. It closes with the words 'Might it not be a fascinating conjecture to think that Homer was inspiried by details of the landscape of both Ithaca and Paliki, and in an act of poetic collage merged them to create the Ithaca where the events of the *Odyssey* take place? Then fortunate readers who have visited both islands, remembering their experiences, could sense the Homeric aura in the interplay of the words and the dual set of images with particular intensity.'

This text will appear in a later publication.

I am extremely grateful to my son Roman Geisthövel for preparing the maps. The representation of the coastline in Map I is taken, with kind permission, from the *Schweizer Weltatlas* (Swiss World

Atlas) published by the Institute for Cartography, ETH Zürich.

[**Translator's note on English versions of Homer.** Dr Geisthövel naturally quotes in this book, in its original German, from several German versions of the *Iliad* and the *Odyssey*, some in verse, some in prose: they are, for the *Iliad*, by Johann Heinrich Voss (Munich 1957), and Hans Rupé (Düsseldorf and Zürich 2001). For the *Odyssey*, he uses Johann Heinrich Voss (Munich 1957), Wolfgang Schadewaldt (Düsseldorf and Zürich 2001), and Anton Weiher, (Düsseldorf and Zürich 2000).

For equivalent English translations I have used mainly the verse translations by Robert Fagles (*Iliad*, New York and London 1990; *Odyssey*, New York and London 1996), and the prose translations of E.V. Rieu, revised D.C.H. Rieu (*Iliad*, New York and London 2003; *Odyssey*, New York and London 1991), with occasional reference to the earlier translations in the Loeb Classics by A.T. Murray (*Iliad*, New York and London MCMXXIV; *Odyssey*, New York and London MCMXIX). Short quotations are in italic in the body of the text; longer quoted passages are indented and set out as distinct from the main text, and I have followed Dr Geisthövel's style of attribution, e.g. (O, F 9, 46) = *Odyssey*, Fagles Book 9, beginning line 46. Line numbers are those of the translations, and sometimes vary by comparison with the original Greek.]

Notes

1. Max Horkheimer and Theodor W. Adorno, *Dialectik der Aufklärung*, Frankfurt am Main 1969, p. 44.

2. John V. Luce, *Celebrating Homer's Landscapes*, New Haven and London, 1999.

3. Armin and Hans-Helmut Wolf:*Die wirkliche Reises des Odysseus. Zur Rekonstruction des Homerischen Weltbildes,* Vienna 1990.

4. Louis Moulinier, in: A. and H.-H. Wolf, *op. cit.*, p. 180.

5. Joachim Latacz, *Homer. Der erste Dichter des Abendlandes*, Düsseldorf and Zürich 2003, p. 168.

6. Bernard Andreae, *Odysseus. Mythos und Erinnerung,* Mainz am Rhein 2000, p. 23.

7. Joachim Latacz, *op. cit.*, p. 67.

8. Armin and Hans-Helmut Wolf, *op. cit.*, p. 93.

9. Johann Wolfgang Goethe, *Italienische Reise* I, Frankfurt am Main 1976, p. 416.

10. Johann Wolfgang Goethe, letter to Friedrich Schiller of 14 February 1798, in: *Der Briefwechsel zwischen Schiller und Goethe*, Vol. 2, Munich 1984, p. 49.

11. Barbara Patzek, *Homer und seine Zeit*, Munich 2003, p. 72.

12. Wolf Hartman Friedrich, Afterword, in: *Homer. Ilias, Odyssee*, Munich 1957, p. 820.

13. Rudolf Hagelstange, *Spielball der Götter. Aufzeichnungen eines trojanischen Prinzen,* Hamburg 1967, p. 40.

14. Barbara Patzek, *op. cit.,* p. 72.

15. John V. Luce, *op. cit.*, p. 76.

16. John V. Luce, *op. cit.*, p. 142.

17. John V. Luce, *op. cit.*, p. 146.

18. Christa Wolf, *Kassandra*, Darmstadt and Neuwied 1984.

19. Peter Blome, 'Der Mythos in der griechischen Kunst. Der Troianische Krieg findet statt', in: *Troia – Traum und Wirklichkeit*, Stuttgart 2001, p. 140.

20. Friedrich Hölderlin, 'Über Achill (1)', 'Über Achill (2), in: *Werke, Briefe, Dokumente,* Munich 1990, pp. 494 and 495.

21. Jonathan Shay, *Achilles in Vietnam: Combat Trauma and the Undoing of Character*, New York 1994.

22. Byron, *Don Juan*, London 1818–1824.

23. Byron, *Letters and Journals*, ed. L.A. Marchand, London 1973, Vol. 8, pp. 21–22.

24. John V. Luce, *op. cit.*

25. Manfred Korfmann, 'Wilusa/(W)ilios ca. 1200 v. Chr. – Ilion ca. 700 v.Chr. Befundberichte aus der Archäologie', in: *Troisa – Traum und Wirklichkeit,* Stuttgart 2001, p. 75.

26. Birgit Brandau, *Troia. Eine Stadt und ihr Mythos. Die neuesten Entdeckungen*, Bergisch Gladbach 1999, p. 183.

27. Manfred Korfmann, *op. cit.*, p. 75.

28. Birgit Brandau, Hartmut Schickert and Peter Jablonka, *Troia – Wie es wirklich aussah*, Munich 2000, pp. 70 and 71.

29. Manfred Korfmann, *op. cit.*, p. 71.

30. Alfred Heubeck: 'Zu Homers Odyssee', in: *Homer, Odyssee*, Düsseldorf and Zürich 2000, p. 697.

31. Uvo Hölscher, *Die Odyssee. Epos zwischen Märchen und Roman*, Munich 2000, pp. 143 and 148.

32. Michael Sommer, *Die Phönizier. Handelsherren zwischen Orient und Okzident*, Stuttgart 2005, p.122 ff.

33. Joachim Latacz, *op. cit.*, p. 69.

34. Armin and Hans-Helmut Wolf, *op. cit.*, p. 101.

35. Herodotus, *The Histories*, trans. A.W. Godley, Book 4, 177, London and New York MCMXXI.

36. Armin and Hans-Helmut Wolf, *op. cit.*, pp. 39 and 102.

37. Ulrich von Wilamowitz-Moellendorft, in: Armin and Hans-Helmut Wolf, *op. cit.*, p. 165.

38. Egon Friedell, *Kulturgeschichte der Neuzeit*, Munich 2003.

39. Bernard Andreae, *op. cit.*, p. 111.

40. Armin and Hans-Helmut Wolf, *op. cit.*, p. 38.

41. Michael Bussmann, *Malta. Gozo & Comino*, Erlangen 2004; Hans Zaglitsch and Linda O'Bryan, *Malta. Kunst und Kultur*, Stuttgart 2002.

42. Ferdinand Gregorovius, *Wanderjahre in Italien*, Dresden 1928, p. 1096.

43. Virgil, *Aeneid 5*, 759, trans. H. Rushton Fairclough, New York and London, MCMXVI.

44. Theocritus, *Idyll XV*, trans. Andrew Lang, London, MDCCCCXXII.

45. Karl Kerenyi, *Die Mythologie der Griechen. Band I: Die Götter- und Menschheitsgeschichte*, Munich 1968, p. 56.

46. Sappho, *Songs*, Book 1. English translation from the German version, Munich and Zürich 1984.

47. Rudolf Alexander Schröder, notes, p. 431, in his German translation of Virgil, Munich 1976.

48. Gerd Gaiser, *Sizilianische Notizen,* Munich 1969, p. 22.

49. Virgil, *op. cit.*

50. Armin and Hans-Helmut Wolf, *op. cit.*, p. 256 f.

51. Uvo Hölscher, *op. cit.*, p. 20.

52. Martin Mosebach, 'Ein Mann mit Geheimnis', in: *Merian Sizilien*, 4 April 1999, p. 78.

53. Armin and Hans-Helmut Wolf, *op. cit.*, p. 48.

54. Armin and Hans-Helmut Wolf, *op. cit.*, p. 48.

55. Max Horkheimer and Theodor W. Adorno, *op. cit.*, p. 68.

56. Uvo Hölscher, *op. cit.*, p. 154.

57. Ovid, *Metamorphoses V*, trans. Frank Justus Miller, New York and London, MCMXVI, p. 265.

58. Armin and Hans-Helmut Wolf, *op. cit.*, p. 60.

59. Johann Wolfgang Goethe, *op. cit.*, p. 386 f.

60. Alban Nikolai Herbst, *New York in Catania. Eine phantastische Reise durch Sizilien*, Hamburg 1997, p. 58 ff.

61. Luigi Pirandello, 'Il Fumo', in *Scialle Nero*, 1922. English version from German translation 'Der Rauch', in *Angst vor dem Glück*, Munich 1962, p. 136.

62. Uvo Hölscher, *op. cit.*, p. 154 f.

63. Max Horkheimer and Theodor W. Adorno, *op. cit.*, p. 55.

64. Bernard Andrease, *op. cit.*, p. 288.

65. Armin Wolf, 'Homer und die Strasse von Messina', in: *Stuttgarter Kolloquium zur Historischen Geographie des Altertums* 7, 1999, Stuttgart 2002, p. 304.

66. Thucydides, *The Peloponnesian War*, Book 4, 24 (5), trans. Charles Forster Smith, New York and London MCMXX.

67. Armin Wolf, *op. cit.*, p. 306.

68. Armin Wolf, *op. cit.*, p. 310.

69. Bernard Andrease, *op. cit.*, p. 303.

70. Virgil, *Aeneid* Book 3, *op. cit.*

71. Ovid, *Metamophoses 13*, *op.cit.*,

72. Ovid, *Metamophoses 14*, *op.cit.*,

73. Johan Wolfgang Goethe, *op. cit.*, p. 403.

74. Johan Wolfgang Goethe, *op. cit.*, p. 403.

75. Johann Gottfried Seume, *Spaziergang nach Syrakus*, Frankfurt am Main, Leipzig 2001, p. 217.

76. Johann Gottfried Seume, *op. cit.*, p. 240.

77. Johann Wolfgang Goethe, *op. cit.*, p. 392.

78. Armin and Hans-Helmut Wolf, *op. cit.*, p. 79.

79. Bernard Andreae, *op. cit.*, p. 321 f.

80. Victor Bérard, *Les navigations d'Ulysse*, Paris 1927–1929.

81. Uvo Hölscher, *op. cit.*, p. 144.

82. Reinhold Merkelbach, *Untersuchungen zur Odyssee*, Munich 1969, p. 717.

83. Reinhold Merkelbach, *op. cit.*, p. 217.

84. Armin and Hans-Helmut Wolf, *op. cit.*, p. 84.

85. Uvo Hölscher, *op. cit.*, pp. 191, 192.

86. Armin and Hans-Helmut Wolf, *op. cit.*, p.86.

87. Ekkehart Rotter, *Kalabrien. Basilikata*, Cologne 2002, p. 305.

88. Armin and Hans-Helmut Wolf, *op. cit.*, p. 87.

89. Armin and Hans-Helmut Wolf, *op. cit.*, p.141.

90. John V. Luce, *op. cit.*, p. 229.

91. Hermann Fürst von Pückler-Muskau. *Südöstlicher Bilderatlas,* Vol. 3, Stuttgart 1841, p. 518.

92. John V. Luce, *op. cit.,* p. 228.

93. Otto Magnus von Stackelberg, *Schilderung seines Lebens ...,* quoted in M. Steinhart and E. Wirbelauer, *Aus er Heimat des Odysseus,* Main am Rhein, p. 2002, p. 67.

94. William Gell, *The Geography and Antiquities of Ithaca,* quoted in M. Steinhart and E.Wirbelauer, *op. cit.*

95. Hesiod, *Theogeny*

96. William Gell, paraphrased as quoted by M. Steinhart and E. wirbelauer, *op. cit.,* p. 58.

97. Matthias Steinhart and Eckhard Wirbelauer, *o p. cit.,* p. 60.

98. Rudolf Hercher, quoted in M. Steinhart and E.Wirbelauer, *op. cit.,* p. 186

99. Rudolf Menge, quoted in M. Steinhart and E.Wirbelauer, *op. cit.,* p. 184.

100. Herrrmann Fürst von Pückler-Muskau, *op. cit.,* p. 529.

101. Heinrich Schliemann, quoted in M. Steinhart and E.Wirbelauer, *op. cit.,* p. 183.

102. Carl Haller von Hallerstein, quoted in M. Steinhart and E.Wirbelauer, *op. cit.* p. 112.

103. Herrrmann Fürst von Pückler-Muskau, *op. cit.,* p. 520.

104. Herrrmann Fürst von Pückler-Muskau, *op. cit.,* p. 521. 522.

105. John V. Luce, *op. cit.,* p. 191.

106. Friedrich Schiller, 'Odysseus', in: Sämtliche Gedichte und Balladen, Frankfurt/Main and Leipzig 2004.

107. J. Cartwright, quoted by John V. Luce, *op. cit.,* p. 201.

108. John V. Luce, *op. cit.,* p. 203.

109. Uvo Hölscher, *op. cit.,* p. 186.

110. Uvo Hölscher, *op. cit.,* p. 203.

111. Friedrich Eichhorn, *Homers Odyssee. Ein Führer durch die Dichtung,* Göttingen 1965, p. 27.

112. Uvo Hölscher, *op. cit.,* p. 54.

113. Jürgen Manthey, *Die Unsterblichkeit Achills. Vom Ursprung des Erzählens,* Munich 1997.

114. Konstantinos P. Komorlis, *Die mykenische Kultur. Mykene – Tiryns – Pylos,* Athens 1974, p. 71.

115. Carl Blegen, quoted in G. Weiss, *Peloponnes,* Cologne 1994, p 212.

116. Pausanias, *Beschreibung Griechenlands,* (Description of Greece), quoted from German translation, Zürich and Stuttgart 1967, p. 242.

117. Thucydides, *op. cit.*

118. Karl-Wilhelm Welwei, *Sparta*, Stuttgart 2004, p. 14.

119. Karl-Wilhelm Welwei, *op. cit.*, p. 35.

120. Wolfgang Hildesheimer, 'Das Opfer Helena', incl. in *Das Opfer Helena, Monolog, Zwei Hörspieler*, Frankfurt am Main 1965.

121. Uvo Hölscher, *op. cit.*, p. 142.

122. John V. Luce, *op. cit.*, pp. 215/216.

123. Matthias Steinhart and Eckhard Wirbelauer, *op. cit.*, p. 190.

124. John V. Luce, *op. cit.*, p. 178.

125. John V. Luce, *op. cit.*, p. 218.

126. Uvo Hölscher, *op. cit.*, p. 192.

127. John V. Luce, *op. cit.*, p. 178.

128. John V. Luce, *op. cit.*, p. 248.

129. John V. Luce, *op. cit.*, p. 248.

130. Carl Haller von Hallerstein, quoted in M. Steinhart and E. Wirberlauer, *op. cit.*, p. 113.

131. Bruno Snell, *Die Entdeckung des Geistes*, Götingen 1986.

132. Ernst Bloch, *Das Prinzip Hoffnung*, Vol. 3, Frankfurt am Main, p. 1202.

133. Dante, *The Inferno. The Divine Comedy.*

134. Ernst Bloch, *op. cit.*, pp. 1201 and 1202.

135. Ernst Bloch, *op. cit.*, pp. 1203.

136. Alfred Lord Tennyson, *Ulysses.* First published in *Poems,* Boston 1942..

137. Inge Merkel, 'Eine ganz gewöhnliche Ehe. Odysseus und Penelope', in *Mythos Odysseus, op. cit.,* p. 165.

138. Lao Tze, translated from German version, *Das Buch vom rechten Wege uind von der rechten Gesnnung,* 47th saying, Frankfurt am Main and Berlin 1990.

139. Hugo Friedrich, *Montaigne*, Berne 1967.

140. Constatinos Cavafy, *A Second Odyssey.*

141. Joachim Latacz, *op. cit.*, p. 64.

Acknowledgements

The publisher and author are indebted to Penguin Books Limited for permission to quote from *The Iliad* and *The Odyssey*, published by Penguin Classics.